VOICES OF THE JOURNEY

"Right always looks like doing right by others. Not only will you invariably find success, but you can always look back on the journey you've been on with pride, feeling that you've navigated through it, with integrity."

— **Will Guidara**
Hospitality Visionary & Restaurateur, Author of Unreasonable Hospitality

"Instant gratification is not something that should be prized. Things that are worth of having generally take a little bit longer and tend to have more value."

— **Chef Nyesha Arrington**
Chef, Television Personality, Restaurateur

"Do it now. Tomorrow is not promised. Take advantage of the time now, of what's right in front of you."

— **Chef Charlie Mitchell**
Executive Chef, Saga New York, Two Michelin Stars

"When you assign meaning to something, people begin to define the senses they're experiencing.
The meaning of your assignment is storytelling."

— **Chef Omar Tate**
Time 100 Next (2021)
Chef & Co-Owner of Honeysuckle, Philadelphia

"May finding wisdom through those with experience, help you to find your own secret sauce — and may it serve as a reminder to always savor your journey."
— **Chef Sakari Smithwick**

Savor Your Journey: Three Simple Steps to Find Your Secret Sauce in Life

© 2025 **Noble Promise Incorporated**. All rights reserved. No part of this book may be reproduced, stored in a retrieval system, or transmitted in any form or by any means—electronic, mechanical, photocopying, recording, or otherwise—without prior written permission from the publisher, except for brief quotations and other noncommercial uses permitted by copyright law.

This work reflects the author's experiences and opinions and is provided for informational/educational purposes only.

Imprint: Noble Promise

Published by: Noble Promise Incorporated

Brooklyn, New York •www.smithwickprovisions.com

First edition • Publication date: December 16, 2025

ISBN (print): 979-8-218-52435-7

979-8-90213-567-8

A portion of proceeds supports the Nourish the Nation initiative.

To my family—
to all the Kings and Queens who have lifted me, guided me, and helped build my foundation as a man. My greatest accomplishment in life isn't found in any accolade, but as being a son, a grandson, a great-grandson, a cousin, a friend and a brother. Because family isn't always defined by blood—it's defined by love, accountability, and the values we choose to carry forward. The greatest gift I've been given is the chance to wake up each day with gratitude in my heart, purpose in my steps, and the responsibility to keep passing these values into the future.

VOICES THAT SHAPED ME

"Never forget who you are, and where you come from. Stay humble, stay strong, and stay true to yourself no matter what life brings your way."

—Nathan A. Moore, My father.

"Life's most persistent and urgent question is... What are you doing for others?"

— Martin Luther King Jr.

SAVOR YOUR JOURNEY
3 SIMPLE STEPS TO FIND YOUR SECRET SAUCE IN LIFE

SECRET INGREDIENTS FROM THE GREATEST CULINARY MINDS

SAKARI SMITHWICK

SAKARI SMITHWICK

SAVOR YOUR JOURNEY

3 SIMPLE STEPS To Find Your Secret Sauce in Life

SECRET INGREDIENTS FROM THE WORLD'S GREATEST CULINARY MINDS

CONTENTS

Join The Journey	xv
AUTHOR'S NOTE: The Moment Everything Changes	xvii
Foreword	xxi
Introduction	xxv

PART I
Part 1 - Passion Craft Your Flavor … 1

1. CHAPTER 1: THE FORBIDDEN KITCHEN … 3
2. CHAPTER 2: COMING OF AGE … 11
3. CHAPTER 3: FROM McDONALD'S TO MICHELIN STARS … 15
4. CHAPTER 4: GOING FOR GOLD … 18
5. CHAPTER 5: COSTA RICA GOLD … 21
6. CHAPTER 6: FOR THE LOVE OF SEAFOOD … 23
7. CHAPTER 7: TEAM ICE CREAM … 30
8. CHAPTER 8: WELCOME TO THE BEST RESTAURANT IN THE WORLD … 34
9. CHAPTER 9: SEARCHING FOR MY ROOTS … 40
10. CHAPTER 10: CHASING THE STAR … 45
11. CHAPTER 11: OPENING A NEW RESTAURANT FROM SCRATCH … 50
12. CHAPTER 12: SETTING SAIL TO THE NETHERLANDS … 56
13. CHAPTER 13: RESTAURANT TRIBECA (EUROPE PART 2) … 64
14. CHAPTER 14: BACK TO THE DIRT … 75
15. CHAPTER 15: MY BIG BREAK (THE DOUBLE ENTENDRE) … 80
16. CHAPTER 16: SIGNS FROM ABOVE … 89
17. CHAPTER 17: THIS IS NOT DRILL! THE FIRE TEST (HELL'S KITCHEN PART 1) … 95
18. CHAPTER 18: THE FINAL TEST (HELL'S KITCHEN PART 2) … 102
19. CHAPTER 19: FULL CIRCLE: Where Dreams and Reality Meet … 107

Part II
HIDDEN GEMS

1. Hidden Gems: The Early Path, Skilled Work, and Cultural Identity — 113
   Chef Roshara: Teaching as Mission, Food as Salvation — 115
   Chef Charlie Mitchell: Breaking Through Identity and Excellence — 129
   Chef Omar Tate: On Finding Purpose Through Hardship, Building Community, and Cooking as Poetry — 141
   Chef BJ Dennis: Preserving Gullah Geechee Foodways — 157
2. Hidden Gems: Adaption, Changes and Transitions — 167
   Chef Nyesha Arrington: Mastering Excellence Through Balance — 169
   Chef Thijs Meliefste: On Transitions, Persistence, and Knowing When to Close the Door — 179
   Chef Camari Mick: Building Her Own Way — 187
   Chef Alex Belew: The Rival Who Became a Friend — 197
3. Hidden Gems: The Path Forward and The Come Up — 208
   Chef Marc Anthony Bynum: The Art of Resilience and Real Hospitality — 209
   Chef Kwame Onwuachi: On Craft, Authenticity, and Why Your Brand is Only as Strong as Your Skill — 219
   Chef JJ Johnson: Cooking Culture, Building Community, and Redefining Ownership — 231
4. Hidden Gems: Building Empires and Taking Ownership — 240
   Alexander Smalls: On Ownership, Legacy, and Making People Feel Seen — 241
   Gary Vaynerchuk: On giving without expectation. — 257
   Will Guidara: On Mentorship, Adversity, and the Power of Relationships — 267
   Chef Josh Capon: The King of Hospitality — 277

Part III
THE TOOLKIT - THE PROMISE

Chef Sakari's Top 5 Kitchen Staples — 287
Food In Season — 291
Recipes — 297
Chapter 20: The Secret — 344
Acknowledgments — 355

JOIN THE JOURNEY

AUTHOR'S NOTE: THE MOMENT EVERYTHING CHANGES

The truth is, when you get to the competition, things never go as planned.

I'm standing in front of Chef Gordon Ramsay! Looking at other chefs around me, right here on the set of Hell's Kitchen. I've gone from preparing to being exactly in this moment. It is one of the biggest stages I've ever seen. The only thing I can think about is winning for my dad. This is competition mode. This is my Mamba Mentality. This is my Noble Promise. I came to win.

As the clock starts, we're cooking our signature dish. Not looking at what others are doing around me, I have to imagine what my signature dish will become on this plate. All the fryers are occupied by other chefs. Some are frying chicken, others fish. I have to create my own fryer. I grab a pot, add oil, and heat it up. Unsure of the temperature, I watch for a little bit of smoke, take it off the heat, knowing it will come back down to the perfect temperature.

There's no time to grab a thermometer. As I take that hot oil right off the stove and let it cool down, I place my fish in the pan. It starts to bubble. Now, let's hope for the best. I'm making my oyster stew. A confit cod with tempura pearls, poached oysters, and caviar. A dish

I've never made in its entirety before this moment. I am trusting everything I've learned.

As Chef Christina comes down and asks what I'm making, I explain the origin of the dish. She stares at me with this combination of concern and excitement, this gaze of "good luck" or complete craziness, to pull this off. My blinders are on. I'm only focused on getting this dish done. I know I have so many components and such limited time. I just hope and pray I can finish.

"Time is coming up chefs! Start plating."

My components aren't ready. I grab the fish with a spatula, hoping it's not too oily. It is not overcooked. I turn the heat down and wait for the cream to reduce by half. I take the liquid of the oysters, then mince the oysters to blend and create an oyster fat. Add leeks, sweat until soft.

Whole peppercorns go in with whole thyme as I hope I have enough time to create the flavors I want. The fish comes out of the oil and I finish with a little lemon zest. I add my oyster stew sauce on the bottom of the plate. I added my oysters, placed my tempura on the top, and almost forgot a garnish. I grab tarragon and sprinkle it on the plate. I wipe the plate and I step away.

That is my signature dish!

Did I do too much? Would the flavors work? Is the fish overcooked? At this point, I'm going off pure faith and my training.

Each chef goes up face-to-face with their competitor, blue versus red. When it's my turn to present, I look up at Chef Gordon Ramsay and the only thing I can think to myself is: I hope it meets his expectations.

"Chef Sakari, describe the dish please? What is it?"

He looks down at my plate, with a fork and knife in hand, pensive, he begins to explore my dish.

Chef Ramsay pauses. "There's a lot going on here. It's a very complex dish."

The next few minutes seem endless...

And then Chef Ramsay says, "I'm just sad..." In my head I say to myself "Sad? What???"

Our dishes were scored between 1 to 5. I eagerly wait for him to complete his thought and when I least expect it, Chef Ramsay says to me...

"I'm just sad that I can only give you a five."

A Perfect score. I couldn't believe it!

To understand how I got here, how a Black kid from Long Island ended up cooking for one of the world's most famous chefs on national TV while grieving this loss of his father—we will need to go back to the beginning.

We need to go back to when I was just a boy who fell in love with food.

FOREWORD

By Chef Marc Anthony Bynum

Sakari came to me when he was still in high school in 2012 — young, hungry, and already thinking about college, kitchens, and who he wanted to become. I've always respected that. Most people don't figure out their path until life forces them to. He walked up to his path early. At that age, that kind of intention stands out. I saw pieces of myself in him.

When he came to intern with me over winter recess, I gave him the same structure that shaped me: clear expectations, real accountability, no shortcuts. I told him what was going wrong in the kitchen and exactly what I needed from him. And I handed him my schedule. We were in at 9 a.m., he left when I left. Stay close. Study everything. If you want to learn, attach yourself to the person who knows how to win.

He showed up. He worked. But he didn't follow me in the way I asked. He didn't walk in with me. Didn't glue himself to my shoulder the way I needed him to if he really wanted to absorb the game. And because

FOREWORD

of that, even though I was fully committed to mentoring him, I couldn't get through to him in those early weeks, not the way I wanted to.

So when we sat down for that closing meeting, I gave it to him straight. I told him exactly what disappointed me. And I told him something I've lived by my entire career:

Never lower your standard.
  Not for anyone.
  Not because of the room you're in.
  Not because of what the next man or woman is doing.

You're in competition with yourself. Beat that opponent every day, and everything else will fall in line. Here's the thing, though, Sakari listened. Maybe not in real time, but life always has a way of making certain lessons ring louder later. And watching his growth since then, I know that moment mattered. Accountability is uncomfortable. But sometimes that's the spark needed.

Over the years, I've watched him fight through things people don't see, carry weight most people don't know about, and keep moving when a lesser man would've folded. From the day he was born, life threw challenges at him, real ones and he's had to grow through all of them in real time.

And that's why writing this foreword means so much to me. Because I didn't just mentor him, I became his big brother. And big brothers want to see the people they care about rise, even when the path is rough, even when the world feels heavy. This book is the beginning of something bigger for him.
  A new chapter. A new level. A new version of himself stepping into the world with honesty, scars, pride, and purpose.

This is the start of his stand, the moment he takes everything life has handed him, everything that he's survived, everything that he's learned, and turns it into something meaningful.

Sakari, I am proud of you.
    Keep going.
    Keep climbing.
    Keep showing the world who you are, who you're
    Becoming, and who you're meant to be!

Yes, Chef.
    Let's build.

INTRODUCTION

What This Book Is Really About.

"When Life hands you lemons, make lemonade." We've all heard that.

Here's what they don't tell you: Some lemons are rotten. Some are underripe. The question isn't whether you'll get lemons. The question is: What are you going to do with them to make that lemonade? This book is about squeezing every drop of juice out of whatever life gives you—the sweet, the bitter, and the unexpected. It's about savoring the journey, not the destination. It's about finding the "secret ingredients" in life to achieve who you are meant to become.

My name is Sakari, which in Swahili means, "Noble Promise".

This book is my promise to you. That your story matters, that struggles aren't obstacles, and that the journey itself—the grind, the setbacks, the small wins nobody sees, is where the real treasure is.

Before we go any further, we need to talk about why this matters.

The food system in America is broken.

We live in the wealthiest country in the world, yet over 34 million people, including 9 million children, live with food insecurity. They might be eating, but they're not being nourished. Black and Brown communities in urban cities in New York, such as Harlem or Bedford-

INTRODUCTION

Stuyvesant, South Jamaica or the South Bronx, and even in Long Island, you'll find entire neighborhoods without a single grocery store, only Bodegas.

We call these "Food Apartheids", referring to the systemic and intentional separation of communities from access to fresh, healthy, and affordable food. Schools are the biggest fast food franchise in America. Over 30 million children eat lunch in public schools every day. For some kids, it's the only hot meal they'll eat. And what are we feeding them? Frozen nuggets, reheated fries, canned fruit, and chocolate milk. This is not nutrition. Meanwhile, those who can afford to, dine farm-to-table with locally sourced and fresh produce, abundant vegetable choices, and lean meats. That's why every copy sold of SAVOR YOUR JOURNEY supports food education and providing nourishing meals to the youth. This book may not provide a solution, but it's a collection of journeys in action from leaders in the culinary space, including myself, that are on the mission to create change and make a difference.

How This Book Works: Three Simple Steps This book is built around three steps to finding your "secret sauce" in life:

PART 1: PASSION - Craft Your Flavor

This first step is about discovering what makes you feel alive. What is palatable to you and not to others. It is not based on what you think you should do or what society may impose. It is not to impress on Social Media. Is it about crafting your own identity, your own menu, the journey, which will ignite a fire inside you. Through my personal stories—from being a fat kid making PB&J sandwiches to competing on Hell's Kitchen—you'll see how I stumbled into my passion, lost it, found it again, and learned to harness it.

You'll learn how to:

Tap into your own story and experiences

Recognize the moments that have shaped who you are Turn obstacles into opportunities Your assignment: While reading Part I, think about your own journey. What moments define you? What makes you lose track of time? What would you do even if nobody was watching?

PART 2: PURPOSE - Words from the Greatest Culinary Minds!
This second step introduces you to incredible achievers who've mastered their craft—chefs, entrepreneurs, and my mentors who've figured out how to turn passion into purpose. These are real conversations about:

How to find purpose beyond just doing what you love

The mindsets and mantras that keep you going

The mistakes and how you learn from them

Your assignment: Find yourself in these stories. Which voices resonate with you? Which philosophies challenge you? What is one insight that could change how you approach your own journey?

PART 3: PROMISE - Serve the World with Intention
This last step is where we move from inspiration to action. You've tapped into your passion. You've been inspired by people who've made it. Now what?

The Toolkit gives you practical, actionable resources:

The Affordable Grocery List

The Replacement Guide

Food in Season and Nature's Calendar

Food as Medicine

Healthy Snack Guide

Recipes handed through from family and through generations

PART I
PART 1 - PASSION CRAFT YOUR FLAVOR

CHAPTER 1: THE FORBIDDEN KITCHEN

I wasn't born a chef, I became one. Before the fine dine kitchens, the TV shows, the interviews and accolades, I was just a fat kid who loved food. Food wasn't something I wanted to master through cooking. It was simply something that I wanted to eat, to enjoy consuming, and to understand it. It was the love language that my family spoke fluently, and I was just trying to learn the first few words. But back then, when I was a young kid, the kitchen was off-limits.

Growing up on Long Island, I split time between the White suburban towns of Amityville and Farmingdale, and the southern roots of North Carolina, where my mom's side of the family was from. We'd drive down every summer, eight hours packed into a car, passing cotton fields along the way. I remember those fields vividly. The same fields where our ancestors once picked cotton. A brutal reminder that while the world moved forward, it hadn't always done so in a straight line.

When we finally arrived at Mother Bell's house, my great-grandmother, who's still going strong at 101 years old, felt like stepping into a different era. No Wi-Fi. Four TV channels. Chickens in the yard.

Everything felt slower, but more alive. And every morning, the kitchen would come to life. The door stayed closed. Always.

You'd hear the sound of oil popping, voices whispering, laughing, arguing. The smell of red sausage and breakfast rice would start to leak out around the doorframe. This was rice you brought back from dinner, kept on the stove, and added liquid again and again until it became a thick porridge. We'd eat it with red sausage, dyed deep and only found in North Carolina, grits, and eggs, straight from the coop outside. But again, I wasn't allowed in.

"Boy, you better get some clothes on before you come to this table." That's what they'd tell me if I came near the kitchen in pajamas. In New York, it was fine to roll out of bed and sit down. But down South, you had to come correct. Full outfit. Shirt tucked in. Back straight. And I respected that.

I'd sit on the couch, listening through the door. My nose would press up against the little crack where the aroma would seep out. I could hear them talking about everything—family, bills, recipes, and pain. That door wasn't just closed because of safety or rules. It was closed because that space was sacred. You had to earn your way in.

Back on Long Island, food was still central. With both my parents working, my mom as a street cop, my dad a full-time corrections officer, I spent most of my days with my grandparents. We'd go to Macy's, JCPenney, and I'd find myself wandering the kitchen aisle. The gadgets fascinated me. Peelers, choppers, and knives. I didn't even know what half of them did, but something about them just felt right.

I remember wanting an Easy-Bake Oven. I was yearning for one, but I was so nervous to ask. I didn't see any other boys with them, because it was obviously a "girl's toy." I wish I didn't let that stop me, because I would have started cooking sooner. But I didn't start too late either.

The very first thing I ever made? A peanut butter and jelly sandwich. I was probably eight or nine years old, and I was so hungry. My grandparents at the time were throwing a Caribbean party. The music was blasting and you could hear Reggae all the way down the block. You could smell the jerk chicken cooking on the grill. My parents would always provide drinks, food, ambiance, and a wonderful experience all around. All of my grandfather's friends from his union job, who were also immigrants from Jamaica or the Bahamas, came over with their families. The one thing about my family is that they know how to host. I didn't know it at the time, but this would be the seed that was planted in me to fall in love with hospitality.

While everyone was getting served, I was a wonder-filled eight year old looking for my mom. They were so busy entertaining guests that I had the entire home to myself. This was like real life "Home Alone".

At one point I ventured outside and finally came across my mom, the life of the party. She was taking care of the guests the way you would do in any restaurant and I asked her to make me a sandwich. She said of course, right after she took care of everyone else. That sounded like forever to me. I stormed back inside immediately. I climbed up the counter and found the bread myself. I grabbed a spoon, found the jelly and peanut butter, and made my sandwich. The bread was baked fresh at a local Caribbean bakery that specializes in its hard dough bread. Caribbean hard dough bread is different—it's dense, rich, and filling. Unlike white bread that crumbles under pressure, hard dough bread is resilient, like the people who made it.

The jelly was no ordinary jelly. Normally, jelly on Long Island comes from a supermarket. In North Carolina, they made it from the land. My grandma grew up around fresh ingredients. So, it was a pleasant surprise to find a beautiful grape vine tree growing alongside the house she bought on Long Island. We used this to make fresh jelly and wine. The peanut butter was from a supermarket, but peanut butter in general is a part of Black culture and history. It's a part of my roots. George Washington Carver, one of the most brilliant Black minds in agricultural science, didn't just popularize peanuts, he revolutionized how we think about farming and self-sustainability. He created over 300 uses for the peanut, not just food, but oils, cosmetics, dyes, and medicine. He was born into slavery, yet went on to become a leader, an educator, and a symbol of Black resilience and innovation. And although he didn't technically invent peanut butter, his work laid the foundation for how we used it, and how it came to be a staple in every Black kitchen I've ever known. To me, that spoonful of peanut butter on white bread wasn't just a quick fix for hunger—it was an unconscious link to legacy. A connection to farmers and inventors who used what little they had to create something lasting.

I didn't know it at the time, but in making that sandwich, I was following the path of my ancestors: taking simple ingredients, mixing them with love and struggle, and turning them into nourishment. No cuts, no burns, just bread, jelly, peanut butter and pride. That first peanut butter and jelly sandwich was the best that I have ever had in my life, because I made it myself. I felt freedom, I felt in control, I felt power. It was incredibly rewarding to enjoy my own labor of love.

I ran outside to tell my mom, expecting praise, she laughed but something inside me had shifted. That sandwich wasn't much, but it was mine. It made me want that feeling again forever. Despite the bit of pride my mother showed me for that sandwich, she was still my biggest obstacle to finding my place in the kitchen. You see, as much as someone still loves you, people show love in different ways. And as much as the kitchen made me happy, it scared her. She didn't want me to hurt myself with a knife, or burn myself on the stove, or by any of the other hazards you find in a kitchen.

Eventually, my grandparents moved back down South to take care of my great-grandparents. During my visits, that's when the door opened—literally and figuratively. My grandma finally let me into the kitchen. Despite my Mom's best efforts to keep me out, my grandma welcomed me in.

With grandma, cooking was a gift. The first meal that I learned to cook was breakfast, the first and most important meal of the day. It started with fresh brown eggs from my great grandmother's farm. We would eat them scrambled, hard boiled, or fried. We didn't eat runny yolks around here. We would serve the eggs with homemade breakfast sausage whether it was black pudding sausage, fresh pork country links from Piggly Wiggly, or my personal favorite, red sausage, which was a perfect blend of chicken and pork. My grandmother taught me to cook the sausage in water, all the way through until it started to expand. Once it was fully cooked, then you would put it on a cast iron skillet. You would hear the sizzle. That hot searing sound. You would see the char start to form on the meat. It became the best version of a hot dog you could ever want.

Underneath it all was the foundation to absorb all of that char and smoke—breakfast rice. This was one of the recipes that was passed down from my grandmother's grandmother, Little Ma. Breakfast rice wasn't fancy. It wasn't plated with garnish or drizzled with anything. It was rice from the night before, brought back to life with water, butter, and patience. Stirred low and slow until it transformed from leftovers into something warm, thick, and familiar. We'd pile it next to the eggs and sausage, soaking it all in, like a sponge for flavor and feeling.

That bowl was love, it represented survival. It was tradition to pass through a pot instead of a lecture. And it taught me something that stuck with me: the best food doesn't come from a recipe—it comes from resourcefulness, memory, and intention. That's why, in our family, rice held the morning table more often than grits.

Grits might be the Southern cliché, but breakfast rice was the heartbeat of our mornings, quiet, filling, and soaked in flavor and history. But breakfast rice doesn't whisper—it remembers. It remembers using what you had. It remembers kitchens with no recipes, just rhythm. This all became sacred, staples passed down through generations. In our case, 5 generations. From Little Ma, to Mother Bell, to Bootjack, to my mother Valerie, to me Sakari.

Now Bootjack was a nickname for my grandmother. Bootjack. Feels gritty, grounded, and blue-collar with soul. It sounds like a person that doesn't ask for attention but commands respect. As I got older this mentality and homage to my grandmother, became part of how I manage my co-workers and fellow cooks in the kitchen. I learned to command respect without instilling fear.

In the kitchen, my grandma was open to my ideas even if they were odd. An omelet with more cheese than eggs or my decision to churn ice cream to make a homemade version. These memories later became the foundation for the stories that helped me get onto Food Network's Chopped.

When my grandmother wasn't watching me it was my Aunt Mavis, my grandfather's sister. One thing our Aunt Mavis made sure of was that my grandmother knew how to cook Caribbean food. She said, "If you're going to be cooking for my brother you need to know how to make curry, oxtail, and rice and peas." My grandfather, a Jamaican immigrant who became a welder in New York City.

For dinner, we wouldn't always have southern meals like our breakfast, we would also have Caribbean meals. I would spend hours learning how to devein shrimp, removing the dark colored membrane, and rinsing the shrimp thoroughly. This became the first foundation or first step for my grandmother's curry shrimp. We would also have Jamaican Bammy. Bammy is a traditional Jamaican flatbread made from grated cassava (yuca), soaked in coconut milk and typically fried or toasted. It originates from the Arawak and Taino peoples, the Indigenous communities of Jamaica, and has remained a staple in Jamaican cuisine for generations. Now typically, it wouldn't be served with molasses, but because my grandmother is from the South, it became the perfect dipping sauce or companion to this light crispy delicious flatbread. We would take the homemade molasses that was made from the sugar canes on Mother Bell's farm and we would pair it with this flatbread and it became the perfect sweet and salty snack.

Now, as adventurous as I might seem today, back then the only things I truly loved were chicken and seafood. If it wasn't one of those, I probably wouldn't touch it. I was also sensitive to spice, so my grandmother made sure to hold back on the Scotch bonnet—that fiery little pepper that gives Caribbean curry its signature kick.

Grown throughout Jamaica and the West Indies, Scotch bonnet isn't just hot—it's floral, fruity, and sacred. A single pepper can change a dish. A single pepper can remind you where you're from. My grandmother always made sure we said grace before every meal. On the table, there was always Pickapeppa sauce—a kind of Caribbean A1 made with sugar cane, molasses, vinegar, and mango. It was bright and bold, and it made everything taste more alive. Next to that, we had fish and meat sauce—a cousin of Pickapeppa, but even more versatile. And of course, there was the Scotch bonnet hot sauce. I never touched that one, it was too intense. Instead, I'd drown everything in Pickapeppa or fish and meat sauce—thick, tangy, and rich with memory. I copied my grandfather, who poured sauce over everything—maybe because the food didn't taste like home without it.

I didn't know it at the time, but I was learning something bigger: Flavor isn't just taste, it's memory. It's identity. It's where you're from. We'd hold hands at the table, my grandmother leading grace in a calm, steady voice. Then I'd dig in. There was never a shortage of food in her house, seconds and thirds were expected, not requested. But that night, the curry chicken tasted different. It was fall-apart tender, rich, almost earthy. At the time, I didn't even know what "gamey" meant, but whatever this was, it had me scraping the plate and going back again. By the time my grandfather and I were nearly licking the pot clean, I turned to my grandmother, wide-eyed and full.

"That was the best curry chicken I ever had," I said.

She smiled and tilted her head like she'd been waiting for it.

"Oh yeah, Kari? That wasn't chicken. That was curry goat."

My jaw dropped. Goat? From Aunt Volvonia's farm?

The same aunt who lived nearby with a yard full of roaming chickens, goats, and lambs? I froze, stunned. But more than anything, I was curious. If this was goat, what else had I written off too soon? I was a little mad she hadn't told me sooner. But looking back, I get it. She wasn't just feeding me. She was teaching me. To stay open and challenge my taste. To trust that something unfamiliar, might be exactly what I needed.

She always used to tell me that travel was the best education. She took me to islands like St. Martin, St. Lucia, Dominica when I was just a kid. I don't remember the beaches, or the flights, we just have the photos. But I remember the flavors. And that goat unlocked something. That one plate taught me more than any passport stamp could.

Later, I found out Aunt Volvonia wasn't just a farmer—she made legendary candied pickles. Thick-cut, sweet and fresh. You could throw them on anything—hot dogs, chicken salad, burgers, egg salad—and they'd elevate it. They were the kind of pickles that stayed with you. So when she passed, I made sure we held onto the recipe. Some flavors are worth keeping alive.

CHAPTER 2: COMING OF AGE

*R*esilience isn't born, it's built. I was never the strongest, not even close. When I joined the track team, I wasn't there to run sprints or rack up medals. I was a shot putter, short, stocky, and totally unqualified by most standards. Some thought I was just looking for an easy gym credit, but I wasn't there for a grade, I was there for a shift.

Shot put is one of those events people overlook. You're not the main event, you're the side act, but even as a thrower, you're expected to condition like everyone else. This meant laps, drills and weight room. My legs would burn, lungs on fire, sweat pouring down my back. I'd finish dead last every time.

Still, I came back, everyday. One practice I'll never forget was a Saturday. I had just wrapped up a weight room session. In the shot put, I was still throwing the same distance. My coach noticed too but he didn't say much. My dad was running late. I was the last kid on campus and my coach couldn't leave until every student was picked up. "Smithwick, let's go, where are we?" he paced. Eventually, my dad finally pulled in and picked me up.

The next morning I came in expecting a normal practice. I stepped into the gym and didn't even get to drop my bag before Coach turned and yelled "Smithwick, dammit!" It wasn't just about me being late, his dog had made a mess of his backseat, which he had to clean because he had waited for me to get picked up by my dad the previous day before.

"You're not throwing shot put anymore. You're running with them. Today, and from now on. You don't like it? Quit."

I was the heaviest boy on the team, not built for speed, not dressed to sprint. That practice was a warzone. Sprint after sprint, my lungs burned and begged for mercy. Every time I felt like giving up, I'd hear it again in my head.

"Smithwick, dammit!"

IT WAS NOT RIDICULE, it was the sound of someone refusing to let me coast.

My coach didn't just change my workout that day, he changed my mindset. I don't know what it was, shame, pride, adrenaline, but I started running better. The team started clapping as I crossed the finish line, barely standing. I didn't feel broken, I felt seen. That shout, "Smithwick, dammit!", became a mantra. Every time I wanted to quit a shift or a competition, I heard it.

They say school is supposed to be the best time of your life. For me, it was survival. If you've ever watched the movie "Mean Girls", you know that line: "You can't sit with us." That was real and that was lunchroom life. When you grow up being different, you learn real quick that "us" never includes "you."

I went to a predominantly White school in Long Island. My parents moved out there in search of a better life. Safer, quieter, cleaner. I was always "too something". Too Black for some, not Black enough for others. I existed in a void, floating between the lines, never really landing, never blending. So I found pockets of people. Misfits like me, but even those friendships came with a side of teasing that cut deeper than even I knew. Therefore food was my safe place. The place I felt love without conditions, but love came with a price. I was short, stocky, and heavy. But with shoes, I was fly. My dad represented that Harlem fresh fit and I inherited that.

My favorite movie growing up was Willy Wonka and the Chocolate Factory, but all I heard walking through the halls was: "Oompa Loompa doopity dee..." That stuck, because it wasn't just about weight, it was being made fun of from someone who looked like me. That hurt the most.

So Senior year, I trained. I put in the work every day: cardio, weights, and track practice. The goal was to have a six-pack by senior cut day and I did. Senior cut day came and it rained. I ripped off my shirt proudly and with confidence. That moment wasn't for anyone but for me, and being proud of myself. School breaks you, then builds you, and breaks you again. It is in those moments that matter, when you choose to show up for yourself, that is the "Golden Ticket."

I survived high school. I wasn't a great student, I wasn't even a good one, but I found my loophole through choosing an elective. That elective was "Foods" and that was where I met Ms. Hecht. She tried to figure me out the moment I walked through the door. Her demeanor was cold and stoic and I matched it, until one day, everything shifted. I was sautéing vegetables, nothing major, flipping the pan simply doing a move that I had seen my family do often. Ms. Hecht locked eyes with me and asked if I had cooked before. Completely uninterested, I continued cooking until I responded that I did. She had told me that I was a natural at cooking. For that moment, again in my life, everything changed.

Then came the parfait competition. The assignment was to take leftovers from the fridge and make a parfait. It helped that I was working at McDonald's at the time making parfaits on a regular basis. I knew how to finesse one and our team won. When the last week of school came, Ms. Hecht recommended me for Advanced Cooking. That was the first time I remember making a real-life decision, choosing a new lane. If Ms. Hecht hadn't recommended me for advanced cooking, who knows where I would've ended up? That class set me up for college and gave me a foundation, it gave me confidence.

In Senior year, my Advanced Cooking Class Teacher, Mrs. Akeson was everything you'd want in a teacher. She was smart and generous. She taught us how to break down a chicken, how to make a mother sauce, and to develop the proper recipes: Béchamel, vinaigrettes, breads, and salads. The game-changer? Her mom's sweet potato pie recipe. I still use a version of it to this day, but rooted in what she taught me.

During career day, the room was filled with white coats and chefs talking about culinary school. That's when I decided to go to SUNY Delhi. Not just to survive, but to try to find something I might actually love.

CHAPTER 3: FROM MCDONALD'S TO MICHELIN STARS

My mom and I had a deal. If I'm being real, it was more like law. If I didn't have a job, I had to go down South every summer. My mom grew up that way and she decided I would too. At first, I didn't mind, but by the time I got to high school, I had track teammates, friends, and a life I didn't want to leave behind. If I wanted to stay home, I needed a job. But no matter how many interviews I went on, I'd hit the same wall.

I was "too" young. Turns out, nobody wanted to hire a fifteen-year-old. No one, except McDonald's. I saw a commercial for National Hiring Day and I'd heard they hired people as young as fourteen. When I told my mom I wanted to apply, my parents suited me up. They grabbed one of my church suits, cleaned it, pressed it, and put me in it like I was about to run the company. I walked into McDonald's, sat down for my first interview with Tony, the hiring manager, and he gave me this strange look. "You're hired." "Really?" I asked. "You're the only person who's ever shown up in a suit," Tony said.

McDonald's became more than a job. Training started at the front counter. Orders, upselling, and always smiling. My trainer Steven was strict. He drilled execution and consistency into me, lessons I didn't know I'd carry for the rest of my life. The real turning point came in the back kitchen. The grill lit me up. The rhythm, the creativity, even making nuggets and wraps. I'd experiment. Turning snack wraps into quesadillas and eating fries straight from the fryer. I saw how tiny details, like cooking nuggets fresh, could completely change the flavor.

My General Manager Sarah taught me how to be fast and efficient. Her movements were graceful but minimal. Every small step had purpose. Burgers flew off her station with half the effort. It showed me that skill wasn't just about speed, it was about flow. At this moment, I decided to build a future at McDonald's, perhaps even become a franchise owner.

When I told my manager about college, they advised me to stay at McDonald's and become a manager. Why would anyone discourage me from an education? It felt wrong, that's when I knew I had to go to college.

I packed up for SUNY Delhi, in the Catskill Mountains. Truth is, I picked Delhi because of the McDonald's next door, but I think God had placed me there for another reason. A student named Diane had told me I was actually in one of the best culinary programs. Our Hot Foods team just won a championship. When classes started, I noticed I had an edge. I had already learned concepts from my advanced cooking class in high school. Still in the other subjects, I tanked. Math, accounting, and history, my GPA sank to a 1.9. Only a point away from being kicked out.

When I spoke to my mom on the phone, she yelled, asking me if I wanted to come home. I declined and promised I'd figure a way to stay in school. In October, on my birthday, I went to a roller-skating party where the Lambda Alpha Upsilon fraternity was handing out flyers. As I headed out, one of them slipped a flyer into my hand. And the more I learned about them, the more I realized I wanted to join. Their requirements was to hold a 2.5 GPA, the highest requirement for an organization on campus. Mine was still at 1.9. But I wasn't shut out, I was mentored by my brothers. They helped me focus during the week and have fun on the weekends.

Around the same time, I joined the Escoffier Club. One of the biggest rewards was paying for club members to experience food at a fine-dining restaurant. I'll never forget that trip to Lincoln Center. At Lincoln Ristorante, run by Chef Jonathan Benno, who was fresh out of Per Se, felt like stepping into another universe. At the time I thought Red Lobster and The Cheesecake Factory were the pinnacle of fine dining.

The first dish was a strawberry, balsamic, and mozzarella salad with arugula. Course after course blew my mind and every plate was art. It was unforgettable. On the ride back to campus, through the mountains, I realized this is what I want to do. I pulled my GPA from a 1.9 to a 3.3. I pledged Lambda Alpha Upsilon and crossed into the brotherhood.

I set my eyes on the Hot Foods team with a mission to become the best of the best. I was ready to compete!

CHAPTER 4: GOING FOR GOLD

Two years of college under my belt, I had McDonald's experience on my résumé and enough confidence to fill a stadium. I walked into my advanced competition class like I owned the place. The coach took one look at my station and walked out. When he came back, he didn't even look at me, simply turned to my partner Mark Garcia and said, "Mark, show him how it's done." That's when I realized I didn't know shit about real cooking. It was a moment that stuck with me longer than I wanted it to. Walking out of class that day affected me greatly. I had to make a choice that would define everything. After finishing my associates, I had three options staring me in the face: Go work, transfer to another school, or stay at Delhi and get my Bachelor's.

My advisor James told me to keep it at and not to consider going to another school. He told me that I was talented and that he'd give all the guidance and support to become successful. I could have taken the easy way out. Finish my two-year program and go straight to work. Instead, I chose to trust the process.

The Hot Foods Team walked around campus in their green jackets, looking like varsity athletes. Knife bags slung over their shoulders. These weren't just students, they were the elite chefs, Delhi's best and

I wanted to join. But wanting something and deserving it are two completely different things. That lesson hit me hard taking that advanced competition class. I could cook but did I cook well?

I partnered with Mark, fully expecting to lead while he assisted me. We were making curry, something I'd made a thousand times with my grandmother. The coach watched me fumble through my mise en place. After the coach had returned and asked Mark to direct me, I learned a lot. Mise en place means "everything in its place". Clean stations. Sharp knives. Measured ingredients. Mark became my instructor. How to fold a towel properly and measure ingredients with precision. How to stay organized and clean as you go. All the details I never thought about, details that separated amateurs from professionals. Our first competition was a cold food platter. We had to set gelatin, create pâtés, and show off classical French knife cuts. I made pâtés with a Caribbean flavor, seasoned with turmeric. We walked away with the bronze medal. My parents came to watch that day and for the first time since high school chorus, I saw a look of pride in their eyes. They were finally getting it. This wasn't just cooking, this was a craft that I loved.

The real test came when Hot Foods Team tryouts rolled around. The doors closed at exactly 4:55am on Saturday morning, I showed up five minutes earlier, knife bag in hand, determined to prove myself. First assignment, break down a chicken, execute knife cuts. I made the team, as an alternate. My ego took a hit. Alternate meant I held trays, prepared mise en place for the starters and learned everyone's position in case someone got sick. I practiced every chance I got. Tourné cuts, seven equal sides, with potatoes. Fluting mushrooms into perfect caps. I bought my own Shun knife and learned to sharpen it myself.

That's when Marc Anthony Bynum changed my life. Three-time TV's Chopped champion and a fellow Long Island native. A Black chef making moves in the same neighborhood where I grew up. I visited his restaurant Hush, in which the motto was "Let the food speak". It was the best meal I'd ever tasted on Long Island. Yellow and red watermelon with feta, balsamic, and basil. Duck. Chicken. And a cornbread that spoke to my soul.

The next day, I drove back to Hush. I walked straight into Marc's kitchen before service started and told him I wanted to learn and will work for free. The entire kitchen went silent. He pulled me aside and said come work whenever you're free. He needed R&D on some new recipes. Two days later, I was cutting tomatoes at the James Beard Awards in the Hamptons. Jeffrey Zakarian landing in a helicopter. Chef JJ Johnson was hosting. And I met Chef Carla Hall who shared her story and encouraged me to never give up.

When I returned to SUNY Delhi, I felt different. Rejuvenated and hungry. Coach Victor announced something that I almost walked away from.

The announcement was for the first time, SUNY Delhi would compete internationally representing Team USA at the Culinary Olympics in Costa Rica. I almost did not try out, having been Student Chef of the Year has already made me feel that I'd proven enough. But I tried out anyway and made the team. Team USA is going for gold.

Standing there in my Team USA jacket, I realized something: the journey from McDonald's to real competition wasn't about natural talent. It was about choosing growth over comfort, mentorship over ego. Progression over outcome. The work was the prize.

CHAPTER 5: COSTA RICA GOLD

My teammates were Paris, Tom, and Oboseoye as our alternate, Alex as an assistant. The most important thing isn't individual skill, it's chemistry. We had to spend hours together, figuring out who would create each dish. We practiced every weekend and I wanted to win the gold.

We created a shrimp roulade recipe, Southern inspired, paired with technique and elegance. Seafood was the perfect choice and something I loved. We placed the shrimp on top of a corn sponge cake, the cake was light and pillowy. Then came the Newburg sauce, a classic seafood sauce, paired with a corn succotash mixed with clams and vegetables.

For me, it was the perfect dish to represent my Southern roots and my Long Island upbringing having been surrounded by water. We were ready and packed our bags for Costa Rica. I'd never been to Costa Rica before. I'd brushed up a little on Spanish and knew a few words here and there.

Whenever I travel, food is the priority. That's when I had my first experience at Pollo Campero, a fast food place. It was some of the best fried chicken I'd ever had. With my teammates, we stayed up all night before the competition, glazing vegetables and getting our cold food platter ready. Tom and Paris, perfected the cold platter first course. When it was my turn, I went through my preparations, cutting, slicing, and steaming. I got my mousseline ready, set up my sponge cakes, and placed my perfectly sliced roulade on the plate. I was proud.

We started chanting, "Team USA! Team USA!", with pride. Now dessert, it was Paris' time. Dessert is like science, you can't just taste and adjust. But this was his wheelhouse. He finished his canal with grape sorbet, peanut butter crumble, chocolate cake and fresh fruits. It looked amazing. This was definitely the highest level of competition for us.

The awards ceremony began. They called each team: top ten, top nine, top eight and so forth. You don't want your name called until the very end, because if it's called early, you didn't win first place, or for us, the gold medal.

They called second place. It wasn't us. And then they said, "Team USA, you have won gold." Just like that a near perfect score, only missing two points. We got our gold medal. I couldn't believe that we came all the way to Costa Rica and returned home as champions. The first team from our school to ever do it. My culinary journey was just starting.

It was time to work in New York City, the best city in the world.

CHAPTER 6: FOR THE LOVE OF SEAFOOD

Growing up on Long Island, surrounded by water, the Atlantic Ocean to the south and the Long Island Sound to the north. There was Oyster Bay, The Great South Bay, and the Peconic Bay. Water was everywhere. My parents would drive out to Montauk Point on weekends and hit the docks when the boats came in. Local fluke, striped bass, and scallops were so fresh they were still moving. Something about seafood spoke to me. Maybe it was growing up surrounded by all that water or maybe it was the way my grandfather would crack open blue crabs on the newspaper and spread them across the kitchen table.

Lobster became our celebration food. Birthdays, graduations or any excuse to make it special. My mom had this way of cooking it, steamed with Old Bay, served with clarified butter and fresh corn. So when I was looking at the best restaurants in New York City, I knew I wanted to work somewhere that specialized in seafood. There were some serious options. Per Se with three Michelin stars by the legendary Chef, Thomas Keller. The Modern with two stars. And the highly reputable Eleven Madison Park with three stars, rated the best restaurant in North America at the time.

I had my teachers reach out everywhere and heard nothing back. I couldn't get an interview to *stage*, which is an internship or apprenticeship, either from Per Se, Eleven Madison Park, Jean-Georges, or Le Bernardin. No one wanted a culinary arts student with no real experience. What I decided to do, was to go eat at these restaurants to get a sense of where I wanted to work.

With the recommendation of Alexis, an SUNY Delhi alumni, I was able to stage at The Modern. I recognized Chef Tom Allan from the young mentor competitions, he now ran the kitchen. Chef Abram, who came from Eleven Madison Park, was the executive chef. The Modern, was a two Michelin star restaurant inside the Museum of Modern Art.

When I walked in with my knife bag, everyone kept referring to me as "Alexis's friend." She was a beast in the kitchen, who worked hard and earned respect. I put my head down, picked herbs, and cut vegetables. I did whatever I could. Chef Tom dropped a piece of fish in front of me and told me to prepare it however I liked. I was actually making a meal for this chef. I made a simple pan sauce, grabbed some vegetables from the walk-in and did the best I could. "Delicious", said Chef, "This is great." He pulled me into his office to tell me my flavors are great and offered me a position. I told Tom that my dream restaurant was to work at Eleven Madison Park, which he understood, having worked there. He replied if I work here, he'd help me get in there.

There was another two Michelin star restaurant I'd eaten at called Marea, it was Italian. Specifically, Italian seafood. I called up my friend Jakari, who I met in college, to join me to go back for dinner. We were greeted by a woman with a distinct African accent whose name was Darnell. She was gracious and attentive. We told her we were culinary arts students and she inquired if I wanted to work here. As we both indulged in their famous fusilli pasta she returned back with the Chef's email. Little did I know that years later, she'd be named the general manager of New York City's best restaurant in 2025, Tatiana, by Chef Kwame Onwuachi. Life, as I learned, was about building relationships.

After emailing a few times, I finally got a call back with an invitation to come in for a trial. Marea was the complete opposite of The Modern, they had two different aesthetics. Upstairs had a beautiful kitchen run by Chef Lauren DeStefano. She was firm and required the best. I watched her and Chef Gadbaw, the chef de cuisine, work together to put out the most amazing, beautiful, delicious seafood. They let me sit back and watch service after prepping all day. They had me cut chives, do knife work, but they didn't make me cook nor clean up at the end of the night.

"Sakari, we would love to have you." I now had a choice between two Michelin star restaurants. French brigade at The Modern with a young chef pushing hard, or this gem of an Italian restaurant with one of the best Italian chefs in North America. The choice? I decided to go with Marea.

And just like that, I started my culinary journey, commuting from Long Island every day to the city to work at Marea. I worked my way through garde manger, the crudo station, and even the risotto station. This was production. This was a factory. This is what it took to get two Michelin stars. Tony the butcher who'd been cutting fish for ten years, used to work for Daniel Boulud. Pastas were made like a machine by a full pasta-making team every morning. I failed and failed again, not knowing anything about making fresh pastas or sauces. I didn't understand service flow, how tickets worked, or how to set up each order. I just knew I was passionate and wanted to cook.

I burned myself every single day for the first few weeks. I made family meals when I could, bringing Caribbean classics like carrot juice, mac and cheese, and cornbread. A fellow Black chef, Daryl focused on hot appetizers. He taught me by being stern and didn't hand-hold in the kitchen, we were doing 400 covers a night. He showed me how to position my body and stand up straight. "Sakari, you have to sing a song in your head. Whatever your favorite song is, sing the beat. Having that beat in your head can create that flow during service." Cooking is like dancing, you have to create a flow. I'd cook whole Branzino, throw them on the hot line, put them in, salt-baked crust with egg whites, rosemary, oregano, and lemons. Push them in the oven and burn my right arm every time. But I still had a flow and I still have those burns.

I learned an incredible amount from the chefs on the team. Greg, who was White had an ease for Japanese cuisine and had the sharpest knives in the kitchen, which he used intricately to slice fish. Morrow-san, a talented chef, was a sushi master who came from Japan to learn pasta because he loved Italian food. Morrow-san taught me how to break down fish and avoid bursting the liver using the sharpest knives in the kitchen. For him, breaking down fish was boring because wanted to learn pasta. And so did I. Everybody wanted to learn pasta, that was the position. That is what the restaurant was known for.

I SAT down with Chef Jared Gadbaw to ask if I could work pasta, the hardest and busiest station in the restaurant. He laughed and told me that if I couldn't cook fish properly, how could I cook pasta? Pasta had two people, one running the board and tickets and dropping pasta, while the other worked sauces. I was not doing anything wrong, but I simply needed more experience. That was my first taste of needing patience. I had a good work ethic, good attitude, and progressively got better.

Another Chef from Cuba, Mikel, was another young cook, from the French Laundry. He could run circles around all of us. He took me under wing, shared insights about José Andrés, and Brooklyn Fare, which was a gourmet grocery store and market. He opened my mind to fine dining culture and told me which books to read and which chefs to learn about.

On my off days, I'd come in and work pasta with Mark, another mentor, and learn how to butcher with Tony. I took all the skills I'd learned and applied them. Working on those days, I'd learn step by step what I couldn't learn during the high-speed service when 400 guests would come in. The head chef saw my eagerness and eventually I was working at the pasta station.

Working pasta at Marea, surrounded by all that beautiful seafood, reminded me why I'd fallen in love with seafood in the first place. It wasn't just about technique or prestige, it was about that connection to the water and to those early mornings on those Long Island docks. But there was drama creating ripples in the kitchen. Another seasoned cook, Rafa, got promoted to sous chef. We didn't get along. The lesson, never sh!t where you eat. Rafa and I were dating the same girl at different times. He didn't like that at all. It spread through the entire restaurant. I felt uneasy working there and him being my sous chef made it worse. I'd give him my plates and he'd send them back every single time. He did it so much I started taking it personal. Maybe it was personal in the beginning or maybe he wanted me to produce the best. He wouldn't talk to me, wouldn't shake my hand. He'd play pranks, put vinegar in my oil bottles, salt so they wouldn't pour, and he changed the temperatures of the oven. I learned the lesson, I messed up. Personal relationships got involved with the professional ones. Eventually I got frustrated and thought it's best that I go. Where do I go next?

Daniel Humm, owner of Eleven Madison Park, decided to come into the restaurant one day. I talked to one of the servers and asked if they'd tell the chef I want to come work for him. I'll do anything. The server refused and said he'd lose his job. After being there about a year and change, I sat down with Chef Gadbaw. I asked again to be considered to work at Eleven Madison Park. Still, with more experience needed, the Chef asked me to reconsider and told me I still had more to learn. At the same time, I got an inquiry about a television show called Chopped. I was familiar with the show but why would they choose a 21 year old cook? I decided to apply while figuring out my next moves. I told them the story of making ice cream with my grandmother. They were looking for a butcher, so I said I could. I mean I kinda could, did it on my off days and sliced fish. I made it to the next round and they loved my personality. As I talked about my love for making ice cream, I got a call back. You've been confirmed and will appear on Chopped."

Just like that, a young cook from Marea, not an executive chef like the other contestants, was going to participate on one of the biggest TV platforms in cooking. The Chopped team came in and filmed me.

I put on a proper chef coat and we sat outside Marea with cameras rolling, walked through Central Park, sharing my story. This was my big break.

Filming took a long time and I still needed to figure out where I was working next. I wondered again how to work at Eleven Madison Park? I decided to just walk in. I walked in, resume in hand. Found the back entrance somehow and was let in by a security guard. All I heard was "Oui, Chef!" and big shouts. I found the closest chef and introduced myself. I had said that I work at Marea and handed in my resume. I mentioned I had worked for Chef Marc Anthony Bynum and this is where I want to work. Although I was told I'd receive a call, no call ever came. Back to square one.

I decided to go on Instagram and followed every single person that worked at Eleven Madison Park. Cook, dishwasher, and followed the entire executive team. They all received a direct message, introducing myself and where I worked. Hoping to make a connection, I sent the same message to a Chef, who also worked there, named Vincenzo "Vinny" Loseto. Vinny went on to do amazing things, Top Chef, worked in California with Chef Phil Tessier as a CDC, or Chef de Cuisine for a Michelin star restaurant. But at this moment, we were both just aspiring chefs. He was from Massapequa, Long Island and I, from Farmingdale. Neighboring towns and track team rivals. Realizing we had all of this in common, his kindness was encouraging and gave me the email of Chef Brian Lockwood, who at the time was the sous chef at Eleven Madison Park and went on eventually to become the CDC at The NoMad.

I contacted him and received a response. He called me in. I was asked to score and cut eggplant, hit it with salt to reduce the texture, and other small jobs in the kitchen. Lockwood liked me since the moment I came in. Spots were filled for Eleven Madison but I asked to keep calling. To keep trying.

At the time, Eleven Madison Park had just become the best restaurant in North America. With renovations in the Summer, they needed people to reopen the restaurant from scratch. I never stopped calling and finally got the green light to come in. I gave my two weeks to

Marea and made my way to Eleven Madison Park. I actually didn't take a break between jobs. My dream had come true. There was this sense of anxiety, trying to learn the difference between two and three Michelin stars restaurants or the difference between Italian food and French food. All I knew was that my new journey at the world's best restaurant was about to begin.

CHAPTER 7: TEAM ICE CREAM

I had watched Chopped on TV many times, but it's different when you're actually going to compete on it. It just so happened that my appearance was scheduled on my second official day of the opening of Eleven Madison Park. I had been training for the past two weeks, getting the restaurant in order as a commis, a junior chef, and learned about the culture and understanding of different phrases in the kitchen like "Oui Chef!"

By the time I entered the Food Network studio to film Chopped, I was only 21, the youngest competitor there. The night before, I was able to see an old friend who was a pastry chef at Marea. We stayed up late to practice the "mystery basket ingredients", which as you may or may not know, are the surprise ingredients you have to cook with on Chopped. We went through random ingredients and my food came out pretty good. My friend then asked me if I was going to practice making ice cream. I was confused but it was the last thing I thought that would ever be included on the show. She looked at me and shrugged her shoulders. That night, we did not practice ice cream.

The next day, I got to meet the other competitors. There were three. A young woman, 29, who was a pastry chef and owned her own restaurant in Brooklyn. Another young woman who also specialized in pastry but was also a line cook. And an older gentleman, about 40 or so, who'd been an executive chef for many years. He seemed the most seasoned. As we came out, we were greeted by the host Ted Allen and chef judges, Scott Contant, Chris Santos and Tyler Malek. I was amazed by the studio, with all the cameras and pantry items. It was exactly what I saw on TV.

As I stared at the host Ted and looked at my chef castmates, he announced, "Welcome, chefs! Welcome to Team Ice Cream episode, where every single basket will have ice cream included and you are also required to make ice cream in the final dessert round. My jaw dropped to the floor. I could not believe it. All I could do was look up at the ceiling and talk to God. What are the odds that the one thing I didn't practice, was the theme of today's episode. We opened up the baskets and the competition started.

The first basket was an ice cream burger. That's right, a burger with a scoop of ice cream between the bun and patties, covered in cornflakes. The other ingredients were a Mexican crema, canned tomato sauce, and asparagus. I decided to make a taco salad, taking the buns and cutting them up into little croutons. I transformed the patties into a taco topping and took the ice cream and made a crema. The lettuce as well as the other vegetables were made into a beautiful, warm salad. I had my dish.

As the judges tasted my dish, I was so nervous but they loved it. The flavors, crunches, and the textures all worked really well together, they exclaimed. During our first shoot break, I asked a fellow contestant what the ration for ice cream was. He refused to answer me. This was a competition. I felt a little embarrassed that I even had asked. All I knew was that I needed help. As we waited for deliberations, I listened to the other contestants as they spoke about ice cream, trying to look out for that ratio answer, but truthfully, that answer was never shared. That same gentleman who refused to help me, was the first to be eliminated. Karma, I guess.

The second round involved "Ranch" ice cream as the surprise basket ingredient. Again, I could not believe that this was the theme for the whole competition. I wish I could have seen my friend's face right now, she did warn me. I tasted the ranch ice cream and decided to make a risotto, for grain was also included in the basket. Marea was in the back of my mind. I added the "Ranch" ice cream, Parmesan cheese, with a little bit of basil and a good amount of butter. Whipped up the risotto perfectly and paired it with a beautifully cooked duck that I knew how to score the skin, and created a delicious sauce, a lesson I had learned from culinary school. The judges were stunned and very happy with the dish.

If I make it to the next round, my concern was how to make this ice cream. I should have practiced making it with my friend when I had the chance. As the result for the second round came in, one of the female contestants was eliminated. We were down to two. Me and the head pastry chef from Brooklyn. Feeling confident and energized, it was time to battle off in the final round. As we got the ingredients, one standalone that stood out was the horseradish. I got my milk, cream and eggs, and tried to figure out my ratio. I took the fruits and compressed them with horseradish juice and decided to make a parfait, something I grew up enjoying when I worked at McDonald's. I put my ice cream in the machine and it came out liquid. My competitor's ice cream came out better. At the time, I didn't realize that I didn't put enough eggs or create the proper ice cream base or cook the eggs. Instead, I just mixed everything together. I looked over at what was a cold griddle, similar to what they use at Cold Stone and decided to use that. I took the base and spread it out on the cold griddle, took the scraper and rolled it off the best I could, and put it inside my ice cream cup. I put it in the freezer and hoped for the best. I added the other ingredients and put it in a parfait.

Not feeling great about my dessert, I awaited the verdict. As the judges tasted my ingredients, the first question they asked was: "Did you taste this? The horseradish was pretty strong. They started to give me constructive criticism on ways I could have used it better. The ice cream was set and cold, but the dish itself still didn't work. Still, I had hoped that maybe my other two rounds were strong enough to gain the win. My competitor and I were at even odds with our successful dishes, the dessert round would make it or break us. When they called out her name, she had won. I could not be mad. The judges were proud of everything I did and how I conducted myself today.

I had lost the competition, but the loss taught more than any win could have, the universe gives you exactly what you need to grow. I have to learn how to make ice cream, I have to learn how to make desserts.

CHAPTER 8: WELCOME TO THE BEST RESTAURANT IN THE WORLD

I was moments away from working at "the best restaurant in the world." Me! At the best! White shirt, black socks, black pants and clean shaven, that's what they asked me to wear for my first day at Eleven Madison Park. I was walking into a two Michelin star restaurant, striving for three, newly renovated and in preparation to reopen its doors. I knew I would learn a series of lessons working there. I had to assist with the opening of this restaurant and discover what it takes to achieve that goal.

I knew nothing about Chef Daniel Humm, his techniques or his cuisine. I only knew he was one of the best. And so here I was. Greeted by a sous chef named Colin (Wyatt), a tall gentleman who'd recently worked for Daniel Boulud for the past few years. He seemed nice but you could tell he could be stern. My first task was to remove the labeled stickers off everything. It was about getting organized while making sure there was no residue from any stickers on cutting boards, containers, and including the new supplies. This kitchen was beautiful.

Many of the incoming crew had already been there for two weeks and started forming relationships. I had just begun to get acquainted with the team. That's when I met Max and to me, we looked alike. I connected with Max not just because he was Black, but because he was determined, quiet, funny at times, and focused. I fed off everyone's energy. People put their heads down and just worked. We didn't do much cooking. Everyone at this level was a commis, basically an apprentice. I just wanted to work at a station. I didn't know at the time that it would take me over a year to get on the line. And even though I had worked at a two Michelin star restaurant previously, I had to work for it. At the same time, Netflix was filming a documentary entitled "7 Days Out", about the opening of the world's best restaurant.

At Eleven Madison Park, all the chefs had one goal in mind, to be the best and to achieve perfection. We'd go over menus and sit with the front of house staff. Will Guidara, the General Manager never wanted to call it "front of house". He wanted no separation between the back and front of the house, he wanted complete synergy. During orientation, he'd give us a field manual and discussed what joining the company would be like. I learned that the culture of the kitchen was important. It was one thing to have amazing, talented chefs from all around the world but everyone should be part of that same mindset, one band and stand behind one brand.

They broke down the measures of what makes something great. It was the four fundamentals. Is it delicious? Is it beautiful? Is it creative? And what is the intention behind it? This experience was reframing the way I learned how to cook. I had to relearn everything, from folding towels to making sure my knives were sharp. One of my first tasks as a commis was the dreaded mushroom tart. It was a potato cut out with a circular mold, then cut in half into a moon shape, scooped out, confited with butter, garlic, and thyme. Filled with a delicious chanterelle puree and topped with chanterelles with cleaned off stems, marinated in olive oil, and sliced very thinly on a mandolin.

The problem was that the chanterelles were so small they'd just rip and break. We had to create beautiful slices that were all cohesive and put on top of this potato tart. This was going to accompany a lobster dish. I sliced for hours. If I wasn't slicing mushrooms, I was picking herbs or buffing tables. Standing on my feet for hours was excruciating. As a commis, my job was to assist every single lead cook. Before each service, I had to organize our walk-ins and the dry pantry.

We had this new Molteni oven, a million dollar stove that was like the Rolls Royce for cooking. I wanted to cook with it so badly. I was approached by a sous chef named Dominique Roy, who's currently the chef de cuisine of Eleven Madison Park. He pointed an egg at me. He needed me to get to The NoMad as quickly as I could. We needed eggshells for the next course and we're right in the middle of it. I had this bizarre look on my face. Why choose me out of everyone in the kitchen? I stepped out of the kitchen angry and annoyed. All the emotions you could feel because I just wanted to cook. I walked, I did not run. I walked all the way to NoMad, got the shells, and came back. I was greeted by Chef Dom who looked pleased. "You're the man, bro, Thank you so much for getting this. And you came at the perfect time, when we needed this." At that point, my outlook changed. My whole demeanor changed.

I realized I was playing on a team, regardless of the role of MVP or who was the star shooter. This was a team sport. This was about playing your role to get to the common goal. There was a sense of morale, a sense of acceptance from that chef. One of the best things about being at Eleven Madison Park was this sense of excellence all around. Every single person was there with a purpose. I met amazing, talented chefs and cooks. My friend Julian from Germany had worked at a two Michelin star restaurant. He was super young, not even 21 yet. They used to call him "Hasselhoff" because of his nice hair. Julian was a beast and moved with such speed and precision. There were chefs from London who'd worked at Restaurant Gordon Ramsay. Chef Buddha Lo eventually went on to win two separate seasons of Top Chef and now has an amazing restaurant in New York City called Huso. I was surrounded by greatness and was just trying to keep up.

Another task as a commis was reorganizing the walk-ins after every shift. A sous chef would come check to see if it fit their standard. The walk-in had to be cleaned and maintained, especially during an intense day of service. It's so important to know exactly what you have in your restaurant. It helps with waste, where to put food, or if more produce needs to be ordered. Tomatoes were left outside the fridge to continue ripening. I remembered that from a former chef I worked with named Lauren. Never put tomatoes in the fridge.

Strawberries and blueberries were laid out on blue trays with parchment paper underneath so if one went bad, it wouldn't catch the others. Same with mushrooms to spread out with constant airflow. Floors were swept and mopped every single day. Twice a day, if not three times.

Family meal happened around four o'clock. It was the worst and best part of the day. The best because we got to eat the food, but the worst because we didn't get to eat it properly. We were so busy managing a million things that we scarfed down chicken thighs, all while thinking about our mise en place or what task was left to do. Some days we'd try not to grab food if we were in the weeds. But I still continued to work, bagging up vegetables and cleaning down stations.

I finally got my big break. I headed to garde manger, the cold line, a cool well-ventilated area where savory cold dishes are kept. Little did I know I had a rude awakening coming. It was Christmas time and I continued to hope to make the line. I met a good friend, Matt, who was from London and he was one of the most talented chefs I ever came across. He easily shifted through garde manger to hot line to lead meat cook and eventually being offered a sous chef position. Me? I thought I was about to have my big break on the garde manger line.

During Christmas, every guest was gifted upon arrival and received a decorated salad. This was my second chance to assist in prep because it was going to be the easiest time to be part of garde manger. For the shift, you'd cut your vegetables for the next day, take the vegetables already cut, blanching them, which meant adding those vegetables to boiling water and then placing them in an ice water bath to stop the cooking process. This was the preparation for the salads and potentially for the next day.

My first chance with a specific task was actually about the legendary sturgeon cheesecake. I'd watched the chefs work on it for hours. This delicious savory cheesecake was thinly sliced with smoked sturgeon. They wanted to see if I could handle it. It took me hours just to create one pinwheel. You had to slice the sturgeon into perfect circle shapes to put on top of the cheesecake. We were supposed to get 10 to 12 pinwheels for the day. I completed one, maybe two. I had done so poorly that I was sent back as commis the next day.

Just like that, I was back to square one. Reminded me of my position when I was on the track team, "Sakari, you're not going on garde manger. You're going back to commis." I had another opportunity to do knife cuts, which had to be perfect. I had a partner where she and I would cut vegetables, blanch them, then mix our salads. We'd do a play on potato salad with perfectly cut small-diced potatoes and brunoise onions. A cucumber salad with perfectly cut cucumbers. As I'd cut and cut again, I could never get it quite right. The chef would come over, look at my mise en place and yell at me to start over. It got so bad that right before service the chef was tasting our salads, looked at the knife cuts and decided not to serve it. Our entire mise en place had to be thrown out. The entire kitchen was now cutting my vegetables. As they quickly banged it out without issue, I was instructed not to cut anymore. This might have been one of the most embarrassing moments of my life.

The next day, I cut my cucumbers with a laser focus. They must be perfect. One of the chefs noticed my progress and instructed me to keep going. Finally, some recognition and a sense of hope. Problem is, when I started speeding up, my knife cuts started being off. I looked at my partner's knife cuts and saw that hers and mine were two different sizes. My choice to mix the sizes would be a decision that I'd later regret. As we were closing out for the day, the chef asked to see our knife cuts. The chef takes the cup and spreads it out across a blue sheet tray. I was doing so well before, but by Chef's expression I knew he was disappointed. It wasn't ok and I was asked to start over. "You are not going home and we are not leaving this kitchen until you have your mise en place finished," said Chef. I had the meat cook, line cooks, and all the sous chefs helping me at the commis table. I couldn't believe this happened again. Everyone was laughing because they had all been there before. Still for me, I was pissed. We finished our cuts and got ready to leave.

The next day, I had a new partner named Ahjesh from Chicago. A cool chef of Indian descent but little did I know I was going to get thrown back into the commis ring again. I had been replaced and placed in the back of the kitchen. Other chefs had to focus on the knife cuts. I felt like I was never going to leave the commis station. I was stuck taking care of sauces, the jus, and the stocks. I was approached by one of the chefs and asked to go grab something from The NoMad. Super familiar with these runs at this point. As I was about to leave, I saw a sauce reducing with a sign that said, "Do not touch." I didn't touch it and headed to The NoMad. Upon my return, I was greeted with screams and words of disappointment as to why I let the sauce burn. That same sauce with a sign that said, "Do not touch."

That sauce had burned and had to be thrown out. The Chef, who was irate, asked me why I let it burn. He lashed out with obscenities that I will never forget hearing. "If I drew a D..., would you suck it?, and he walked away. I don't think chefs spoke like that, but I'll assume his point was for me to have taken initiative to have saved the sauce. Chefs shouldn't burn things. After getting in trouble, the solution at this point was for me to be sent upstairs to the private dining room. The kitchen upstairs moved at a slower-paced. I was in charge of parties of 10, 15, 20 and I wasn't happy about it. I felt like I was losing on all fronts.

On one specific cold day, I headed to The NoMad once again to grab something from a chef. As I entered the kitchen in my big fluffy FUBU jacket, I was greeted by a chef who said I looked like a robber. Another example of passive aggressive racism? I didn't know what to think of that and I still don't. Sometimes we deal with things that don't sit well with us but don't know how to communicate or address it. As a Black man, I used this example to showcase the importance of choosing your battles and the importance of not reacting. This was just another test. Another chance to prove that I belonged in this world where passion meets precision and my mission to set a standard and a precedence of who I was to become.

CHAPTER 9: SEARCHING FOR MY ROOTS

*A*fter two years, many seasons passed, many menu changes, my journey at Eleven Madison Park was coming to a close. I remember the day we received our third Michelin star, after the Netflix documentary "7 Days Out" Eleven Madison Park, had just been released. It was an absolutely joyous day. We were one team celebrating this major win and achievement. Still, I was ready to figure out what was next for me.

I sat down with Chef Lockwood to let him know that I was thinking of heading to Seattle to work with Chef Eduardo Jordan. At the time, Eduardo Jordan was on the rise, receiving two James Beard Awards and doing amazing things with Southern food and Thai food cuisine. He'd also worked for the French Laundry and Per Se. And anybody who worked for Chef Thomas Keller was a big deal and earned major respect in the industry. As I was telling Chef Lockwood about departing, he had this look of acceptance but disappointment. Not disappointment in me, but disappointment within himself. He apologized for not giving me enough time as he had promised. He thanked me for my hard work and told me that I was solid, like a rock and to continue to have a great attitude. Chef Lockwood then asked if I could give him one more month of work and I did.

I really wanted to learn about my roots. I wanted to cook food that I was excited about, that I could relate to. So I traveled to Seattle. I took the trip with my parents and went to the restaurant where Chef Eduardo worked. I was greeted by the sous chef who took me under his wing for that day, along with Eduardo. They gave me a full tour of the kitchen. It was a small kitchen, but you could tell everyone enjoyed working there. Eduardo had two restaurants at the time, JuneBaby and Salare. Salare was an Italian restaurant, which was elegant and JuneBaby had Southern soul and even had a bar next door. He owned this entire operation and the food was incredible. They offered me the position to come work, but they wouldn't cover any cost for travel or housing. Though it seemed like an amazing opportunity, something just didn't sit right with me fully. I wanted to keep looking.

My next stop was DC. There was a young Black chef with an emerging restaurant called Kith/Kin. I wanted to meet Chef Kwame Onwuachi and see what he was up to. I drove out to DC with my family. I was greeted by the chef de cuisine at the time, Martel Stone, who was very friendly and personable. He interviewed me, not knowing my resume or who I was. I told him I worked at Eleven Madison Park and the interview was over. "Come on in", he invited. What I didn't realize was that once you worked at Eleven Madison Park, it opened doors to many opportunities. You could literally work wherever you wanted because you'd worked at the best. Kwame had worked there in the past as well.

I entered the kitchen to see so many cooks that looked like me. It was incredible and emotional. I was greeted by a pastry chef, Paola, who was baking cakes and testing out new dishes. Little did I know she was going to create an amazing name for herself as well in the future. As I continued to *stage*, hopping in and helping where I could, Kwame came in with a piece of fish and dropped it right in front of me. Similar to that feeling when I had to cook fish for Chef Tom at The Modern. Kwame gave me one hour to cook whatever I wanted. Instantly, all my experiences started coming back about my time at Eleven Madison Park, my time on Chopped, and cooking competitions in culinary school. I grabbed whatever vegetables I could find, roasted mushrooms, made a beautiful sauce to go with the mushrooms, and cooked the fish the best way I knew how. I served the plate with time to spare.

Chef Kwame tasted it and was pleased. "It's delicious," he said to me. He then asked me to come into his dining room and we had an amazing conversation. He didn't offer me the cook position I came there for, he offered a sous chef position. Chef Kwame saw something in me that I didn't see in myself yet. He saw my potential for leadership and my ability to add value to a kitchen. But once again, something told me to continue my quest on my journey. I politely declined and headed back to New York. It was my hope to maintain that relationship with him through mentorship.

Driving back from DC, I had to figure out what was next. I remembered being at Chefs and Champagne with Marc Anthony Bynum, where I met Chef Joseph "JJ" Johnson. Chef JJ was doing some cool things at his restaurant called Henry located at LIFE hotel in New York. I wouldn't have to relocate. He created Pan-African cuisine with his own flair. I decided to give it a shot.

I was greeted by Samantha Davis-Allonce, who's now the CEO of Hot and Saucy, which has been featured on the show, "Hot Ones". She was very impressed with my resume and introduced me to the sous chef Omar Tate. Omar Tate walked out with an apron, a full beard, and shoes with that worn war room grit. He put in that work. I just came from working at Eleven Madison Park, where everything was about a spotless appearance, cleanliness, and a clean shave. So I instantly doubted anybody who didn't mirror that same image. Big mistake, because Omar was one of the most hard-working and passionate chefs that had inspired me. He was the backbone of the restaurant, working alongside Chef JJ. JJ would come in and out when needed, but he was so busy managing the property that Omar was the heartbeat of the restaurant. In partnership with Chef Sam, they both led with kindness and put out delicious food.

I'd cook right next to another line cook from Jamaica who taught me how to cook rice and peas. We'd cook things like festival and lemon pepper wings, all foods I grew up on and loved, but cooked it in a restaurant format. JJ always started all his sauces with bird's eye chili, garlic, and ginger, his Holy Trinity, that became the basis of everything he cooked. We did roasted chicken, jerk chicken with Guinness, suya beef, and braised short ribs. This food was different. It had a story and deep roots. I realized I was home.

After working at Eleven Madison Park, I wanted to learn about the roots of cooking and humble myself by cooking alongside Sheldon to learn about all Caribbean food and its flavors. I remember Omar would coach me through service because we had to be faster. I was moving with very intentional precision, not wasting a minute of time. We had to get the food out.

I had to learn how to make choices on what was okay and what was not. Things didn't have to be perfect, but they had to be delicious. That in itself was an adjustment. They operated so differently than Eleven Madison Park. At most fine dining restaurants, you have a chef de partie, a station chef, who is in charge of their mise en place and dishes. If you're the fish cook, you're in charge of everything that goes with the fish. Chef JJ was different. Cooks would come in around three o'clock and have all their mise en place mostly prepared. I wanted to learn about the essence of how to make these delicious purees, like the beautiful purple yam potato puree or these curry sauces that went with the dumplings. As much fun as it was cooking the food, deep down I wanted to learn more.

An old friend from Marea named Mikel reached out to tell me that they were looking for a chef to work alongside a chef on the Lower East Side. It was with the former chef of Brooklyn's Chef's Table, Marco Prins. Marco was Chef César Ramirez's right hand and he'd eventually leave to start his own restaurant called Ukiyo. So I decided to *stage* there with Marco before having a serious talk with Chef JJ. As I arrived in this small chef's table kitchen created by Marco, after tasting each dish, I knew this was a place for me.

He had an orange granita with fresh mandarin oranges and meringue that melted in your mouth. An oxtail and beef tongue soup that was delicious and a mushroom noodle dish where the sauce must have taken hours to cook. I tasted each course as I got to know Marco better. He knew I worked at Eleven Madison Park and worked with Mikel, and told me he'd love to have me.

I was so nervous to tell Chef JJ that I had wanted to move forward. It was one of the hardest conversations. He was not happy and wanted me to stay. He was happy with my work, my discipline, and how I maintained the kitchen. I had made the decision to leave but I was just hoping we could maintain our relationship because he was someone I respected very much. He was one of the first few chefs I saw cooking incredible food who looked like me.

Before I left, Omar stopped me. We had a common thread. He would talk to me about his dream restaurant, Honeysuckle, and I would talk to him about my dream, Noble Promise. We connected through our aspirations over what we wanted our restaurants to be like. He would educate me on Black chefs such as Patrick Clark, Edna Lewis, Jessica B. Harris, Leah Chase, names I didn't quite know yet and opened my eyes to a whole new world.

When I was leaving, he was open to continuing to work with me. Omar had worked hard to make his dream restaurant come into fruition. I never forgot his openness to mentor me if needed. I left JJ's restaurant feeling at peace and happy, especially after being exposed to our food culture of cooking. From JJ's to Kwame's to Eduardo's. I became more well-versed in my culture's cuisines than I had ever felt so before.

But I missed fine dining and the level of excellence. I missed the multi-course dinners. It was that feeling I had on my first fine-dining experience with the SUNY Delhi student Chefs. I knew the next step was to push for a Michelin star.

CHAPTER 10: CHASING THE STAR

In the midst of the streets on the Lower East Side of Manhattan, close to Chinatown, a block or two away from The Bowery, I found myself in a basement. Not just any basement, a cooking basement below which housed the chef's table. I was working with executive Chef Marco Prins. He'd opened Restaurant Ukiyo about a year prior. The outside had a red and black exterior, right next door to a notable Michelin star sushi omakase restaurant called Jewel Bako, both of whom were owned by a lawyer named Jack Lamb.

I got introduced to Marco from my friend Mikel. Mikel and I had worked together at Marea where he'd worked alongside Chef César Ramirez and Marco. Mikel would tell me stories about how Marco was one of the only three-star chefs still cooking in his kitchen. He was known as being both a team player and a coach. He'd coach his staff, but would be there right alongside them, every single day. This is very common in Europe but in some New York restaurants, it wasn't as common.

Mikel had told me that if I wanted to go back to fine dining that was the place to go. Chef Marco was someone I could learn a lot from, like how to make desserts. As soon as he said desserts, my ears perked up. I'd just lost battling it out on Chopped maybe a year ago. I knew desserts were something I really wanted to master. If he was gonna be the chef who could teach me everything from first courses to desserts, I was in.

This was different from most kitchens in New York. There was no prep person to make all your mise en place. You were going to make everything you needed for that day and you better be ready for service. The difficult part was the adjustment between Marco and me. Marco was from the Netherlands, spoke very good English but had a heavy accent. The sole common denominator between us was food. I remember Marco following me on Instagram and him telling me that he understood why I was there now. He saw that I had a deep love I had for food.

On my Instagram, everything was about food. Him and I would reminisce about us working at Eleven Madison Park at two different times. He'd tell me stories about how intense cooking with César Ramirez was and he found a home there. One of the challenges with this kitchen was that there was no gas oven or stove. We had two induction burners and an Alto-Shaam. An Alto-Shaam was the oven of ovens. It was able to steam, heat, and cook precisely to what was needed. It was an open kitchen with very limited cooking supplies, so we had to make sure every detail was ready.

We'd sear our steaks, then wrap it inside a cloth and add brown butter. This is how we'd hold our steak throughout the entire service. It was crucial to sear enough steaks perfectly for the entire service, because we couldn't just fire steaks à la minute. Dishes like oxtail and beef tongue soup were perfect for the wintertime and would be poured tableside. The same went with cauliflower soup. When it was mushroom season, beautiful morels would come in from our local purveyor. We'd clean them, cut them, and cook them with delicious brandy. We'd have this mushroom stock that would go on for hours with this incredible sense of umami.

Marco liked combining French cuisine with Japanese and other international cultural influences, which worked great because we were right next to the sushi omakese restaurant. Some days I'd go to the Jewel Bako and just watch everyone slice fish. Their knives were super sharp and the attention to detail was unlike any other. It was masterful how they broke down fish. Sometimes we'd share fish and create a crudo dish with tomatoes and basil.

Every guest that came in would have a beautiful experience. They'd leave us 4.5 or five-star reviews. As time went on, it ended up being just Marco and I. We'd have only a few covers a night sometimes, but every single guest had an amazing experience. The problem was we needed more guests. Marco would get frustrated, wanting for more people to come in. As Marco's right hand, I was okay with having little to no customers. That's only because I didn't truly understand how a business ran. Not understanding that we needed to fill these seats to make money, I quickly learned why that was so important.

It was one week where I didn't get paid that I realized how business actually ran. Jack the owner could not pay us because of how slow it had been. We still came in and prepared the best we could. Jack would take funds from the sushi restaurant just to be able to float our side. We weren't strong on social media and Jack was old school. Even though we put out great food and had two talented chefs both coming from Michelin star backgrounds, it was still difficult. We had to switch things up. The chef prepared an à la carte menu to make it more user friendly for people to come in and enjoy. À la carte made our service more difficult. It was very challenging for people to sit down and have a two-hour, seven-course meal, even though we offered affordable prices. There was a little fluctuation, but it wasn't enough.

I recently bought a new camera and spoke to Jack and Marco. I wanted to shoot some content for the social media pages. I came in with my camera and shot photos and videos for the Instagram page. One day, as I went downstairs to look for my camera to take photos of our new dish my camera had gone missing. I looked everywhere. I knew it couldn't have been Marco, but maybe it had been someone else. That type of experience makes me look over my shoulder a little bit. As I continued to work, my feelings started to change. Marco would ask me questions about payment and the differences of getting paid in America. I was frustrated. For me, being paid on time was non-negotiable. It was something we shouldn't even have to talk about. It should be expected. As I addressed Jack about our back pay, it turned into a heated argument. Once again, this left a dishonest and distasteful experience for me. As time went on, we understood that the restaurant was going to close as much as we tried to fight it.

A chef friend of Marco's came in named François. Marco's ears perked up like a deer, he was laser focused and made sure every dish would go out perfectly. François was a two Michelin star chef from the Netherlands. I had told Marco that my dream was to go to Europe. Marco, being a man of God and faith, had promised me that he would help me get there if I stuck it out with him a little longer. When François came in and had this amazing meal, Marco took time to pitch me as a chef to go work with François in the Netherlands. François, looking like someone who could have been my father, of similar complexion and possibly of Caribbean descent, looked excited. He gave me his card and invited me to come when I could. I was finally able to make the next stop of my journey, to travel to Europe.

After my camera had been stolen, I was distraught and figured we could only do our best with the Instagram page. But slowly the Instagram page suffered and we continued to focus on the food. Marco and I had a serious conversation. He saw that I was visually upset. He stopped me and told me that my happiness was important, if not, why be here? He understood the payment issues were extremely difficult and that I worked in the basement. Still, we had an opportunity here to work towards a Michelin star and we strived for it. I looked at him with this level of seriousness and amazement. We're going to go for that star.

We knew the Michelin guide was coming out and we just wanted to push through. The star was a way to change everything for us. At this point, it was just Marco and I. We continued to work hard, but still the restaurant closed. At this point, we all felt it was for the best. When Marco welcomed a new baby, I had an opportunity to take over the kitchen for that night. I was at the reins of the kitchen and I experienced what I felt like to run one on my own.

We also had amazing servers, Abe and Caitlin. Abe had the personality and knowledge of some of the best servers in NYC and Caitlin was effortlessly wonderful with our guests. They both brought this je ne sais quoi to the restaurant and strived for perfection. Again, getting a star is more than just food, it's about the team and the chemistry. We all did not want to give up. After Jack told us this was the last night at the restaurant, we all needed to figure out our next steps. For me, I was considering opening up a new restaurant, The Tavern, with another chef named Eli Kaimeh, who was a previous chef at Per Se. I looked at this opportunity to learn how to open a restaurant and get that experience I needed under my belt. Marco decided he was going to go back to Europe.

The guide came out and I received a phone call. The most exciting tone I'd ever heard in Marco's voice. We did it. Uyiko received a Michelin star. Jack had just contacted Marco, who then called me and asked us to come back. At this time, Marco was still unhappy with the hardship he faced at the restaurant and decided not to go back. I posted on Instagram and congratulated Marco on the star, but it still didn't feel right. To my surprise, Jack had decided to use this as an opportunity to run the business again. He hired a new chef that came from three Michelin stars and ran a similar playbook for food and service. It still faced difficulties and even through hiring a new chef, the restaurant would eventually close again.

Marco decided to go back to Europe with his family, back to Rotterdam. For me, I held onto his contact and decided to save up my money and get ready for my next venture. If I was going help open up this restaurant with Chef Eli, I was going to save all my money. What I learned was valuable. It was about the work itself, this pursuit for excellence, and the importance of searching for life changing experiences. I was looking to join a team I could truly learn from and that was the true reward, not chasing stars.

CHAPTER 11: OPENING A NEW RESTAURANT FROM SCRATCH

Hudson Yards was a beautiful place in New York City, some called it the new Times Square. A restaurant called WS was opening up in this location. It would be a private members only club where all the top athletes and celebrities could join. One of my former chefs I had worked with from Marea reached out to me. Chef Eli Kaimeh had taken the position for sous chef and was looking for other chefs that would be a great fit. Ukiyo had just closed and I was in need of a change. I had to save up money for my initial plan to go to Europe. Still, I was enthusiastic about the potential to open WS as it would be a great opportunity.

At this point, I decided to move back in with my parents as my lease was ending. I needed to save as much money to make the major move to Europe. I continued to commute from Long Island to NYC again. I slept on the train, worked a 12-hour shift, went home, rinse and repeat. I was dedicated to opening up this restaurant. For me, this was really reminiscent of my first Michelin star experience at Lincoln Center. If Eli's kitchen was going to be anything like the experience I had at Lincoln Center, then I knew I had to be part of this. This would be the first time I'd be working with chefs directly who had worked under Thomas Keller. Thomas Keller was arguably one of the best

American chefs in the world. If Thomas Keller mentored Eli, I'd learn a great deal. I interviewed with the chef de cuisine Michael, who looked at my resume and saw that I had worked at Marea and Eleven Madison Park. He extended the invitation to work with him. This would be my first time working in a kitchen that did not have a Michelin star.

There's always this sense of what standard is the right standard. The details were important. Orientation came fast as we learned the ins and outs of the restaurant. The sous chef team was and included those who had worked with Eli in the past at Per Se. One chef that really stood out was Max, who'd worked at French Laundry. He walked with such grace and confidence and his food was superb. Another young chef named Zane, moved at a lightning speed and always anticipated the high paced environment in the kitchen.

Another sous chef, Kelly, who now owns Radio Bakery, one of the best bakeries in New York City. Then there was Peter, another former chef from Marea. He taught me how to work the line and how music helped you focus. Peter would always give me tips like the importance of icing down our fish and changing the ice on oysters, both day and night. He'd anticipate and look at the time of each ticket and knew exactly when the next set would be fired.

Peter was a stickler for time with tickets, which challenged the other chefs. That attention to detail was a lesson I valued. We became good friends and shared many experiences about working in the kitchen. Our goal was to set up this restaurant for success. We visited the restaurant while it was still under construction, showcasing the view and learning about the owners, Stephen Ross, an investor in Hudson Yards and the Miami Dolphins. We learned all about Stephen Ross and his new adventure and the booming expectations of what Hudson Yards would be. When building a brand such as a restaurant, it was really important for everybody to be invested in this brand they intended to create.

Our first kitchen tasks were doing minimal things like making garlic oil, homemade hot sauce, or house-made pickles for the burgers. Chef Eli almost resembled a football coach. He was New York style, super down to earth with a strong build. He was always locked in and focused. They'been working on the menu with the chefs and recipe books for quite some time as they were getting ready for this project. I was very excited to work alongside Chef Eli to see what I could learn.

I learned how to pick up on the language as it was quite different from Eleven Madison Park. The culture Eli brought to the kitchen was about communication. At Eleven Madison Park, it was super quiet, but here, it was louder. I started off in garde manger and made sure the cooks around me worked well. I really wanted to work at the fish station as I didn't get so at Eleven Madison Park. This could be my opportunity to work on the hot line at the highest level. I made sure that every paycheck I got, I just put a little bit away. The real goal was going to Europe.

As I hoped to join the hot line there was some pushback. I was doing a great job as a garde manger and the chef didn't want to change pace. They spoke to me about being on the meat side as they needed a meat cook but I didn't have enough experience. I had little from working at Marea, not as much at Eleven Madison Park, and not at Ukiyo. As I deemed it important to always be transparent, they put me on fish. We did plays on American classics, like a crab cake, but instead of a crab cake, it was a "Krabby Patty." A crab mousse with scallop mousseline folded in with crab.

I'll never forget the day I cried. And no, I didn't cry from cooking, but I cried from what I had just learned. My idol, Kobe Bryant died. I was shattered. Kobe was an inspiration to me, an athlete who motivated me on my journey greatly. He was the 13th pick but worked endlessly to become one of the best players in the entire world. I never was the most talented chef, but I tried to reflect nothing less than hard work and resilience. I related to Kobe in that facet. Through putting in the work, the last could lead first someday. When it was shouted that Kobe just died from a helicopter crash, I couldn't believe it. I walked off the line into the bathroom to go through my phone. As I saw the news and the crash, I saw that it was real. I couldn't believe someone who I looked up to, who I saw on Instagram the night before had suddenly passed along with his baby girl, Gigi. I came back to the line distraught.up all the picks. My sous chef Kelly, noticed the change in my demeanor. I was quiet, head down. Her eyes twitched a little bit, but she still didn't understand how I could be so affected by a celebrity I had never met.

That was the influence of connecting with someone from afar who motivated you. Kobe had such an impact on me that I decided to get a tattoo that week, the words "Mamba Mentality" on my chest, as an honor to him. We had a big event coming up that we had to prepare for. Carmelo Anthony, another great basketball player, was also a big foodie and wine enthusiast. And the guest of honor who was also coming to dinner was the "TK". Chef Thomas Keller was coming in for dinner.

He'd be coming in and cooking alongside us for a special sponsored event. The cooks were all going to be sent home, only the sous chef team remaining, to work alongside him. We had zero room for error and this was truly important to Chef Eli, being that Thomas Keller his mentor. I decided to stay the entire time and didn't ask for permission. I was relentless in my pursuit to see and learn from the best. Chef Eli knew that I wanted to be there and allowed it to happen. It's now me, another fish cook and all the sous chefs cooking with Thomas Keller. An experience of a lifetime.

The other fish cook was searing a piece of fish, burned it and plated it anyway. At a glance, Chef Keller walked over and deliberated why the fish could not be served. I had witnessed why Thomas Keller was one of the best chefs in the world. His presence in the kitchen was unlike anything else. You could not read his expressions, he simply moved with intent. At the end of our seven-course tasting, he would go and fist bump every single chef, giving us positive feedback and telling us all that we did a great job. From then on, he would come into the restaurant and order the same thing: a confit piece of salmon, sautéed spinach, with a little bit of mustard on top of the salmon. I paid attention to as much detail as I could with TK because he resembled the perfection that young cooks wanted to achieve.

As time went on with the restaurant, I continued to save money.

While I was working, I had constantly reached out to Chef François in Europe, waiting for a reply for when the best time to travel would be. The restaurant had been open for about six months, with framed reviews from major food critics hung on the walls. I was cooking on the hot line when I was told that Peter Wells had arrived. He was the New York Times food critic, but also a reviewer that Chef Eli had a past with. Peter had written a review of Per Se, where Chef Eli had worked at. The review had affected him greatly. Chef Eli started to give all the chefs specific instructions and tasks for the kitchen. He had asked me to make this the best soup of my life. I witnessed Chef Eli go from a chef to a conductor to a coach. Dipping into each station, tasting, guiding to make sure every dish went out exactly as he'd designed. He'd ask if I tasted all my ingredients, to ensure that the food was hot, and of course, to make sure that it tasted well.

As course by course went out to Peter Wells, we felt like we were feeding the Michelin star inspector. We waited for the review to come out and it was published a few weeks later. More stars, but this time a rating as a review. We received a two star review, although we hoped for three. The most you can get is four. It wasn't a bad review and had been better received than what had been written in the past for Chef Eli's previous work at Per Se. It was a full circle moment and showed me what is required when cooking for a reviewer of a notable publication that is going to critique your food. Service and reputation is key.

I finally got the message I'd been waiting for. A response from Chef François Geurds, owner of FG in Rotterdam, Netherlands and to whom I'd met during my time at Ukiyo. FG was a two Michelin star restaurant. All I knew was that his openness was all I needed and I was told I could come to Europe and housing could possibly be provided. I was so thrilled. The only thing left was to inform Chef Eli.

Six months in business, we had just served one of the biggest food critics, Peter Wells and now I'd be leaving. It was an extremely hard decision but I had to chase my dream. I had to continue my journey. I told Chef Michael that I was giving my two weeks. In his shock, I had shared my plans to move to Europe. Again, he stared in disbelief and did not take the news well. They had given me opportunities for growth and I was preparing to leave. Chef Eli was also confused and perhaps disappointed. The energy shifted as well as how we interacted. I felt as though I did not exist in their eyes anymore.

Although it was a great experience and I had learned a great deal, I needed to go to Europe. I made the announcement I'd be leaving and a small gathering and going-away party was thrown for me. I wanted to take another opportunity to speak to Chef Eli again. I shared with him that he had been a huge influence on me. Through his teachings, advice, and the opportunities he had bestowed to me, I asked for any parting words of advice he could share with me. We sat for about an hour as he told me about his life and lessons he'd had. "Never burn bridges," he said. Treat everybody with respect and have respect for yourself, you'll never know when you'll connect with them again. I held onto that and used that as an experience.

Eli was a masterful executor. He was intentional and detailed, and I was grateful to have worked for him. As this new chapter was closing, another was soon to be written. My dreams were about to come true. Netherlands, here I come. Sometimes the best experiences are met with the hardest decisions, I was going to learn that in more ways than one.

CHAPTER 12: SETTING SAIL TO THE NETHERLANDS

I follow the motto that it's better to ask for forgiveness than permission. I waited to hear from Chef François to reconfirm that I'd be able to work at his restaurant in the Netherlands. We had such a positive conversation about it all on the phone weeks ago. So I continued to get ready and pack. Everyone around me asked if I was sure, and although I wasn't, I said "yes, absolutely". Truthfully, I didn't get an exact invite to go to the Netherlands or a confirmation as to where I'd be living. I'd heard stories of people just backpacking through Europe, so worst case scenario I could do the same.

I had a feeling that François was just busy working at FG restaurant and would get back to me about housing. I did not want to wait around in New York, so I made the hasty decision to go, not having a single plan as to where I'd live. I looked into Airbnbs or any place with residence, even a hotel. My parents had both decided to come with me. This for me, was one of the proudest and most terrifying moments of my life. Traveling had always been a love language for my parents and this was an opportunity for them to see a different part of the world. This would be our first time in Europe together. So we set sail, got on the flight, and decided to figure out the rest when we got there.

I was never fully comfortable with flying. I felt uneasy and in no control. I was fearful and the loss of Kobe and his daughter Gigi was still heavy in my heart. After eight long hours, we landed in the Netherlands. I knew that we were going to fly into Rotterdam, which was a major city pretty close to Amsterdam. My intentions were to show up at Chef François's restaurant and that is exactly what I did. As we finally found a hotel to stay in, settled in, my parents and I went on to sightsee. Still I stayed in tune with my mission to go see Chef François. I arrived at the restaurant and proceeded to greet Chef François, who met with confusion. To my fear, he had stated we had never confirmed and was shocked to see me standing in front of him. I assumed from our conversation it was a confirmation, it felt that way to me. He continued to say that we have a process for new hires, a system we follow. He had sold the house that was meant to be a chef's residence and did not have a place for me. I was faced with another challenge and a humbled lesson of what a confirmation truly was. I had the hotel secured for a few days, for four or possibly five days. After our conversation, we made a deal. If I found a place to stay in Rotterdam, he would help me retain a visa.

The energy was strange. I remembered when I was at the hotel, sharing with people my hopes that I was going to work at the restaurant with Chef François Geurds. FG was well known and had two Michelin stars, but François, on the other hand, was known for not being the most gracious man. He had a reputation that I wasn't familiar with, but held my future in his hands, so all I could do was trust this process. I had to look for a place to live, somewhere close to the restaurant and somewhere that I could afford. I had to move within the week. I looked on different apps, asked everyone that I knew around, the hotel clerks, guests, and even locals I saw in passing while I explored Rotterdam. I was stressed out. All my bags were packed as if I had a place secured. After reaching out to countless listings, I started to get some inquiries back. The problem was that most wanted me to have a bank account set up here in the Netherlands. And with that required a working visa. Almost all the available housing that I saw that was affordable or approachable needed proof of my citizenship and I did not have that.

I came across another listing close to the city center and a short bike ride away from the restaurant. I met a Dutch man who was a local taxi driver in the Netherlands. When I got dropped off, the first thing he said was how much he hated Ubers. He felt that Ubers were taking his job away. Little did I know that this nice but talkative man, who spoke limited English, would provide housing for me. He had a wife and potentially an Indonesian partner who would take care of cleaning and cooking. This was Europe and seemed like a different way of living, but it wasn't my business. I wasn't able to show him a bank account of any sort, but I was able to secure the first payment. Paired with the fact that my parents were with me, he had a good sense of my seriousness and was open to the idea of me paying in cash. This place was a two-story apartment, and I'd be on the second floor. There were renovations to be done in the bathroom, no sink or mirror. I would be using the single shower bathroom on the first floor with just enough room for me to be able to stand and clean up. I was greeted by four other roommates: an Italian, two Dutch, and one from Spain. My room was small with a twin-size bed. I looked at my mom with a look on her face of concern, disgust, and hesitance on my decision to stay here, alone. I'd be crazy to take this apartment and live with people that I didn't know. I looked around and simply said "This will be great. I'll take it." I had a place to live and my mom was able to sleep knowing I found a place too.

I took my parents shopping and ate some food later that day. My mother was so excited. We discovered that they had a Chinatown, similar to my New York Chinatown and the food was delicious. Shopping was one of my Dad's favorite things to do. He always said that you can always find clothes of great quality whenever you traveled abroad. He set out to buy a Hugo Boss jacket that was made of all leather and was super excited about it. He also bought a few souvenirs. As we took Uber to the airport, a look of sadness appeared on my parents' faces, tears coming from their eyes, knowing that I was going to be on my own. I was to face the unknown, with only myself to depend on. I hugged and kissed them both goodbye and watched them board the plane. My entire drive home to my new apartment was filled with excitement and energy as to what my next, first steps would be.

My first task living in a new country, I needed something to eat. I went down to the fridge and saw that it was stacked and packed with my other roommates' food. I looked on Facebook Marketplace and bought myself a fridge. I bought meats and hams, and other produce that I knew wouldn't spoil. I bought myself a little hot plate and acted like I was back, living in my college dormroom. I lived off of sandwiches, peanut butter and jelly, being that was my first true love, but also salamis, pickles, some condiments to make sandwiches daily. I ate sandwiches for breakfast, lunch, and dinner, but occasionally went out to experience the food of the Netherlands.

I decided to go back to the restaurant to let Chef François know that I found a place. When I met with him and to my surprise or how I interpreted it, he was shocked that I had found an apartment. It felt like he didn't want me to succeed. I met with his assistant, who didn't speak any English. She seemed very frustrated with the process of having to try to get me a visa. She would give me instructions on what to do and what paperwork needed to be submitted. Once all the paperwork was entered, we had to wait. I had asked François if I could work at FG while I waited for my visa. He was very hesitant and wouldn't allow me to work without it. I'd be a liability without the work visa and he could not afford to put his restaurant at risk. I had to wait.

Breaking news struck, COVID-19 hit. As mass craziness set out in New York, as I watched through the lens of social media, not knowing that Europe would be affected, if not worse, as well. Masks became prominent, and this plague would spread rapidly around the entire world. They stated that those in underlying conditions would be the ones most affected, along with elderly people. Unfortunately for me, my closest family members all had underlying health issues, including my grandparents. We were all instructed to stay inside, New York, Europe, the world. Restaurants began to close due to outbreaks and no one went outside. Then Chef François restaurant FG had to shut its doors.

As I biked over, I met with François one last time. I asked if there was anything I could do. My visa hadn't gone through yet but I still wanted to be of assistance. Angrily, the chef had shared that he spent thousands of dollars between my visa and the restaurant's needs and now had to close the doors. He dealt with the stress that most restaurant owners were dealing with, closing the restaurant. I was stuck in the Netherlands: no friends, no family, no job, barely any money, along with this terrifying and life-changing plague.

The only thing that was open was supermarkets, that's where I would find my meals. Deli meats mostly and an attempt to make different meals with what I had. Coming from restaurants where I spent most of my time, I had hours and hours and hours that were now free, paired with the pressures of how I was going to survive. I reached out to my former Chef, Marco who lived in Rotterdam, since moving back from New York. Although our relationship was strained, he apologized that things didn't work out with François and offered to come up with a new plan together. Perhaps a chef in Belgium, Brussels or Amsterdam would be open to give me work. Nothing could be promised of course with COVID-19 at the forefront. Still, I remained hopeful.

I was greeted by my roommate Alberto who was from Spain. He spoke broken English but we were able to communicate. As we played 2K, we started to get to know each other. We would get competitive and play video games for hours to pass the time. Eventually, he was able to go back to work, while me, on the other hand, had no luck. He introduced me to his friends: Yele, Sergey, and some others, slowly I had a small tribe of new friends. They were heavily interested in what New York had to offer, as I was interested in what the Netherlands had to offer. And so we exchanged cultures and learned from each other. Yele would teach me about coffee shops and Kapsalon, which in Dutch means "hair salon" or "barbershop". Kapaslon was a dish with fries, shawarma, vegetables, Gouda cheese, garlic and chili sauce, similar to the NY chopped cheese without the bread. Rotterdam was also famous for classic dishes like stroopwafels, kibbeling, Indonesian rijsttafel, herring and patat frites.

Essentially the go to order was the Kapsalon. It used to be the order of a person that used to cut hair right across the street, and then get some shawarma. I also got introduced to Surinamese food from Alberto, because his girlfriend was from Suriname. Suriname was right next to Guyana, which is a small little island that serves curries and a mix of Chinese. I was so amazed that Suriname had cuisine that I resonated with, like curry chicken and goat. Alberto put me onto bara bread, which is similar to how Trinidadians had fried dough, but this dough was different. It was a roll that was fried with curry and herbs and spices. The Netherlands have delicious food.

Trying to figure out my next steps while passing time, I turned to YouTube to see what I could learn. I was a visual learner and wanted to know more about running a business. Although it felt like some "Buy This!" or "Subscribe to this!" platform, I continued to research, hoping to stumble on something or someone I could connect with. That's how I came across Gary Vaynerchuk or who is better known as "GaryVee." I remember being told about Gary at a party almost a year ago. His aunt saw the way that I was working and said that I had got grit like him and should look him up. I discovered videos dating back years, The #AskGaryVee Show or the DailyVee series. I watched every single episode. He was an entrepreneur, an author, a speaker, and clearly a major internet personality. He gave helpful advice to other entrepreneurs and it was all readily available, for free. He didn't want anything in return and that connected to me.

I've always had this idea of starting my own restaurant and developing my own brand. I was going to call it Noble Promise, for Sakari in "Swahili" which means "Noble Promise". I dreamt that one day Noble Promise could be a fine dining restaurant and I'd be one of the first Black chefs to win a Michelin star. Now was the time for me to create content and start posting. People in the past had shared with me that I should have a YouTube channel and this was the perfect time to start.

The plan was set in motion. I called up a friend of mine, Kelsey, who later became a business partner of mine, he was a talented painter. He had been in charge of a fashion show while I was in college, so as an artist, I knew that he could create the perfect logo. I want to create my own logo for Noble Promise. After talking in length, he created the logo that I use to this day, an "N" locked into a "P", like the Superman "S", that'd I wear on my chest or the simplicity of the Nike swoosh. I would use this logo and what it represented on me and shown to others for the rest of my life. I started to create a plan for my cooking and I knew I needed to build a strong online presence. Through hours of research on Julia Child, Emeril Lagasse, Gordon Ramsay, Marco Pierre White, I studied. I learned the importance of charisma on camera, how to be authentic, and how to educate viewers. What I know now is inspiration, information, and demonstration. What you could demonstrate to people and instruct on how to do certain things. How to inform and inspire communities.

I remember, prior to going to Europe, I hosted a pop-up in Miami. I remember shooting what for me was going to be my first video on camera. I stayed up all night, prepping and cooking, and shot footage with my friend Michael's cameraman until three o'clock in the morning. It was my first video speaking into existence about what Noble Promise would be. I still have this video and I watch it as a reminder to see how far I've come.

If I'm going to be in Europe, it's time for me to start making videos. Malik, who was great at videography and reached out to my cousin Franklin, who was an emerging artist. I wanted him to write my theme song. The track "Cooking with Sakari," came into existence. My logo was designed, song produced, and video ideas were captured. I was running out of money and I needed to pay my team and secure a job. Luckily, at the time, stimulus checks were sent out and I was able to receive some help. I paid for my logo, my theme song, and my S-corp, all during COVID-19. Nevertheless, the money lowered, my struggle arose, and my parents were concerned.

There was this level of anxiety, not knowing what was going to happen, but I'm stubborn and giving up was not an option. Time continued to pass and a decision needed to be made. I considered going back home and after a few months, I was going to return to New York. As I decided to call my mom, I received a WhatsApp message from a former chef, Jan Sobecki, who both Marco and I had reached out to. It had been weeks and I hadn't heard anything back. The message was an invitation for me to come in and do a trail at the restaurant. A hotel would be covered. I dropped to the floor in shock that I was given another opportunity. I was on my way to a new but unknown part of the Netherlands to work.

CHAPTER 13: RESTAURANT TRIBECA (EUROPE PART 2)

I was greeted by Chef Jan who picked me up and brought me to his restaurant, Tribeca, ironically named after the New York neighborhood, which currently was across the other side of the world from me. The name reminded me of home and served as a positive reminder that a new start was ahead. I was amazed to see a private residence that also doubled as the restaurant. The chef lived upstairs with his family. It was a small team of about eight but the way that the restaurant was designed was truly beautiful. There was an open kitchen from the front, a chef's table, and then a reserved kitchen in the back for the main kitchen. We did lunch and dinner service. Not knowing what to expect, I was ready to go all in but the chef wanted to have a conversation. I've staged and trailed many times without hassle, but this was different. Chef Jan wanted to get to know me and hear my story. I told him my story of how I came here from New York with the vision to learn as much as I possibly could. I had shared my story about how I lost the ice cream episode on the American food competition Chopped and how that loss pushed my interest to learn pastry cooking.

Chef had spent some time in New York as well and worked with Chef Tom Colicchio, celebrity chef judge on Top Chef. He learned about pastas and related to me about being a foreigner in another country. I started working the day, not knowing Dutch, and struggled to communicate. I paid attention to the ticket flow coming in and watched how to anticipate every chefs' move. Even though there was a language barrier, cooking was the central language. Vegetables had to be peeled and picked, cuts needed to be done.

We started our day by heading to the garden. It was a five-minute drive, 20-minute bike ride, and where we were able to connect with the farmer directly. The farmer would tell us what's in season and we would pick our flowers and garnishes every day. The farmer would show us what was plentiful and we got some of the most beautiful products that I'd ever seen. We would then head to the restaurant and be greeted by the chef. The chef, in his shorts and a T-shirt, would come from downstairs, a towel over his shoulder, glasses on, ready to work. He would bake bread, make macarons or break down seafood that had arrived while all the other cooks and chefs collected produce.

Chef Jan introduced me as his guest and that I traveled all the way from New York. I was excited to work with them. We spoke of how many covers we had for the day, what menu we were to execute, and if any special guests were coming in. We'd do enough prep for lunch and dinner. My job as the *stage* was to help where I could fit, be it with the mise en place, pick through vegetables, peel and wash. Real entry level, but this is what I'd done for years.

After a few days of staging with the chef, he sat me down and offered me a job. He arranged to have me live at an Airbnb which was a five-minute bike ride. All I needed was to move out of my current apartment. My new housing would be covered. With a blend of all the emotions, amazement and also confusion, I looked up and was grateful that I didn't quit. I asked Marco if he could help move and he agreed without hesitation. He felt bad because the François opportunity didn't work out and we rented a truck and drove to the Heeze. It felt like it was in the middle of nowhere.

I packed up my stuff and let my landlord know that I was leaving. I said my goodbyes to everyone I met in Rotterdam and journeyed forth to another part of the Netherlands, a new place unknown. I was happy to be cooking again and surrounded by the beautiful land. Marco and I arrived at the Airbnb, I was greeted by a woman who was in charge of the house. I had my own flat fully covered by the chef. It happened to be on a farm which was very reminiscent of the time that I spent Summers with my family in North Carolina. I said farewell to Marco and thanked him for his help and support. This would have been impossible to do without him. I set up my bike that I had bought and rode it to the middle of Heeze, where I would ride into town and pass the farmland and the animals. The food that we put out at Tribeca was incredible. We had langoustines with sea beans. Lychees mixed with shrimp or other seafood. We would make a cold crudo with foam on top. Fried shiso leaf that worked as a beautiful crumble or Tempura batter to form balls to top on the fish.

Halfway through my shift, he told me to go change for a menu tasting, compliments of Chef Jan. I had a truffle and fish dish that was out of this entire world. The fish was so fresh, and the earthiness of the mushrooms worked very well with truffles. There was a perfectly cooked steak then a strawberry dessert that was accompanied by caramelized white chocolate and a sorbet that was made with leaves that were found in the garden with a lemon gel. I was so inspired to work there that I would do it for free, and I did, for a few months. I worked for free, with Chef Jan covering the cost of my flat. That was our deal. I worked on the hot line because that's where I was most comfortable and how I knew how to maneuver. I would help plate the langoustines or the duck, venison and steaks. I did whatever was needed. It was such a small kitchen and we would hop from station to station. All hands on deck to garnish, plate the first course, and then the second, third and so on. We had a pastry chef that was in charge of the macarons, ice cream and sorbets. He was an older gentleman who decided to leave after some time. That was my opportunity. This was my chance to take on the open position and learn about desserts and pastries. I wanted to earn the money and invest in myself.

I spoke to Chef Jan, sharing how grateful I was to have this opportunity. I had asked if I could be paid to cover living costs and to be able explore the countryside on my days off. He understood and started to pay me in cash. With reluctance, I asked if I could take the open role for the pastry chef position. The chef had been pleased with my work thus far with the meats and entrees, but was unsure if pastries would be the right fit. I had never done pastries before but I was eager to learn. He trained me, working both as a garde manger and then began to work on some pastries. The breakdown included making mango, passion fruit curd and chocolate spheres. We made macarons and fresh bread. We used sourdough with our starter that was already a few years old. We made donuts from scratch that were paired with vanilla bean and citrus glaze. And I finally learned the ratios for sorbets and ice cream! We used a Pacojet to be able to re-spin and have the perfect consistency for whatever we didn't use. I wrote down notes of all the recipes and all the measurements in my chef's book. I used the back of my clipboard to make a list of my labels for the day. I was extremely organized. I had taken all my experiences that I'd learned throughout the years and applied them to this new position. This restaurant was different and smaller. Our fridge would get so packed that at times, we would barely be able to get in. I learned the greatest lessons working here. You have to make the best with what you have and savor your journey in the process. Chef Jan created one of the best restaurants out of this house and with minimal resources. I was inspired by that. On my off days, I would come in and prep for my upcoming shifts. We had three days off, worked for four days because shifts were 16 hours or more for lunch and dinner, and included all the kitchen clean-up and prep for recipes. We were both the cooking and cleaning crew, which was different from New York.

As I started to make an income, I had three days off to rest and make content for my YouTube and social media pages. "Cooking with Sakari" was live and I made my first YouTube video. It took hours trying to emulate other chefs that I had seen online. After some hours and a few takes, I was able to find my groove. My first video was about razor clams, something that was very popular in the Netherlands and what we had been serving at the restaurant. At Restaurant Tribeca, we would clean the razor clams and cook them a la plancha with a little bit of lemon. I wanted to create my own clam basket using ingredients that I was learning about. I decided then, that on my days off, I would cook recipes and create content for my page.

All the tickets would come in Dutch. Service would be run in Dutch so I had to maneuver around it. During post-shift meetings, we would talk about how to improve and although I tried to learn the language, the Chef would speak in English to make me feel comfortable. I was grateful to the chef for making me feel at home in a new country.

On hectic days, I'd pick up Dutch words like "verdomme" which meant "dumbass." That'd come in handy to know for future shifts. No matter where the kitchen was, New York or the Netherlands, a head chef would expect the best out of you. I would learn that through my mistakes. I was always used to being the youngest in the kitchen. At times it could be an advantage and sometimes it wasn't. But this time, I wasn't the youngest. Fifteen and sixteen year olds would work at the best restaurants here in the Netherlands. I wished I had started that young! Lessons I'd wish I'd known when I was younger like the importance of tasting your food! At the restaurant, our strawberries had arrived but were under-ripe, they needed to be perfectly sweet for our dessert as they were supposed to be in season. I didn't taste them, so I wouldn't even know the difference.

I wasn't a cook anymore, I was a chef. Chef Jan randomly walked by to taste a strawberry. Me, not thinking anything of it, he spits it out immediately. "Sakari, did you taste this? You must taste your food. How are you supposed to know if it's good or not?" That's what he said in Dutch and walked away. I waited to hear the word "verdomme" at any moment. I felt like I let him down. Something so simple, something so basic, I mistakenly didn't think to do. When products come in, you must inspect them. I had to learn about our products. Sometimes the produce would be under-ripe or over-ripe, so I had to inspect each one.

I never made madeleines before. It was my first time and they were delicious. It was like a cornbread cake without the corn part. They were fluffy, light, and sweet, a perfect ending to most dinners.

They paired perfectly with coffee as well. The problem with madeleines is that they took time, effort, and technique. We had to brown the butter, lots of it, and we had to slowly fold that into the batter and whip it. The chef explained: "You have to whip it until you hear a helicopter motion. That's how you know that it was properly mixed. You should be able to look at the batter and it should look all cohesive, all together. My batter was all broken and didn't come together. The brown butter might have been too hot or my ratios were off. When the chef looked at the butter, he told me to put it away. I thought he meant to get rid of it and put it in the garbage. And that's exactly what I did. I put about 40 pounds of butter into the garbage. Now, if you're a chef, you know that that's very expensive butter, especially dairy products being one of the most expensive products. I did not consider the cost, I didn't ask questions or double-check, I just tossed it away. I was embarrassed that I had messed up the batter.

The next day, the chef comes in and asks for the butter. He went through the fridge and couldn't find it. I was so confused. The night before, I had "gotten rid of it", as asked, but I never assumed it meant something else. In my confusion I had told the chef that I put the butter in the garbage. He was shocked. "You put 40 pounds of butter in the garbage? You're kidding, right?" I saw his face and instantly I knew I had made a mistake. Although he wasn't specific, reflecting on it, he did not specifically say to toss it out. The chef explained that the butter could have been fixed, re-emulsified. Waste was not an option. His temper exploded and started shouting, yelling in Dutch with words that I didn't understand. Directing his attention to the sous chef, Vitale, the chef had asked how he could let me do something so carelessly. That made me feel even worse, because it was my mistake. I should have known better.

"You'll never be able to open up a restaurant if you're just going to throw away pounds of butter. Your restaurant would close." He told me straight to my face. All I could do was listen and accept this mistake. As a young chef, you need to think about how to save and utilize the products. At Eleven Madison Park, there was tons and tons of waste because we were always trying to make things perfect. And oftentimes, when something didn't work, we would toss it away. Not here. Not in a smaller restaurant like this. Every dollar and every cent mattered. As a sous chef, it is your responsibility to lead and oversee the work of others. In leadership, you have to catch the silly mistakes, even if it's done by the other chefs. Ultimately, we rectified the situation and I never threw products away without asking again.

Living and working in the Netherlands was a cultural awakening. The sous chef, Vitale, was a kind man and a good chef. He grew up in the Netherlands and had spent some time in London. Anytime he spoke in English, he would always say "mate." He was always very friendly towards me. One day, we had all been at work. I was working with my head down and all I heard was "What's up, my nigga?" I looked up as if I had just heard a screeching noise, like a loud bang. I must have imagined it. I continued to work and Vitale said it again, "What's up, my nigga?" Puzzled and shocked beyond belief, he had no sense of remorse. No level of understanding that this was a racial slur. I don't think he even knew what that word actually meant. I had to decide whether or not to address it, but as minutes passed, I couldn't let go. I pulled him outside and calmly told him he could not say that word. Like a deer in headlights, he told me he didn't mean anything by it. I was stern. "No, you don't understand. That's not a word that's okay to use." I explained to him the history and pain behind it and as a White person it will never ever be ok to say that to any person of color, specifically a Black person.

"But I hear it in all the rap songs." Now, I had been placed in a situation where I needed to choose whether to explain why the word was used in rap music. I've only heard this word used once before by my landlord. He had been talking to me and the other tenants about a movie. In this moment, he had said the words that "nigger guy", when pointing to a Black actor on the screen. When I approached him, he quickly tried to lie and continue to defend the he had said "negro". I heard loud and clear exactly what he had said. It didn't matter, I was highly offended and like explaining to Vitale, I had warned my landlord not to say it again. This was one of a series of racial instances where I had experienced a major culture shock in the Netherlands.

My craziest encounter was with a colleague named Felix. Felix was a chef but worked on the construction of the restaurant. Heeze was a small town in the Dutch province of North Brabant. I was one of the only few African Americans for sure, within a hundred miles. It wasn't common to see a Black person in town. Felix and I would work alongside each other sometimes. He was usually quiet but on this specific day he had a lot to say. As I prepared to start the day and begin to peel vegetables I overheard him share his thoughts about Black people. He had no intention of lowering his voice. He was bold in relaying that having Black people work in the restaurant would prevent the guests from coming into the restaurant. There was a sense of assurance in his words. He actually believed what he was saying. If a Black chef was cooking at the chef's table, people would not come in. He was serious. And was this being addressed to me passively? "I wouldn't go to that restaurant. I wouldn't trust them. They might steal something." I was completely stunned. As I looked around, all eyes were on me. Waiting for me to react or cause a scene. Some chefs awkwardly placed their hands in prayer signaling me to keep calm. I wasn't going to react badly, I couldn't. It was my only job working in a foreign country who knew no one. "You really believe that?" Felix responded "Absolutely," with no fear in his heart. "It's a shame that you believe that someone's skin color would distract people from coming to a restaurant, and that they're not worthy of cooking at this level." That's all I could say and walked away. The kitchen turned cold, not by temperature but by energy. Everyone assumed I'd cause a big commotion. But I'd been in situations like this before in a work space and always had to remind myself of where I was. It was not the cowardly way out, it was a decision. If it happened again, I would address it differently.

As COVID-19 continued to get worse, we received the dreaded news that we were to close the restaurant again. It was spreading like wildfire in both small towns and across major cities. The restaurant would close for a few weeks. Unsure of what to do, I used the time as an opportunity to explore other options. I turned to Chef Jan and told him that I was unsure I was to return back to New York. I was grateful for the experience at his restaurant, but with its closing, options were limited. I'd ask him for the recommendation to stage somewhere else. When he asked me where I wanted to go next, I said "Paris." The chef did not have a lot of connections there but anywhere else in the Netherlands, he could oblige. With his strong reputation, I'd be able to secure an opportunity somewhere else in the Netherlands.

I thought of places that I had heard of and one place that came to my mind was a two-Michelin-star restaurant with a Surinamese chef. The food had been very similar to the type of Caribbean food that I had grown up eating. They had curries and their own version of roti. They even opened up their own little roti food truck, if you will. This could be a great way to explore more about my culture and learn different flavors. But everyone's face when I mentioned the restaurant wasn't super excited.

Another restaurant that came to mind was the oldest three-star Michelin restaurant in all of the Netherlands, De Librije. I heard stories about this restaurant, endless hours, quiet kitchen, and cameras everywhere, very reminiscent of Eleven Madison Park. I've been in that intense environment before, so I could do it again. Chef Jan had reached out on my behalf, but after days we had heard nothing. I later found out, to my surprise, the chef at De Librije was reluctant to hire me because I did not speak Dutch. Although disappointed, I knew finding a place to work would not be easy. But I continued to remind myself that everything happens for you, not to you.

Chef Jan had recommended a new restaurant in Zeeland. They did not have a Michelin star but the head chef was young and talented. The chef's position would include menial tasks, picking vegetables, cleaning, and doing just odd jobs. Chef Jan wanted me to be open-minded so I could learn differently. Trusting his judgment, I decided to pack my bags from Heeze and make my way to Zeeland.

Zeeland was the primary place where all the seafood, or most, came from in the Netherlands. The Netherlands were known for the mussels and the majority came from this one strip in Zeeland. If you thought Heeze was in the middle of nowhere, Zeeland was even smaller, but how was I going to get there?

Ironically enough and with major hesitation from my end, I accepted the invitation for Felix to drive me. He had volunteered, go figure. The same Felix who had shared his cultural perspectives, publicly in the kitchen weeks prior, about his resistance to having Black chefs work in the restaurants here. I looked over and thought to myself, what other opportunity in my life will I have to sit with someone in a three hour ride who does not view me as an equal. The entire drive was eye opening. He, without having been asked to, openly wanted to continue our last conversation about race. I did not necessarily feel his hatred, I just genuinely believed he felt his beliefs were valid. I wanted to learn his story, about how he grew and why he felt the way he did. It had been uncovered that he'd been abused and had a pretty tough life. He lived on his own for quite a while, and had different jobs. He was trying to make a living and make something of himself. I was more curious than frustrated, more empathetic rather than disgusted. My job was not to change his perspective about how he viewed people, it was to share different perspectives and tell my story while listening to him. Whether accepted or not, I believed to lead with kindness, because overall, he wasn't a bad guy. And at the end of the day, he was offered his help and I accepted. We learned a great deal about each other that day. I believe we crossed paths with one another for a reason.

It's so hard in our country or in our lives when someone has a strong opinion about something you don't agree with. It's almost impossible for people to speak on complex issues without aggression and even without violence. This was an opportunity to see my patience and my growth. To those reading this, ask yourself how you would respond in these situations. They are tests of character that will happen in life, in one way or another. How you respond will define you, especially when you have to work with others. I thanked Felix for the ride and moved forward. I switched my focus on what would be another stop in my journey. I was about to embark on a whole new adventure at a Michelin starred restaurant called "Meliefste" with

Chef Thijs Meliefste, whom I'd never met. It overlooked a beautiful view of the marina and the Veerse Meer lagoon. Chef Meliefste's cooking style was characterized by intricate details in his dishes and showcasing a wide range of techniques. We'd cooked with fresh seasonal vegetables from Zeeland. Fresh fish and shellfish straight from the waters and wild herbs and plants forged daily from the surrounding fields. There was a deep respect for using resources from the natural environment, which was the hallmark and mission of Chef's philosophy.

CHAPTER 14: BACK TO THE DIRT

My feet were planted back on the New York streets, firm on the ground, I was home. As I reflected on my time in Europe, I knew that coming home was an opportunity to really execute what I wanted to and who I wanted to build with. I was in deep thought about what my next steps would be, my next stop along this journey. I listened to hundreds of podcasts, researching and learning on how to build a business and how to hone in on your craft. You started from the dirt.

Gary Vaynerchuk also known as "GaryVee," is one of the top, notable entrepreneurs, an author, speaker, and online marketing phenomenon. There was value in listening and watching all his podcast episodes. He shared and often spoke on his philosophy about the "clouds and the dirt." The dirt, where I believe the magic happened. Gary had said in one of my favorite episodes, "that your success would be predicated by the "dirt." The dirt was a mixture of having the work ethic to get your hands dirty and that the experience was predicated from actually doing the work. If you're not working on your craft, you lose." To me, that craft in which you build from humble beginnings. He shared, while standing outside on a city block, "that all it takes is one thing to get the momentum going." And I was ready to work.

I had a new sense of humility, a superpower, sometimes fear, but a strength that I had after working in the Netherlands. I knew what I wanted to bring to the table, but the reality was, I had to start again, from the ground up. I was back in the dirt. No job or apartment. I reconnected with my parents back home and they were so happy that I made it back in one piece. After settling in, I was restless and I decided to take an impromptu drive into the city. I parked somewhere to look at the cityscape and views from the water. All I wanted was to make it in this city.

A few weeks in, I got a phone call from my old mentor and friend, Chef Marc Bynum. He told me that he was going to be delivering meals to hospital workers and that he could use my help. It was in the back of this Chinese restaurant called Danny's in Massapequa, Long Island. As I walked through the restaurant, I was greeted by my old chef in the back. We would be in charge of sending out hundreds of meals to frontliners working selflessly, assisting those affected during the COVID-19 epidemic. This was important work to me.

When I had time, I ate in the restaurant. I wanted to learn about Chinese food and understand why it was a "go-to" staple in communities. The food was good and it was consistent. Chicken and broccoli was one of my favorite dishes. The chicken melted, covered in sauce, the broccoli was steamed and blanched, inside a pot known as a "Wok." I learned that cooks would freeze the chicken breast so that they can easily shave it. The chicken was then hit with baking soda with a technique called "velveting" to help break it down, make it more tender, almost transforming the texture of the chicken. When giving meals to the frontline workers, we served cauliflower, chicken, and rice.

Being back home and serving meals influenced me further to start my Pop-Up, Noble Promise. I had this vision of having a fine dining restaurant but I wanted to start by interacting with people and sharing my food personally. I wanted to find purpose in my cooking, be proud of its presentation, and connect with those who loved good food and service. That's what Chef Omar Tate taught me, as well as Daniel Humm and Will Guidara. I wanted to create a space to showcase my food, be it in a restaurant or in someone's apartment. I was going to create my place in the dining industry. I partnered up with a company called Resident, where we were able to transform studios, penthouses, apartments and retail spaces to host private dining experiences. This became the first step to planting the seed.

My friend, Mo, had a company called "Peace in Parmesan", a lifestyle and clothing brand. I wanted to incorporate his decor and artistry in the events I was hosting. I ordered pillows and plushes, mats, pitchers, and even created a signature dish inspired by his work. Mo was one of the most selfless people that I've met in culinary school. He was Jamaican as well and after culinary school, he got into graphic design and making art.

Kelsey, another partner of mine, and Hamza, who was Omar Tate's brother, worked together to build the concept of "Nobel Promise." We moved at 100mph having meetings, ideating through dinners, formulizing the plans on what this experience would be. We even spoke about my dream to write this book, which became a reality. And for that, I am grateful.

We created dishes that were soulful and could tell a story through food and culture. I thought of my life thus far. About the cotton fields that I passed as a child, driving down to North Carolina. I wanted to represent the ancestors at the table through the textures, place settings, Mo's art, and the room's aesthetic. Hamza was able to capture snapshots and I started to document.I create dishes in honor of people that inspired me, Leah Chase, Patrick Clark, and Edna Lewis. I also made a dish inspired by Harlem's culture connector, Ethiopian and Swedish Chef, Marcus Samuelsson. We created up to 30 dishes.

COVID-19 was still running rampant in New York. I couldn't foresee its ending, but I continued to work and tried to remain encouraged. I'd serve my Mother Bell's, my 101 great-grandmother's recipe. I found this hand-written recipe, rummaging through all of her books she'd given me. It was her legendary "mayonnaise cake". It combined raisins, mayo, vanilla and flour, creating the most delicious and moist cake. It was unlike anything I'd ever tasted. I paired that with snow cream, an ice cream I had when I was young. As kids, we would collect snow and mix it with yellow food coloring and vanilla. We'd then freeze it again with some evaporated milk and that became our version of "snow cream". I wanted to remix it. Now that I was well versed in ice cream, I made a vanilla bean ice cream, added turmeric to get that golden, yellow hue. I did this as an alternate to using yellow food coloring and paired this with our raisin and mayo cake. It is dedicated to my great-grandmother. I shared this handwritten recipe with our guests. Additional dishes, influenced by Mo's artistry, was potato gnocchi with tomato jam, similar to what I learned to make in the Netherlands cooking with Chef Jan. We partnered this with a parmesan fondue and tomato powder right on top, and parmesan crisps. The flavors of basil and tomato had such a sweetness to savor with just the right saltiness and umami.

"My Dutch Travels," was a curry shrimp dish inspired by my grandmother. The shrimp was marinated in a curry ketchup. I learned to make it in the Netherlands. I made a chive and shrimp oil, took the shells and roasted them. We created a broken emulsion on top of the plate, and served the shrimp on with Spring salad, peppers and avocado. Spices, like coriander, were used to make a vinaigrette. You could almost taste this depth of flavor in the orange and the citrus.

We hosted pop-up after pop-up. I'd enjoy interacting with guests to gain their feedback. I learned which meal was a fan favorite and which dishes needed some work. I connected and network, really putting myself out there for guests to enjoy that type of food I wanted to cook. In addition to showing them who I was as a Chef. I wanted the experience to have an impact like that of my first time having a fine dining meal. I met a sommelier that was inspired by the food and what I was doing. He wanted to introduce me to Chef Marcus Samuelson. I didn't truly expect for him to make it happen but the next day, he had put me in a group chat and connected me with Marcus. We then scheduled our first phone call.

I shared and presented everything I wanted to do to Marcus. I told him about my ambitions and goals for Noble Promise and what, at the time, was an NFT project around food and fashion. He listened, gave advice and told me he'd be in touch. I was hopeful but tried to streamline my expectations. On the same day of the call., I got an interesting text message from one of the associates at Resident, saying they had an opportunity for me. It was to cook for artist Jidenna, the hitmaker behind the song "Classic Man." I remembered being in college creating step shows to that song. Jidenna brought in the swag, the culture on how to be that classic man. He was coming to New York to host a celebrity event. The team got on the phone with him and his people and started to lay out the menu that was to be based. He shared stories about his LA roots and how tacos were super important to him. He'd spent some time in Nigeria and loved jollof rice. I created an oxtail lamb taco with pickled vegetables and a homemade tortilla. A beef and cow stew that was classic in Nigeria. And of course, I researched and learned how to make jollof rice. This is a different level of pressure for me. I was the head chef and leader for my team, working with a celebrity foodie that had given me the opportunity to make dishes tailored to his life and culture.

At the end of the meal, we shared a special moment and I believe he understood how much I wanted to cook and succeed in the industry. We joked about how nervous I was to make jollof as I wanted to impress him. Referring to how his mother made it, I wanted to be as good. He shared that this was not about making a better jollof, it was about making it with my personal influence, what I wanted the dish to be. That's what made it special. I was moved to then get an invite to his album release party and we kept in touch. Another stepping stone, connecting and cooking for someone who inspired me so early on in my new culinary journey.

It had been a nonstop grind and I needed a break. No perfect time then to celebrate my mom's upcoming 60th birthday. This celebration turned out to be special, but also an awakening in more ways than one. My entire life was about to change, personally within the family, and at the same time, in work.

CHAPTER 15: MY BIG BREAK (THE DOUBLE ENTENDRE)

The Florida Sun and crystal blue water, that's what I saw when we landed from the plane. A celebration was to be had. My pop-ups were making traction. I was building relationships with major powerplayers in the industry. I was grateful for the growth. My grandma rented out a beautiful home with a pool to celebrate my mother. My dad was still working and couldn't fly down until a little later, so we arrived first.

As I settled, my phone pinged. I received a direct message from a producer of the reality show cooking competition, Hell's Kitchen with celebrity Chef and TV personality Gordon Ramsay. Earlier in the book, I shared that experience but it's important to entail how it started. I thought it was a joke at first, but it turned out to be real, no pun intended. My online presence was growing, I was documenting everything for my YouTube channel and social pages. They were impressed by my cooking and my content depicting it. I'd never really watched Hell's Kitchen but I knew that Gordon Ramsay was a respectable chef and he was someone I admired. I responded to the message with interest, put my phone away, and continued my vacation, celebrating my mom.

My grandfather layed on the floats and enjoyed the water as my grandmother watched him. Music and warm sun took over most of the day. We visited different restaurants and ate all types of different food. The anticipation and the excitement of my mom's big birthday was all we spoke of. All we wanted was to eat seafood, the family loves seafood. My dad was unsure if he wanted to fly down with COVID-19 still hoovering over. Even with his hesitancy, I wanted him to be here with us, and ultimately he made the trip. I was absolutely thrilled to be together as a family. It felt complete.

When he arrived, he greeted my girlfriend at the time, who came with us on the trip. We put on our best fits and ate seafood by the pier. My mom wore a glistening tiara on her head, smiling from ear to ear. She was so beautiful and happy. I had a family photoshoot and took this beautiful photo of me, my mom, and my dad by the poolside. Traveling back from Europe and jumping right into hosting my pop-ups made me realize how much I missed this feeling of being together. Through me growing as a chef and now having the time celebrating the big joys, it felt like things were aligning. Still, the reality of the present state of the country gave me a sense of fear. The vaccine wasn't something that I wanted to consider nor my dad. There was too much uncertainty, different opinions of the effects, so I genuinely couldn't decide. When we went out, we tried to be as vigilant as possible. Making sure everyone around us was safe, especially my grandparents.

For fun, we decided to visit and experience an Escape Room. A locked room with games, clues, and puzzles seemed like it'd be an interesting experience. Having a time clock made for a perfect opportunity to see what my parents would do. Both of my parents were retired police officers. Being able to see how we all were under pressure, filled the room with laughter and jokes, making it a great time. It just flew by. It was one of the best and craziest experiences with my family.

The next day, to my surprise, I felt gloomy. I started to feel badly with a cough and a splitting headache, I had gotten COVID-19. I quickly locked myself in my room and stayed away from everyone. I had no idea how I contracted it, especially having been as careful as I was. My dad had to return to New York to work after we celebrated my mom's birthday. I had to stay in Florida and recover.

I received a phone call that placed my world on a halt. My dad had gotten COVID-19. He was positive with no symptoms, no fever. I pleaded with him to take all the necessary medication. As I was stuck in Florida, my mom called me to tell me that my dad's symptoms had started to develop. It started as a slight sweat and cough. My dad was resourceful and made his own elixir to try to suppress the symptom. He would mix ginger, garlic and lemon in hot water on the stovetop and create his own vapor system. I had to get home to him. I battled with an internal guilt that I had gotten him sick. Though there was no proof, it stayed with me. My only thought was to get back to help him.

When I got back to New York, my dad looked drained, different from the superhero-like presence I had seen in my entire life. He would sleep in his room with one blanket, tossing and turning, coughing back to back.

As men, we didn't really show a lot of physical affection but we loved and respected each other. He was my dad and I hated seeing him sick, I wasn't used to it. I knew something was different, something was wrong. It'd be two o'clock in the morning and more hours passed as his cough continued. Still tossing and turning. I wanted him to go to the doctor and called him by his first name Nathan. I always did, that was just our relationship. He did not want to go to the doctor but he didn't have a choice. I took him myself. At the hospital, doctors had informed us my dad had pneumonia. All I could do was be grateful we had taken him in. My mom was still in Florida and was updated daily. We were still coming off the energy of her birthday.

Due to strict COVID-19 rules and regulations, I couldn't stay with my dad at the hospital. The hospital was adamant on the concern of germs spreading and family members were to be sent away. Before I took him to the hospital, I was trying relentlessly to heal him myself. I'd make spaghetti with herbs but he couldn't eat anything. I would try any and every holistic blend to make him feel better, but nothing worked. The hospital had to be the next choice. My dad told me that the doctors had put him on steroids to help with his breathing, but breathing became harder and harder for him. Luckily, my mom had come back from Florida and was here with us.

As we both waited home for my father to get better, he would send us pictures in the hospital, trying to show his strength. He felt like he had been there forever and was trying to get stronger. One day he would feel better. The next day he wouldn't. Doctors would come and go, saying contradicting things between one another. Constant inquiries as to what type of insurance would be better and who would cover what. I felt that the healthcare was broken and became so frustrated and increasingly angry.

Doctors had placed my dad on the oxygen machine. They helped him stay mobile. They tried to get him better. As he improved, within a day he would be worse. It was an endless cycle of emotions. Doctors advised him to go home because they believed they did everything they could. Being released would leave him with no oxygen but they informed us that he would be ok.

I picked my dad up from the hospital. He was put in a wheelchair with an oxygen tank attached. He was breathing and feeling normal, feeling okay, but the moment that oxygen tank was taken off, he fell weak. He was slowly starting to recover upon being back home. My mom stayed by his side at every single waking minute. Walking up the stairs strained his energy, so we made him comfortable downstairs on the couch. I had mixed emotions, concerned but hopeful, making sure I monitored his progress. He started to eat breakfast and start to do daily things, move around a little bit, and smile.

My dad was my sole focus. I was so affected with everything going on at home that I was completely surprised by an unexpected phone call from Chef Marcus Samuelsson. I could not believe he was calling. I answered. We exchanged greetings and before I could even surpass saying that I was doing OK, I had updated Marcus that I was taking care of my father, who was still recovering from COVID-19. I asked Marcus what he had been up to and how things were on his end. He shared with me that he was hosting an event in Aspen and invited me to come along. I was conflicted and excited, but unsure of what to do. I ran down the stairs, placed Marcus on hold and told my parents the news. I was serious and valued their opinion, especially as it concerned my dad. I wanted to do well in life and knew this opportunity may be the next inch forward, but I was worried about my dad. I asked them both and directed my attention to my dad. He was doing better and told me to go. He reassured me he'd be ok with this look of strength and positivity. He gave me the blessings to go, he supported me so much.

I released this line and accepted Marcus' invite. It looked like everything would be ok. My dad was getting better, my mom right by his side, I was going to go and make them proud. The next day, I woke up a little later than usual, feeling okay because my mother was going to take care of my dad. As I was upstairs, I took a moment to get some business in order, writing the information down on the business credit card I had just got an approval for. I heard a scream. My mom was yelling, telling my dad that we were going back to the hospital. She ran upstairs to get me. My dad's oxygen numbers were below the normal levels. I was so confused, he had been ok the day before. Wanting to see him, I ran downstairs but I could not find him. He wasn't sitting in his usual spot. He had moved. Looking in every room, I had found him on the floor of the bathroom. The Ten Commandments that we had hung on up had fallen and broken. Undressed, my dad had passed out on the floor. My mom found us in the bathroom. "Nathan, no! What—you have you," trying to get my dad up. Pleading for him to get up. I had called 911 and was directed on how to give my dad CPR. Mouth to mouth, pumping his chest, I repeated in my head, trying so hard to wake him up."You're doing so good, Sakari. Just keep pumping. Don't stop pumping," my mom kept saying to me in tears. The medics finally arrived for what seemed to feel like hours. The longest collection of minutes I had ever felt. They came inside, rushed through the door, asking questions like if he had diabetes, about if his blood sugar was low, checking for a pulse. As best as we could, barely calm, my mom and I tried to explain everything that had happened. Medics carried out my dad and put him inside the ambulance. One of them said that they have everything that they need right here in this ambulance and they were going to do absolutely everything they could to save him. The ambulance stayed parked outside for about 10 minutes and the second they drove off, my mom broke into tears. She was uncontrollable, calling out my dad's name, "Nathan, No…Nathan." We got in the car and I am racing behind the ambulance, driving for what now felt like the fastest collection of minutes in my life, felt like seconds. I was going to be right behind this ambulance.

We all arrived at the hospital, medics came out, pulled my dad out from the ambulance and rushed him straight to the Emergency Room. Pacing, I kept asking out for updates, then seconds later, asking again. I needed to know what was happening with my dad. Hospital staff told us that we'd have to stay in the waiting room. And so we waited. Frantically. Waiting. The doctor came out and before they could even speak we kept asking what happened. What is going on? What is the situation? We need to know. We needed to see him.

"We tried to revive him with no luck. I'm sorry, but there's no heartbeat." My mom and I instantly dropped to the floor. Shock in complete disbelief. I have just heard the ultimate worst words of my life. My dad had passed. They kept him on the ventilator machine and needed our permission to take him off of it. "We need you to go say your goodbyes." As I entered the back room, I saw my father connected to a machine trying to pump air into chest, pumping to get him to come back to life. I looked at him and my mom in shambles. I went over to his body and I cried. Us two, with physical touch. Laying on him, all I could do, all I could tell him, was that "I'm going to make you so proud" repeating it, over and over and over, "I'm sorry, I'm going to make you so proud, I swear, and I love you, Nathan. I love you, Dad. I promise I'm going to make you proud." My mom was torn into pieces. I couldn't speak. Nurses would come in and ask us questions about COVID. I would turn them there way angrily "Are you fucking kidding me right now? Are you fucking serious? I can't answer these questions right now. I just lost my fucking dad. What's wrong with you? Have some fucking decency. We just lost someone." My mom was beside him, begging him to wake up.

An important reminder: Losing someone is never easy for anyone

—not for the doctor, not for the nurse, but especially not for their loved ones.

Barely containable, I knew I was going to have to make those calls. Firstly, my sister, my dad's firstborn. She had been asking for updates from time to time about how he was doing. At the time, we had been waiting to hear and hoped that he was doing ok. My dad was known for showcasing such strength during the hardest times. And so I called my sister, "Kateesa. We lost him." The call dropped. Moments later, my phone rang and my sister's boyfriend was on the line. I had to explain the situation. As best and strongest as I could. "What are you talking about? What happened?" I struggled to say the words: "His breathing went down and we had lost him."

We would start to make phone calls to deliver the news to the family. My grandfather would call me, my grandmother would call me, trying their best to comfort me and figure out what to do next. At this moment, the only thing that I could think about, other than my dad not being here, was just taking care of my mom. I had never seen my mom broken in tears like this before. She looked so lost and helpless and I just wanted to be able to be there and comfort her the best I could.

The ride back from the hospital was one of the quietest, loneliest rides, in my entire life. Even harder, was opening the door to an empty house. We had just lost our favorite person. My mom was unable to even make it upstairs. She slept by the couch, tossing and turning and crying throughout the night. She lost her best friend, her partner that she had loved for so many years. I lost my hero, my true hero, my true mentor, and the closest to me. My relationship with my dad was something unlike anything else. Nathan was extremely easy-going, calm and patient, respectful and kind. He was stern but caring. He was loving. He was Noble. I couldn't believe I lost him.

I felt like I was navigating on autopilot, trying to figure out arrangements and be there for my mom and family. Everyone was in shock. I still couldn't fathom losing him. He did everything to remain healthy. He didn't eat meat, he didn't smoke, he didn't drink. He had diabetes, but there was never a time where I thought I was going to lose him. I had dreamt of him being at my wedding. Be a grandfather and watch the kids grow. Watch me work hard and see my success. The reality was too harsh, that he was not here. My great-grandmother is 101 years old. How did I just lose my dad?.

As I continued to operate on autopilot, I had to let Marcus know that I could not go to Aspen. He shared his sentiments and told me to be with my family. Though sad about missing this dream opportunity, I couldn't think about anything else but my dad. I had to be there for my family, for my mom. Everyone grieves differently. I needed to act, to keep busy. I decided to message Hell's Kitchen on the same day to share the news that my father had passed away from COVID. I needed to be on the show. I had to do it for my dad.

Preparing for my dad's funeral was the toughest thing I ever had to do. to navigate Everyone was overcome with emotions and me trying to hold everything together. I sat in this pool of what ifs: "I should have been there," or "I should have done this better," or "What if I didn't do this?" or "What if I did this?" I kept telling myself all these different scenarios, but as I sat at my dad's funeral, the preacher said one thing that stayed with me that I will never forget: "Put God first. If you don't take away anything from today, take away to put God first." And that's what I decided to do. Following that day, I decided to pray and speak to my dad in heaven, the angel that God had blessed me with. I started to look for signs or ways to be able to communicate and understand the lessons that were trying to be taught to me from God.

I remember being in a room after dealing with all the emotions and people of this day. The constant "I am so sorry for your loss." I could hold it back anymore. I cried. I screamed. Screeching sounds and tears running down my face. I dropped down to my knees and began to pray. Letting all my emotions out that had been building inside of me. I reflected on the stories I heard from everyone he had worked with. My dad had two lives. One was "Andre", which is his middle name, which people from Manhattan and those people from corrections would know him by, and then Nathan, the Long Island native who worked in Lowe's helping people and loved listening to

R&B through his headphones in or on his speakers. He also displayed many acts of kindness, as my neighbor shared when my dad lent him a leaf blower or a snow blower. Countless stories about how kind of a human he was.I tried to show the same kindness, I hope my dad is who I got it from. There was a sense of love, a true sense of love inside that funeral, as we celebrated his life.

I needed to figure out what God was trying to teach me. So I went searching. I went searching through all of my dad's things, trying to understand the man that I had known my whole life. He was taken from me way too soon. I would go through old articles and old books as I started to create this bin of things. I found his old menu, Ads, and pieces from the restaurant he owned. Yes, he had a restaurant back in the day. I would start to see how eloquent he would write to others, how deep his love was for his family, and I would find books with highlights and notes. It started to all make sense. All of the lessons he was trying to teach me as a young boy were all coming together. Everything was intentional, his values and his virtues, his acts of kindness, how to act as a man and how to treat others the way they want to be treated. All these things were documented in all the resources of books, articles, and letters that he had written.

As I continued to go through my dad's letters, I tried to put together letters in his handwriting to spell out the word "legacy." I got it tattooed on my body within days. I wanted his legacy to live on through me and I wanted to create a legacy for him. With time, I conceptualized an animated character in his honor called "Noble Nate", because my dad was the most noble human being I had ever known. And in that moment, I realized what my purpose would be, what I had been put on this earth to be and to do. Food, health, wellness is medicine. How you take care of your body is important. I vowed never to chase accolades, but to chase impact.Make the world a better place through food and education. I made the noble promise to harness that mentality but largely in honor of my dad's life, love, and legacy. Soon, I'd begin to start writing this book.

CHAPTER 16: SIGNS FROM ABOVE

Therapy is something I never had considered. I just remember listening to Charlamagne tha God speaking about how important mental health and therapy was. Having just been through losing my dad and grieving, I sought help and guidance. I found a therapist. She was a kind Black woman and someone I hope to connect with. I wanted my mom to join, but she wasn't very open to it. I had to respect her time in grief and how she felt. It was still so difficult to sleep in the house.

My friend Ahjesh from Eleven Madison Park had called me. Time had passed and I was mentally trying to prepare to start working again. He told me that there was an NBA basketball player for the Brooklyn Nets that was looking for a private chef. What is the first sign to get back at it? Was it a blessing from my dad? I needed the work because I had stopped doing the pop-ups. I had to push myself, with no avoidance of what I'd been going through, but transfer that energy into being productive and purposeful. I accepted the role. It was one of the most beautiful homes I've ever seen. I cooked from day to day, focused but feeling this hole in the pit of my stomach. My heart was missing my dad so much. I knew I wasn't ready to take on this opportunity. I knew that it was too soon. I simply hoped that it was a sign from God and my dad to give me an opportunity to make some income. It was the most amount of money that I'd ever made and cooking for a superstar athlete was definitely on my list of hopes to accomplish. In time, as I worked as hard as I could, emotionally it became tough, and I had to step away.

Some time passed and I had received another unexpected email. Gary, who I had mentioned previously was coming out with a mentorship called the Sorcerer Scholarship, where five applicants out of the thousands were going to be chosen to get exclusively mentored by Gary. This also included receiving a valuable collectible, one-on-one meetings with him, and an introduction member within his entire network. This is exactly what I wanted.

Let's take it back to why I needed this mentorship. Prior to leaving for Europe, I had this crazy plan. I had gotten into collecting. When I had the opportunity to come across Gary in the past, he was sharing his passion about sports cards and the next trends. His dream was to own the NY Jets one day. He advised, to start collecting sports cards. Sports cards were to be a hit! I never knew collecting could be so profitable, I'd collected them when I was younger. So I researched and wanted to invest in a 1948 George Mikan rookie card, a card that I heard Gary wanted as part of his collection. That was the master plan: get this card and sell it to him.

I thought it was the highest grade of the George Mikan rookie card. I believe it had been a PSA eight or so, not realizing that the grade that was actually on it was from an old grading company prior to PSA. The PSA was like top of the line, if you will. I got the card. I used credit to pay for it. I couldn't even afford it, but I thought it was such a good deal. I wanted to show this card to Gary, pitch to sell but even if I couldn't sell it, I just want the mentorship.

Well, I tried to get this card in front of Gary. Whatever I could do, I reached out to Ryan Harwood, his business partner and general manager. My intent was to get this card in front of him. I was overly confident, partially running on adrenaline, telling myself that I'm going to be able to sell this card in exchange for a mentorship and it's going to be great. Ryan answered my email after my countless

SAVOR YOUR JOURNEY

attempts to reach out. I even attempted to reach out to Gary's entire network. I did exactly what I did with Eleven Madison Park, follows, DMs, and follow-ups. I finally got a response, I heard that Gary wasn't interested in the card. I was torn that I failed. I looked at the card grade and I decided to get it re-graded. It came back from an eight, which I had mentioned earlier, to a four—PSA four. I thought I had the highest grade George Mikan. I thought it was a million-dollar card but once it had properly gotten rated by PSA, it went down to just being another card. Now, it's still a rare and interesting card, but it didn't have that same validity to it that I believe it did. A lesson was learned. I prepped for my final attempt to gift this card to Gary. Gary was hosting an impromptu pop-up. I had just finished a Residence pop-up the night before and asked my parents if I could use the car to drive to the city. I had one hour to get to his office, as he had a big surprise for all of his supporters.

Now, at this time, Gary didn't come out of his office that often and didn't have any impromptu fan meetups. This was super rare. Half tired, half asleep, I documented the entire journey, racing to be able to get to him. It would be my first time meeting Gary Vaynerchuk, also known as "GaryVee". As soon as I got there, I saw him and made my way to greet him. He was giving out Manga books, comics or graphic novels, from Japan. I stood in line, eagerly but patiently, waiting to meet him. I think he thought all I wanted was a picture but I presented the George Mikan rookie card. "That's a sick card." I was so excited to finally gain his reaction, in person no less. I continued to tell him that I wanted him to have the card. We spoke briefly on the history of how I got it. He seemed shocked by my gesture. I had to thank him for serving as such an inspiration to me. From his podcasts, to running his business, and his books! Gary was definitely an influential figure to share my story and write a business book. Or in the least write about my journey to achieve success. He held up his famous high five, grateful for the conversation, we then went our separate ways. I left inspired and relieved that I completed this personal mission.

Fast forward to a year later, here I am, thinking about how to get considered for this mentorship opportunity. I remember seeing Andy Krainak on the street at NFT NYC. I knew Andy was Gary's right-hand man. Gary was at the event, connecting with people but I wanted to share my story and meet Andy. I told him my story, damn near my full story and he stopped me halfway through the conversation and said that he read my essay application and that I had an amazing story. I hope I get this scholarship. I said it without hesitating. Andy nodded, signing that he had heard me and politely walked away. Later that day, an email was released on who made the next round. I'm so sorry. Even though you made it to the next round, you decided to not move forward with your application.I didn't get it. I couldn't believe that it wasn't enough.

I decided to take this opportunity as I was able to see Andy later that night and approach him. I told him that I received the news that I wasnt selected, even though we just connected earlier. I told him that I was going to show him why I was going to be at that table one day. That I'd be working to make it happen regardless how long it took. One year, maybe two, however long it takes. I needed to get it off my chest. I wanted him to know that I could accept the rejection but I was not going to give up. I was going to continue to push myself. I stayed and enjoyed the rest of the party.

The following day, as I'm scrolling through Twitter, I see the exact same George Mikan rookie card that I had gifted Gary tweeted, saying that he was "obsessed with this card." I commented below relaying that I was happy to see he was enjoying it. No one needed to know that I gave it to him or what I wanted. I was just thrilled that he acknowledged and shared his thoughts on the card that I knew I personally gifted him. It didn't go unnoticed and I believed that I did the right thing, being relentless in my pursuits for him to have it.

A few days later, I got an email from Veefriends Sorcerer Scholarship committee, reading the first line saying, "Sakari, it's so good to talk to you. We wanted to know if we could set up another meeting. You have been reconsidered for the Sorcerer Scholarship." There was no way! All the thoughts in the world of why I wasn't accepted or why I wasn't able to get it had gone away. For continued context, part of the Sorcerer Scholarship process was to make a video of what you would do with the prize money that came along with this huge opportunity. And I told them I would give it to my mom, as my dad just passed away and wanted her to be taken care of. That was my honest and true answer.

At the time, I didn't realize that they were looking for specific people that had a plan to do impactful work and make the world a better place. That had clearly been my goal, throughout every single thing I had gone through. All of my work experience. All of my travels. All of my ideas that came into fruition. I knew I had it in me, but my answer, without a doubt in my mind, was to take care of my mom and family. I reflected on the possibility of that being the reason to get chosen. It wasn't personal, but I was personal. So as I read this email aloud again, I knew I had to take this meeting.

I got in my zone. Listening in my headphones, conversations with all the bosses and inspirational leaders in the business. I watched Will Smith interviews and Dame Dash, and Kevin Hart's as well. I amped myself up and got ready for this interview. And when I did, I left it all out on the table. I gave it everything I had and told them exactly why I deserved to have the scholarship. I left with no regrets. I felt happy and content, not caring what was meant to happen. I had put God first and whatever meant to happen would happen.

The next week, I got an email saying that I had won the Sorcerer Scholarship! I would now have access to mentorship with Gary Vaynerchuk. Access to learning and connecting within his network. The collectible prize was the cherry on the top. At that same exact time, I had got an email confirmation that I had been chosen for Hell's Kitchen. Having it escape me that I had reached back out after losing my dad, I found comfort in the thought that I had the energy to succeed even through my darkest moment. This energy motivated me and now I'd be moving to the final round to be considered for Hell's Kitchen. God is so good. The wheels were spinning and both my culinary and entrepreneurial dreams were coming true. I still had this heaviness in my heart for all I wanted to was share the news with my dad and he wasn't here to see it. I remember what I told him, as I held him that day, I was going to make him proud. I repeated those words again.

I learned about the importance of karma because I told Gary how crazy it was that after a year he posted the card I had gifted him and now gained his mentorship. He told me that it wasn't crazy. I had given it with no expectations. And that was his lesson, to give with love and good intent, and expected nothing in return. When you do good, good things will happen. Perhaps it was good karma, my dad, God or a beautiful combination of all three. My dreams were coming true. I thanked the Heavens but got ready to pull up my sleeves, as I was going to Hell's Kitchen!

CHAPTER 17: THIS IS NOT DRILL! THE FIRE TEST (HELL'S KITCHEN PART 1)

*P*ressure reveals character and there's no greater pressure than competition.

I had competed on TV before. Years back, on the food networks Chopped. Though faint, the memories of initial nerves, unaware of what the results would be, couldn't stop me from preparing for the opportunity to do so again. This was different. The stakes were higher, more contestants, shot over the course of weeks, and having to live and compete with chefs, as hungry as I was for the win. The flame that led the fray, was none other than one of the most prolific chefs and the biggest culinary media personalities on television, Chef Gordon Ramsay.

Known for his fiery temper, brutal honesty, and strict demeanor, Gordon Ramsay showcased to me what achieving success would require. I had to be disciplined, focused, but most importantly cook damn good food. The truth was that I had only watched a couple of episodes of Hell's Kitchen. I was inspired by and known of Ramsay for everything else that he had accomplished. A Multi-Michelin Star chef, nationally and international restauranteur, an accomplished, best selling author, entrepreneur, host, and more. I strive to achieve success like that with my own blueprint, while on this journey and throughout every experience that's happened along the way.

Still on high from the Sorcerer scholarship, it became real that I was going to do this. My first thought was that my number one goal was to win. What followed was the reality that I hadn't been cooking for a while. I was still considered fresh from Europe, COVID had and was still spreading, and the loss of my dad realigned what was important, time, and I had to be there for my mom and family. I would assume that most of the other chefs would have been working in restaurants and staying consistent and my challenge was that I believed I didn't have enough innate, day-to-day restaurant reps.Yes, I hosted successful Pop-Ups but some time had passed. I only knew, I had to get in the kitchen.

Due to COVID, we had to be isolated for two weeks prior before even being able to participate in the competition itself. The competition before the competition. I needed to prepare. I went back on Youtube, did research, tried to organize my thoughts on what I thought we'd be cooking on the show, reminded myself on how to make certain recipes, work with specific produce, meats and seafoods alike. I read cookbooks, even "White Heat" by Marco Pierre White, who worked closely with Gordon in the early stages of his career. I spruced up on my culinary terms, tricks and techniques. During the down time I focused on mentally preparing, reading Mamba Mentality by Kobe Bryant and studied the five pillars Be Passionate. Be Obsessive. Be Relentless. Be Resilient. Be Fearless.

I meditated to find balance. Ensuring the importance of staying focused, even through the grief, my doubts, or what obstacles I would face. Even through the possibility of elimination. I had to be secure and ready in this highly pressurized environment. I had to find my place of Zen and learn aspects of Tai Chi. This had to be my secret weapon.Within my movements, my breathing, and focus. I also reminded myself that through being featured on Nationally TV, I had to be aware and fully confident on how I wanted to present myself to the world and what I hoped for people to see.

I brushed up on episodes of Hell's Kitchen and watched other competition shows hosted by Chef Gordon. I paid attention to contestant behaviors, how to handle the clock, and what dishes or handling of food did Chef Gordon pay closer attention to. I practiced risottos and searing scallops. The difference in handling meats and other types of fish dishes. What was also important was learning the structure of the kitchens on set.

Fast forward back to my winning dish that I reflected on earlier in my Author's Note, I still couldn't believe that I got a perfect score. I had set the bar for Team Blue and potentially put a target on my back. The heat had been raised and I knew I had set the bar high. In the living room, one of the contestants Alex started to break down my dish. Comments on what I used or didn't use were the topic of conversation. I just wanted to cook and didn't have time for confrontation. I kindly walked out and addressed Alex. He asked what I put in my winning dish. Puzzled. Looking for some kind of detailed explanation. I didn't have to explain myself, again I was there to cook. an explanation. True colors and characteristics started to show. This was not the time for fun and games. For winning the first challenge, the team celebrated with dinner on a boat and Gordon's attendance. We learned from Gordon Ramsay, what his story truly was, directly and within inches away from us. A moment, an experience and a conversation I'd never forget. Now I don't get starstruck, but it was a once in a lifetime opportunity to connect with Gordon personally and know that you'll be cooking for him directly on this show. He asked me about my background and asked what I wanted to achieve in life. I shared my story with him and there was a mutual respect for one another. He again congratulated me and I truly cooked a winning dish.

Chef Christina, our chef team lead congratulated me on the win. She reminded me to do the work to stay up from here. I started on a high note and needed to maintain that. I had to be consistent. Our next competition was the wing competition, and I felt eyes were on me. I hadn't made wings in so long. I'd been so used to creating fine dining dishes, that cooking something as simplistic as wings felt harder than expected. I decided to make jerk wings. One of my teammates, Brett, had finished early and openly offered help to anyone who needed it. I asked him to drop the wings and cook them for me. As he did, I prepared the sauce. I returned to the wings to realize they had been still raw. They were not even cooked all the way through. I had to throw them in the oven as quickly as possible, hoping and praying that I had rectified the cook. Brett apologized and assumed that they were cooked. I had no time to panic, I needed to address them and put my food out on that plate. Chef Christina went on to taste each wing and pointed out that the cook on the wings were borderline, a minute less, and they would've been undercooked. I wasn't able to represent my team for that dish. I definitely had one of the weakest dishes there but my favors potentially saved the dish. Chicken is not something that you want to play with and with no excuse can be served raw.The winner of this challenge would win a pass and be exempted from any punishments. The winner was Alejandro. I'd have to look out for him for sure. As we went back to the dorms, I felt almost defeated. I couldn't believe that wings were going to be my near-takedown after just having a winning dish in the first challenge. I could have been easily eliminated. I thought to myself, I have to refocus.The competition was heating up, and I was starting to understand the team dynamic. Teams were always split in two, by color, red and blue team. I was on the red team along side chefs with strong personalities. Our team, altogether, had some strong players: Alejandro with the punishment pass, Sommer, Dafne,myself and others who spoke their minds and appeared to be strong chefs. There are always a few who struggled and often this was a concern for the team to be successful in winning challenges.

 Every single day we would wake up at the crack of dawn, get ready, and head into the kitchen. The pressure was unlike anything I'd experienced before. This pressure felt like working 24 hours in an open kitchen and even a heightened stage with rolling cameras, countdown clocks, and I'll say again, cooking for Gordon Ramsay. The screaming was an added bonus. I can still hear his voice. Our first dinner service was approaching and I could feel the anxiety building. I was assigned to the fish station, my comfort zone. My experience with fish had only increased with my previous work in Michelin starred kitchens. I knew fish but cooking a halibut dish compared to executing multiple at a rapid rate was completely different. Chef Gordon came over and asked to see my scallops. They were perfectly seared with a golden crust, translucent right in the middle. Chef Gordon had looked at me and asked, "Now can you do that every single time, 150 times tonight?" I confidently replied, "Yes Chef," in which he replied, "We'll see."

The pressure was on! This was not a drill. The first ticket was up and Chef Gordon's voice echoed through the entire kitchen. You couldn't ignore it. His tone was iconic. Many had heard it before, most popularly from the comfort of your own home but this voice, this voice commanding respect. It rang louder live and in person. With every ticket call, the pace was unlike anything I had ever experienced. High intensity. Two teams split, with chefs on either other side, crowded together, through overlapping yells. The clanking of dishes, the burst of flames from the stoves, stations were split contestants by role or produce. It was never-ending. Appetizers were up first and I watched as the team started to move. The communication was suffering. Matter of fact, we weren't communicating at all. Chefs overlapped each other and ticket calls were in shambles. The clock was running fast and then came my first ticket for fish. Chef Gordon yelled out my name, requesting two scallops, one halibut. I had to be quick. He asked for time, and I responded, "Four minutes Chef!" My pan was hot, I dropped my scallops, moving in a rhythm, using all my training. I felt I could do this with my eyes closed and then…a yell loud enough for even the guests to hear, raw chicken from meat station. "STOP! Everyone stop! You're going to kill someone! RAW CHICKEN!" The entire kitchen stopped. My heart sank and even though I perfected my scallops, it didn't matter. When one station failed, we all failed. Gordon throws the chicken across the pass, yelling at it to get it together. He had pointed out my scallops were dying from waiting. I was demanded to start again.I had to throw away perfectly cooked scallops, start over, due the team not being together across stations.

As service continued, it became a disaster. We sent dish after dish, but nothing was coordinated. Almost everything had been sent back. Chef Gordon was furious. Yelling at the team to communicate. You could barely tell who messed up individually unless the Chef said so by name. He turned his focus to Chef Sommer who was trying to call out orders, but no one was listening. Miscommunication spread quickly like wildfire. I kept my head down and just focused on my station, as I did my past restaurants. I tried to work with nothing but precision. As I continued to bang out perfectly good fish, again with the timing collapsing other stations, my fish didn't matter. The team could not keep up. After what felt like hours of a revolving clock of chaos, Chef Gordon had enough. Red team, get out! You're done!. The Blue team will finish service! Completely disappointed and angered, I got in the line to follow the other contestants. We were thrown out of the kitchen, defeated. I couldn't believe we'd lost as a team.

Back in the dorms, the mood was heavy. Someone was going home tonight. We had to deliberate and choose who should be put up for elimination.

The obvious choice was whoever sent up that raw chicken. Fingers were pointed, cursing cruised through the walls like an endless flow. I had nothing to say.

Standing in front of Gordon Ramsay, he decided the fate of who would go. I was confident it wouldn't be me but even if you're not up for elimination, you could feel its weight and toll. Chef Gordon grilled both nominees, asking why they should remain in the competition. One crumbled under the pressure, the other stood firm. Both pleading their positions to stay. Gordon had made his decision and requested the jacket of the eliminated contestant. The journey for one chef was over. As we walked back to the dorms, I thought about my dad. I thought about the promise I made him. The pressure was overwhelming. I had tried my best to stay strong.

The following more, a new challenge awaits. I was trying to be perfect, I was attempting to cook perfectly. I wanted more wins than losses. Every chef strived for the same. I ignored the chatter and comments. The best response was no response.

There was a shift. The blue team started losing services. They were in disarray, fighting amongst themselves. Meanwhile, we as the red team began to gel and become a cohesive unit. I believe we had found our rhythm.

The flame of the competition never lowered and things became even more intense. We were down to fewer and fewer chefs, and we even switched teams back to the original girls vs boys. Every elimination was harder because everyone that left was super talented, regardless of the downfalls. The challenges became more difficult. We had to cater events, create tasting menus and cook for celebrity guest chefs. Each challenge pushed us to our limits further.Alejandro still had his punishment pass in his pocket. That punishment pass hung over all of us. He could use it at any time to avoid a punishment, which meant someone else would have to take his place. It created such a tension and nobody wanted to be the one who got stuck with the double punishment.

Then disaster struck. During a challenge, I cut myself badly. The knife slipped while I was breaking down fish, slicing my finger open. There was blood everywhere. Medics rushed over and for a moment, I thought this might be it. If I couldn't cook, I'd have to leave the competition.They bandaged me up and gave me a finger cot to protect the wound. They asked if I could continue. My finger was hurting like hell. But I had my dad in my mind as well as everything I'd sacrificed to get here. I continued the competition. I pushed through. I would see the face of Chef Gordon disappointed with such a careless mistake.

One night in the dorms, after a particularly brutal service, I opened up to some of my teammates. I told them about losing my dad right before coming here and about what this competition meant to me. The room got quiet. Some of them knew loss too. We all had our reasons for being here. In this moment, we were not competitors, we were simply connected through our stories and our struggles.

CHAPTER 18: THE FINAL TEST (HELL'S KITCHEN PART 2)

We were down to the final group. Every service mattered and every challenge was crucial. Tonight Chef Gordon was combining both teams, red and blue. We knew now that we'd be competing as individuals for the illustrious black jacket. The black jackets were a symbol that soon, a select few would join this special collective of final chefs. The symbol that represented that you were one step closer to winning the competition. The next challenge was to create your best dish. There were no restrictions as to what you could create. Show me who you are as a chef, Chef Gordon requested. This was my moment. I looked up at the ceiling as the black jackets descended in glass cases.

This was it. The most important day we'd had so far.

Everyone around me felt the weight of it—the symbolism, the status, the moment. But as I stood there, something surprised me. I didn't actually care about the jackets themselves. I knew they mattered, but they weren't the goal.

Winning was the goal.

The black jacket was just another step.

Chef Gordon broke the silence.

"Welcome, chefs, to the Black Jacket Challenge. Today, there will be three rounds. In each round, you'll cook dishes inspired by some of my favorite restaurants. The best dish in each round earns a black jacket."

Three rounds. Three chances. One mistake, and you're fighting for your life.

I knew immediately what I had to do. I wasn't going to cook safe food. I was going to cook food that spoke to who I was.

Round One — For My Mom

Growing up, every birthday in my house meant lobster. No matter what else was happening in life, that was our ritual. That dish represented celebration, family, and unconditional love—especially my mother's.

A mother's love is your first true love. It's steady. It's forgiving. It shows up whether you win or lose.

So I cooked lobster.

I paired it with butternut squash to bring sweetness and comfort, and a tomato-based sauce to add depth. I wanted balance. I wanted warmth. I wanted memory.

To keep the lobster tender, I poached it gently in beurre blanc.

When Chef Gordon sliced into it, he paused.

"Thirty seconds," he said. "That's all it needed. Thirty seconds more, and it would've been perfect."

That was it.

Thirty seconds.

The flavors were right. The story was right. The execution was just short.

And just like that, Summer and Daphne were awarded the first black jackets.

Once again, I was fighting for my life.

The Night Before

The night before the challenge, Alex and I sat down together.

I asked him why he was doing this.

"For my family," he said. "For my boys. I want to give them a better future."

Alex was forty years old. In that moment, I thought to myself—he needs this more than I do.

That thought stuck with me.

I had come into this competition carrying my dad with me. I wanted to honor him. I wanted to win for him. But as the weeks went on, the exhaustion started to take its toll.

This competition drained everything from you. Physically. Mentally. Emotionally. Some days, I barely recognized myself.

I started questioning how much further I could go—and why.

Round Two — Falling Behind

The second round was inspired by one of Chef Gordon's restaurants: Black Cat.

They wanted something Asian-inspired.

I leaned into something I loved—coconut collard greens. I paired them with salmon, wrapped the greens inside the fish, and finished the dish with trout roe.

The flavors were bold. The dish was me.

But I made a mistake.

The coconut cream reduced too much and became salty. Paired with the trout roe, it tipped the balance. Chef Gordon wanted more texture, more crunch.

The critiques were fair.

Alejandro's dish was near perfect. He earned a black jacket.

Then Alex.

I hugged them both as they moved forward.

That left me alone.

Chef Jason pulled me aside.

"Don't overcomplicate it," he said. "Just cook delicious food. Nail the protein."

At that point, I was completely exhausted. Cooking back-to-back rounds felt impossible. But I knew there was no room for hesitation.

Round Three — Do or Die

This was it.

My protein was pork chop.

I marinated it in green Trinidadian seasoning to bring depth and heritage. I seasoned the carrots with curry spice. Everything on the plate had meaning.

I could feel Chef Jason watching me. I knew it probably looked like I was doing too much.

But I wasn't going to play it safe.

I wasn't there to blend in. I was there to speak.

Then I opened the oven.

Something was wrong.

The temperature was lower than I thought. Medium-low. Not hot enough.

I pulled the pork out and pressed it gently. I wasn't sure.

I sliced it open.

Raw.

My stomach dropped.

All the flavor in the world doesn't matter if the protein isn't cooked. Jason's words echoed in my head—*just nail the protein.*

I put the pork on the flattop, trying to save it.

Thirty seconds left.

I cut the pork in half and plated the piece that had the best chance.

I knew.

I knew it wasn't right.

The Wait

We were sent to Chef Gordon's office to wait.

Minutes felt like hours.

All I could think about was the pork. It wasn't cooked. It wasn't cooked.

Then the twist came.

Chef Gordon wouldn't be making the decision.

The competitors would.

Blind tasting. Peer judgment.

Summer tasted my dish and loved the seasoning. She voted for mine.

The others felt the pork was undercooked.

That was it.

The End

Chef Gordon stood in front of us.

"The chef leaving Hell's Kitchen today and not receiving a black jacket is… Sakari."

He explained it clearly.

"Great seasoning. Strong flavors. But the pork chop was undercooked."

He took my jacket.

"You should be proud of everything you've achieved here," he said. "You did a great job."

As I walked down the hallway, I looked at my watch.

It was the anniversary of my father's passing.

And suddenly, everything clicked.

The Real Victory

I came to this competition to prove something—to myself and to the world.

Out of thousands of applicants, I stood on that stage. I cooked my heart out. I showed who I was.

And standing there, jacket gone, I felt something unexpected.

Peace.

My father always taught me that character isn't revealed in victory —it's revealed in defeat. In how you respond. In how you keep going.

The raw pork chop was just food.

The real test was everything that led me there. Every setback. Every moment of doubt. Every time I chose to continue when quitting would've been easier.

I didn't walk away from Hell's Kitchen empty-handed.

I walked away knowing who I am.

And who you are matters more than what you win.

This wasn't the end.

It was the beginning.

CHAPTER 19: FULL CIRCLE: WHERE DREAMS AND REALITY MEET

When two worlds blend.
    It's been a year into my scholarship and Gary had launched his modern hospitality company called the VCR Group, founded with his partners, David Rodolitz, Josh Capon, and Conor Hanlon. I now had the opportunity to witness the company's new sector and its growth from the inside. The coincidence of having both my inspirations merge, food and business, with GaryVee at the forefront, actually felt more like perfect timing. Relationships were the basis of what you'd gain working with Gary. I was one of the lucky few.

As I was scrolling through Instagram stories, I saw an ad for the US Open. They were looking for a cook to help with the production. I saw that the message came from Conor Hanlon, a partner and operator from the VCR Group. I immediately reached out but received no response. As time went on, I decided to follow up once again. This time I got a response. Your superpower can often be your confidence to step forward as well as your to have a diverse portfolio of work experience. Fine dining, Pops-Ups, small scale restaurants or concessions, consistency in the delivery of great work is all that matters. I got the job. I met with Conor and Capon to go over the seasonal menu. This was also the opportunity to shed a glimpse of the world's first NFT restaurant, FlyFish and the first iteration would be at the US Open. It so happened to be Serena Williams' last year there.

As we moved forward with the program, I was in charge of producing hundreds of pounds of lobster, ceviche, scallops, and shrimp. The US Open was a massive operation, attracting over 700,000 attendees across the span of two weeks, generating more than $400 million in economic impact for New York. They would serve over 500,000 meals and go through 135,000 bottles of wine during the tournament. The scale is staggering. We would come in day in and day out, working to make sure the quality was up to standards. Excellence scales when you understand its fundamentals.

During my preparations to work at the Open, I got a phone call from Marcus Samuelsson. He wanted to check in to see how I was doing since my father's passing. He also had seen my appearance on Hell's Kitchen. He noticed my work and my talent. I told him about all my plans and hopes for the Summer. We connected and exchanged words. And then he said the magic words—the words that I'd heard from Tony Hawk, which resonated with me deeply: You have to work on your craft. Marcus had told me to let him know when I was ready. He had plans to open up a restaurant in Chelsea, called Hav & Mar, featuring sustainable seafood. They were looking into prospective chefs to open the restaurant and I was one to be considered. I thanked Marcus but I honestly needed time to carry on my personal goals I had set forth for myself.

For me, it just didn't feel right. I always enjoy working with people, but I knew that I wanted to focus on my goals and chase my crazy dreams of having pop-ups, products, building my brand and writing my book. Conor had also inquired if I wanted to be a chef de cuisine. I was not ready to make that decision and so I politely declined. The doubt crept in as I went back to prepping hundreds of pounds of seafood for the next days of service. There was an internal struggle as to whether I was making the right decision. The questions swirled in my mind as I watched the crowds flow through the US Open grounds. I pondered as I watched guests flow into the stadium seats, all of them there to witness greatness, or at least witness the pursuit of it.

You can have hopes and you can have dreams but the best way to make your dreams come true is by working with people who have already made their dreams come true. Be it a Marcus or a Conor or Gary, keep the connections that inspire you. Continue to build that rapport, but also understand what it takes to actually run a business. There will be Yes' and Nos, declines and reconsiderations, life challenges and life changes. If you're a young cook or chef reading this, it's okay to dream, because I've been there and I'm still there. You can not build alone. The essences of expansion are built in the fabrics of relationships. You need people. You need to provide value to people. You need to help people. You have to have good intentions. You need to be kind, lead by example, and put good grace into the world.

And as I watched Serena Williams' last match at the world's biggest stage, all these emotions started to come out. I was not only watching the GOAT in tennis or her last performance, I was witnessing the hard work that led her to savor this moment of her journey. The crowd gave her a standing ovation that seemed to last forever. She had lost but so gracious in her defeat, acknowledging every person who'd been part of her journey. Even at the end, she was thinking about others. Greatness isn't just about individual achievement. It is about impact and intention. It's about lifting others as you climb, creating opportunities for the next generation, building something bigger than yourself.

I had to do the work to help open the Flyfish Club, not just for me but for every young cook who needs to be inspired to go for their goals. For every kid who gets told their dreams are too big for where they come from. For everyone who's been counted out before they even got started. The vision crystallized in that moment, watching one legend pass the torch: I wasn't just going to be a chef. I was going to be a bridge, connecting worlds that rarely meet, bringing access to places that seem unattainable, creating opportunities where none may have existed before. The young chef who started peeling carrots in a community center had evolved into someone who could see beyond the next service, beyond the next job, beyond even the next restaurant. I could see the movement.

Now, if you made it this far in this book, you were able to hear my stories, read about the lessons I learned, and gain real insight into what it was like for me as a chef, as a young cook. But this next section of the book is a collection of insights from the voices who have inspired me on my journey.

This part of the book is dedicated to the greatest culinary minds in our generation. Featuring different philosophies and actionable steps that can implement influence in your life. Remember it begins from the dirt. From the ground up. This will depict the personal stories of: early careers, the come ups, building empires, and transitions. Relatable regardless of the industry that you are in. If you love food, become a chef, or if you love medicine, become a doctor. All professional ambitions can relate or be connected under the same philosophy. Hear all the voices, learn from their lessons. Let this serve as a reminder to live in the moment and Savor your journey.

PART II
HIDDEN GEMS

This section of the book will be a collection of interviews with carefully selected people, all highlighted to help you on your journey.

I've come across a lot of amazing people through my journey, people who have affected the way I think and helped me become who I am. What I have learned is that the best lessons don't come in formal settings or planned conversations. They happen in kitchen pass windows between services, over coffee at 5 AM before prep, in quiet moments when someone's guard is down and they share what they really think.

I'm hoping this section provides just one sentence, or one word that will change your perspective on your journey as you go throughout life, whether you're in the food industry or whether you're a nurse looking for some inspiration.

WHY THESE VOICES MATTER

I didn't choose these people randomly. Each conversation reflects a relationship, a moment, a connection that taught me something essential. Some I've worked alongside with and others who became mentors when I needed direction most. This includes: talented chefs, entrepreneurs, and food connoisseurs.

What you'll find here is an array of different perspectives:

- Finding the voice. The grind. The struggle.
- Building your empires. The Cost of the Journey.
- Striving for Excellence.

Success is not about your sole individual achievement, it's about lifting others as you climb.

.

What to Expect

Throughout these conversations, you'll see sidebars with context about how I met each person and why their perspectives matter to my story. These aren't just interviews; they're relationships that shaped how I think about food, business, and life.

The main point: If this helps you, it helps me. Each of these people shared knowledge that took them years to learn. This is the wisdom that makes the work meaningful. Whether you're influenced by these voices, connected to their journey, or simply looking for insight to be inspired by, those revelations are within these interviews.

HIDDEN GEMS: THE EARLY PATH, SKILLED WORK, AND CULTURAL IDENTITY

Chef Roshara Sanders
Chef Charlie Mitchell,
Chef Omar Tate
Chef BJ Dennis

CHEF ROSHARA: TEACHING AS MISSION, FOOD AS SALVATION

"You have to cook food because you love hospitality and you love the art. Don't cook because you want to be famous, because you may never be on the Food Network. You may never meet Gordon Ramsay. You have to do this because you love this."

I met Chef Ro through Instagram, honestly. I saw her work and knew I needed her voice in this book.

Here's the thing—most culinary school professors I've met are cool, but they're not always...real. They teach you the French techniques, show you the "right way," but there's this disconnect. Chef Ro isn't like that. She's a Black woman teaching at the CIA who's simultaneously working 16-hour days at Red Rooster with Marcus Samuelsson while holding down a full-time teaching position. That's not balance—that's grit.

Her story starts in an abandoned building in Queens. Her mom, nine months pregnant and deep in addiction, walked into a soul food restaurant called "Bird's Place". A woman who owned the spot looked at her and said, "You're pregnant. Get off these streets. Come work for me." That decision saved two lives—Chef Ro's mom got clean, worked at Compass Group for 35 years, and Chef Ro was born without the disabilities that could have defined her life.

Food saved her before she ever picked up a knife.

Chef Ro joined the military because she couldn't afford the CIA. She deployed twice to war zones before realizing she needed another path. The military taught her the brigade system before she ever stepped into a professional kitchen—because Escoffier literally created the kitchen brigade from his time in the French army. When she talks about teamwork, about "one band, one sound," she's not being motivational. She's speaking from experience where hesitation gets people killed.

Now she's at the CIA teaching kids who think getting a toque at orientation means they're chefs. She's developing the African diaspora concentration because she got tired of being told French cuisine is the only "foundation." She'll tell you straight up—foundations aren't French or African or anything else. Foundations are science. Heat control. Understanding why shit works. Once you have that, you can cook any cuisine in the world.

She's working with Marcus Samuelsson now because she's been head-down in the diaspora for years—traveling to Africa, researching with Mashama Bailey and Michael Twitty, building something real. Red Rooster's menu has been the same since 2016. They need fresh energy, a new perspective, someone who understands technique and flavor but also understands what it means to cook your ancestors' food with intention.

What You'll Discover:

- How food literally saved Chef Ro and her mother before she ever became a chef
- Why she would never recommend the military route she took, and what alternatives young cooks should explore
- The mistakes culinary students make (spoiler: they don't understand grit)
- Why "foundations" aren't about French cuisine—they're about food science
- How her military training translates directly to kitchen leadership
- The real shit about being a teacher—you're a parent, relationship coach, spiritual guide, and mentor
- Why cooking your ancestors' food isn't just cooking—it's cultural reclamation

This interview is for culinary students who think they're ready to be executive chefs when they graduate. It's for cooks who've been told French cuisine is the only "real" cuisine. It's for anyone who needs to hear that your origin story—whatever it is—doesn't disqualify you from this work.

Chef Ro works full-time at CIA, puts in 16-hour days at Red Rooster, and still shows up at 4:30 AM the next morning. That's what this life actually looks like.

Sakari: You said food saved your life. How did it save your life?

Chef Ro: My mom's originally from Queens, New York, and she's a 35-year recovering addict. When she was pregnant with me—I'm an '80s baby, so I'm a millennial—she was walking the streets of Queens, and she ended up moving to Connecticut. She was living in an abandoned building, and a woman who owned a soul food restaurant called Bird's Place, a woman of God, was like, "Hey, you know you're pregnant. You need to get off these streets. Why don't you come in here and work for me?"

She gave my mom a job, paying her under the table. My mom ended up going to a shelter, trying to get herself clean. She got an interview with Compass Group and just retired after 35 years there.

It was a miracle that I don't have any disabilities because she was really doing the worst things you could think of while carrying me. She was nine months pregnant in an abandoned building. But food was able to get her off the street.

She's a single mom, so coming from that—working two jobs, being able to provide for her child, bringing food home from work—I was raised around kitchens. I was two years old running around the back of restaurants.

Food gave me the opportunity to see where it could not only save my life and my mom's life, but when I was in the military too, putting so many people on the ground, I was like, I gotta find another path. Food was an opportunity for me to get out of going to war. I deployed twice and was about to be on my third deployment when I decided to take a chance on culinary.

I credit food with giving me purpose to navigate through life. If my mom didn't walk into that restaurant, the way she was doing drugs, there's no way I would have been born. She would have—I would have come out stillborn, probably. Honestly. It was bad.

Sakari: What made you want to join the Army?

Chef Ro: I just couldn't afford to come to CIA. That was the only school I knew about. They come to your school in high school and talk about the GI Bill. I was like, well, if I can't afford it through financial aid, then the military would be the smartest step for me. Because realistically, our industry doesn't make any money. Me working to pay for school wasn't realistic. And if I did do that, I would have to work 100 times harder. That's why I joined the military—to get the GI Bill.

Sakari: What advice would you give to people in that same situation? A kid who can't afford their dream school?

Chef Ro: I would never recommend the military, especially in today's climate.

I just wasn't educated enough to understand what scholarships were, how to apply for scholarships. I didn't know—like, oh, I can get a scholarship for being a Black woman, or I can get a scholarship for being left-handed. I don't know. There's just so many different things I didn't know.

I did my own FAFSA. My mom never graduated from high school. She's in the eighth grade reading level so she couldn't help me. I had to figure it out on my own. So I just didn't know.

I would tell them: try to get scholarships, try to get grants. I went to a vocational high school, but I was lazy and I didn't want to compete for Skills USA. I could have done stuff like that. I could have done ProStart. Churches have a lot of grants and scholarships, and I was really active in the church, but as a high school student, I just didn't know how to ask for help. I didn't know where to go for help.

But the military? I would not recommend.

Sakari: What got you to that place where you could ask for help throughout your career?

Chef Ro: I think it was the military. I've had two deployments under my belt, so it's one band, one sound. We are a unit. You walk, I walk—we are together. It's a dance.

War, the military, taught me teamwork. Somebody could be saving your life right next to you. You could be saving somebody else's life. We have to be locked in. It's a battle buddy system. You can't go anywhere by yourself. You can't sleep, you can't go to the bathroom alone, you can't shower alone. I'm bred in that environment.

And the military is very much like the kitchen. It doesn't matter if *sauté* is ready if the grill is not ready. They have to be ready at the same time because it's table one. It's two plates on the pass. We've got to be very much in sync with each other.

Sakari: The kitchen brigade system is very similar to the military. Was that an easy transition for you?

Chef Ro: It was a very easy transition. Escoffier used to be in the French army, and that's how he created the brigade system—from what he saw during his military time. The brigade system is literally military.

You have the Executive Chef, you have the CDC, all the way down to your line cooks. It is the military. I understood that very quickly. And it helps you structure the kitchen—it's divide and conquer in a good way. I don't need three people making a stock. I don't need five people cutting carrots. It gets the job done at a maximum level.

Sakari: You're a professor now. What are some of the mistakes you see students make?

Chef Ro: I think it's a generational thing. When I have adult students—I've taught a couple of retired Army colonels because CIA is for any age, it's a secondary career, whatever—adult learners are good. They understand life, they have a lot to offer, and they understand hard work.

This newer generation does not understand that this is not an easy job. They think, "I'm going to be on the Food Network," and "When I graduate, I'm going to be an executive chef and own a restaurant."

It's like the NFL. Only a few people get drafted. You have to play football because you actually love football. Don't play football because you want to make the NFL. Same thing with the NBA. You have to cook food because you love hospitality and you love the art.

Don't cook because you want to be famous, because you may never be on the Food Network. You may never meet Gordon Ramsay. You have to do this because you love this.

This is very costly. There's a lot of hours. There's a lot of holidays. You're going to miss the birthdays. You're going to miss the baby showers. They come in with the mentality like they're ready-made. A lot of faculty say the one thing we've done recently is give them a *toque* ceremony in the beginning. When I was a student, you got a toque when you graduate. Now you get a toque ceremony during orientation. So now they think they're chefs.

You have to earn that.

Chef Ro: They don't understand grit.

I'm full-time here. Yesterday I left school, went to Red Rooster because I'm working with Marcus Samuelsson right now. That's the seventh 16-hour day for me. Then I gotta be in at 4:30 the next day. That's grit.

Sakari: Marcus is very big on mentorship. Can you speak about that relationship?

Chef Ro: It's fairly new. I'm the new Chef Ambassador of Red Rooster, taking over menu development and creative innovation. I think Marcus and his team picked me because I've been head-down in the diaspora for about three to four years. I've been to Africa. I travel with Mashama Bailey and Michael Twitty and Eric Williams—these are all James Beard people.

At the school, I've developed the African concentration. Marcus is Ethiopian. Red Rooster's menu has been the same since like 2016, so they need some freshness, some newness, some new faces, a new buzz.

Marcus does this with all his restaurants. You look at Hav & Mar, he has Fariyal over there. You look at Marcus B&P in DC, he has Anthony over there. Red Rooster in Miami—he has a metropolis of people running his vision. But he's looking for people of color. He's looking for people with passion and people who understand technique and flavor profile.

Because of what I do at the CIA, I kind of fell on their radar.

Sakari: What do you look for in a student? Similar to maybe what Marcus is showing you?

Chef Ro: I was really militant. You got to be at the right place, at the right time, in the right uniform. I can tell a student has it as soon as they walk in the kitchen. You don't even have to open your mouth. It's a sense of energy.

I look for people who ask a lot of questions, but it depends on the question you ask. Let me give you an example from today.

I teach *à la carte* right now—this is your first real production kitchen. I told a student, "You need to make polenta. You need two cups of polenta by volume." The student got four cups. That completely messes up the ratio because it's a starchy vegetable, it's cornmeal—it's going to absorb all this liquid.

I look at the polenta and I said, "Why is the polenta so dry and burning on the bottom?"

"Well, Chef, I put two cups."

"You didn't put two cups. I watched you put four cups."

I let her put four cups in because she needs to know that. But she didn't fix it. She just left the polenta cooking and sticking to the bottom. Instead of saying, "You know what, Chef? You're right. I mismeasured. Let me add more water."

I'm looking for solution-based thinking. You can make mistakes, but how do you fix it? The guest doesn't care that the polenta is thick. You need to add more water, get the polenta cooked, then you just keep moving.

I'm looking for people who ask questions, people who are adjustable and adaptable, and people who, even after a mistake is made, just move forward.

Sakari: What are some things that go into being a teacher at the CIA that maybe students don't think about?

Chef Ro: Everything. You are a mentor. Sometimes you're a parent, and you got to really find a balance. Sometimes you're a relationship coach. I try not to do that with my students until they graduate or get out of my class because there's boundaries. I'm your teacher, we're talking about food. But once they move on, people always call me. "Chef, can I get your email?" And I continue the mentorship.

You're a mentor, your relationship coach, your mom, your dad. You provide a lot of wisdom and knowledge. Sometimes I'm a spiritual coach, depending on the student. I don't really talk spirituality, but if some of my students are very spiritual and they ask me questions, and with respect, if they're open to the conversation, I'm always open for the conversation.

You're everything. Sometimes this is the first time people have moved away from home. They don't know anything. They're just deer in the headlights, so you got to really guide them.

We're teaching them soft skills. We're teaching them how to communicate. We're teaching them how to work with a team.

With my military background, I have an advantage. In the military, I'm working with people from all over the country, all different types of backgrounds. So I'm able to mediate when people don't get along.

You're not going to get along with everybody in the kitchen either. When you get a job, how do you still make the food come out quality and the guest experience is good? And then you guys can talk about it later. We're teaching them soft skills as well.

Sakari: What's a test you would give to a student?

Chef Ro: They take quizzes. Allergies—what are the nine allergies? How do you put allergies on your menu? Food safety is a big thing. They don't know how to hot-hold things. They don't know how to pull things down. Cross contamination. What's a physical contaminant?

If you're breaking down a chicken and you leave the wishbone in it, and God forbid somebody chokes on it, that's a physical contaminant. Or your earring pops out.

Food safety, allergens. In my class specifically: ratios. If you're making risotto, what's the ratio? How much liquid to how much rice? Units of measurement.

We have a career fair coming up, so I assigned: go to the career fair, get a couple of cards, and tell me why you want to go to this place on externship.

Key terms. What does "all day" mean? What does "fire" mean? What is FIFO? First In, First Out. It's a constellation of kitchen jargon and allergies and food safety.

Sakari: If a student can't afford to come to your school but they want to learn, what would you tell them?

Chef Ro: You don't have to come to school. I don't know if you finished the show *Not To Just Chef*, but there's people on the show that never went to culinary school, and they're doing really well in the competition.

You go to Sur La Table and take a cooking class. As long as you listen—some people who go to culinary school ain't that good. That's just real shit. Just because you come here don't mean you're really that good.

You just got to have the passion to learn, and you got to be able to read. If you can read a recipe, then you're good.

Sakari: What made you go down the route of learning about the African diaspora and your roots?

Chef Ro: I've been to Africa. You know how they say you got to know where you come from to know where you're going? Same sentiment.

My father is Jamaican, but I've never met him. So how do I learn about my heritage? Through food. Because food gives me history.

What is jerk? Jerk comes from burying your protein in the ground to hide from the colonizers, because the Jamaican Maroons were running. Now you go down this whole rabbit hole, but you were just talking about jerk.

Learning about who you are through food. My mom always makes this okra stew. I'm not a fan of okra because I don't like it to be slimy, but my mom never makes it slimy. She stews it in tomatoes, puts ham hock and neck bones, eating it with rice and peppers and onions.

Me doing research—that's how the Gullah Geechee do it in South Carolina. My grandparents are from South Carolina. So now I just found out that I have Gullah in my family. I do this research at school, writing this class—this concentration. "This is how the Geechee make their okra, but you make it like that." My mom has no idea about her background.

I asked family members, got family trees, and now I know for 100% my people are Gullah. But I learned that through this thing she makes every Sunday.

Food is fun. I've been to France. I'm classically French trained. Obviously I graduated from the CIA. But that food is not my food. I feel like there's a stigma—all Black people cook Southern food, or all Black food is not refined. You see a Gregory Gourdet who's making Haitian food, one of the most refined, top of the line.

I just want to break some glass ceilings. I want to cook my own food. I like a lot of fusion—I love Asian cuisine. But the more I get into Jamaican cuisine, I notice there's a whole population of Chinese in Jamaica. Now it makes sense. Everything is a melting pot, and that's the food I want to cook.

I don't want to cook the food of my colonizer. That's just what it is.

Sakari: There's a fine line, right? There's "I want to cook my ancestors' food," but then there's "I need to learn the basics." What would you say to a student?

Chef Ro: Well, what basics? Because I'm teaching the French basics—is that the only way? You go to Japan, they have their own basics.

For example, we teach students to never boil stock because you want it to be clear and fat-free. You make *pho*—they boil the stock. Depending on where you go, sometimes I've had Vietnamese pho that's super clear. Sometimes I have ramen and it's cloudy.

What basics are we talking about? Whose is the standard? I think that's a whole other conversation.

Foundations are: can you execute what you're taught? That's what a foundation is to me. If I'm telling you to blanch broccoli and keep it green, that's not French, that's not African, that's not Spanish. I'm just telling you to blanch it and keep the chlorophyll. Now this is science—chlorophyll.

A pickle is a pickle. If I want to pickle red onions, it's not French. I just want a pickle. *Escovitch* is basically pickled peppers and onions. A pickle is a pickle.

What foundation are we talking about?

Chef Ro: As long as you can follow directions, to me that's foundation. As long as you understand the *why*.

If I tell you to fry an egg and I don't want any browning, you need to understand heat control, conduction. If I have too much fat in the pan, fat expedites browning. That's not about French versus African. It's not about culture. It's about foundation of food science.

You can learn any type of cuisine as long as you have the foundation of food science, heat control, ingredient functionality. Why does pear go well with fig? Why does kimchi go with whatever? You got to understand the science, and then you can adapt it to any type of cuisine.

Sakari: Growing up, what was your school lunch situation?

Chef Ro: School lunch is tricky for me because I had to pay for school lunch. Some days I wouldn't eat school lunch because it's four or five dollars a day. That's kind of a lot for me when I was growing up.

My mom would bring food home from work. If I didn't eat school lunch, at least I know she worked at Compass Group. I know she gonna bring something home. That's what I looked forward to.

Sakari: One of my chefs always said, "You might not get rich as a chef, but you'll never go hungry."

Chef Ro: That's for sure. 100%. Even if I gotta eat family meal—family meal's the only meal I eat that day, at least I got one meal. That's why family meals are important, because you just don't know people's background.

Sakari: Any last pieces of advice for the next generation?

Chef Ro: Let the food lead you and guide you. For me, it's a spiritual thing. It gets me closer to God. It gets me closer to my community. It opens up many doors. You can travel. You can work in a homeless shelter, a soup kitchen. Look at José Andrés—you could be in Gaza one day. You could work in a restaurant, you could work in catering, you could work at a mom and pop.

It's bigger than just restaurants. You could be a writer. There's so many different lanes. Let it guide you to your purpose and have fun. We forget because we work so hard. This ain't that serious, bro. As long as we don't kill nobody and give nobody *E. coli*, just have fun.

The guests—you will not please everybody. Life is too short, so at least have some fun while you're doing it.

Sakari: How important has faith been on your journey?

Chef Ro: It's everything. It is the journey.

I posted something on Instagram about my garden on campus. Just watching things flourish, planting a seed—that's what life's about. You plant a seed, you have an idea, and then you water it. You nurture it. You watch it come into fruition.

As culinary creatives, I have an idea. This is the recipe, what I want to do. Then I play with it, test it, and it ends up on a menu. Somebody comes to my restaurant like, "Oh my god, this is the best meal I've ever had."

From inception to giving it to somebody—we're giving ourselves to people through this channel. That's energy. That's very spiritual. If you have a bad day, the food's probably not going to be good. I have bad days and I'm like, "Damn, this really don't taste good." On my best days, I'm like, "Damn, I killed this."

You can feel it.

CHEF CHARLIE MITCHELL: BREAKING THROUGH IDENTITY AND EXCELLENCE

"You don't need to lead by fear. Set the standard, hold the line, and teach the lesson. If they grow from it, you've done your job."

Those words hit me hard the first time I heard Charlie say them, not because they were harsh, but because they were true. Charlie Mitchell, the first Black chef to win a Michelin star in New York City. That was a dream of mine, and to see a friend achieve that is something special.

I first met Charlie at Eleven Madison Park. He came in with tattoos and unapologetically himself. He would speak to the chefs in no particular cadence, just full authenticity. You could feel like he was from Detroit, and he walked with a confidence as he had just left Betony, a well-known Michelin star restaurant that was run like a mini boot camp. Charlie always wanted to be a serious chef. He fell in love with the idea of fine dining and went on to continue honing his craft. But when I met him, he was just a cook, just like me. Later on, he was promoted to butcher.

The one takeaway from Charlie for me was always his authenticity. He just was himself. Sometimes we feel like we have to adjust or adapt to people. We don't want to say the wrong thing, almost walking on eggshells. With Charlie, there were no eggshells, and if there were, he cracked them all. There was a level of confidence he had because of the work he put in. When people walk with confidence, it puts others at ease and allows you to trust them. That's something that happened with the cooks, with the other chefs at Eleven Madison Park, when Charlie came in, they would feel more relaxed, like "he's got it," because he had the confidence.

Now Charlie is a young chef making his dreams come true. When I interviewed him, he had just taken the reins at two Michelin starred restaurant Saga because one of the legends, James Kent, had passed. Charlie and I have had many encounters—from him being a cook, to working at one of his first restaurants before Clover Hill, and then of course at Clover Hill where he got his Michelin star. To see him at Saga, taking the reins and leading a real kitchen with a huge team of cooks is inspiring to see.

I didn't choose Charlie just because he's a friend or because of his accolade, I wanted readers to learn from his approach.

In this conversation, Charlie breaks down what it really takes to excel, while staying authentic. He'll challenge how you think about identity, leadership, and the responsibility that comes with success. You'll learn his framework for managing different personalities, why he believes mentorship isn't what most people think it is, and how his Detroit upbringing shaped his approach to fine dining. This isn't just about cooking, it's about the cadence, the work ethic, and the mindset required to break barriers in any field. Whether you're in a kitchen or a boardroom, Charlie answers questions about excellence that I hope will help guide your own journey.

Sakari: When I just saw you walking through the kitchen, it didn't feel like people were walking on eggshells. But you're clearly holding high standards.

Charlie: You don't need to lead by fear. You can lead by fear, you can lead by respect, a little bit of both. They're not afraid of me, they just need to know the standards. I don't want them to be afraid of me, that's not my goal. It's not personal either. Back in our day it was personal—cooks would hit you, pick at you, call you stupid. I don't cross those lines. It's very professional. I'm trying to teach you a lesson, it's not personal. And I only teach this lesson because you want to be a chef. If you told me you don't want to be a chef, I'd let you do whatever you want.

Sakari: Looking for a sense of comfort, you should go in another direction, right? Because comfort breeds complacency.

Charlie: Exactly. It's like teaching your kid how to play basketball, maybe you want to work on their left hand, so you make them tie their right hand behind their back. They don't see value in it at that moment, but eventually they will. And that's all it is. It's not about being mean, it's about teaching them something they don't understand. You have to be willing for that person to not like you because they don't understand. And one day they will.

I have a method where I'm very sour and sweet. I may come down on someone about something, but then I'll explain why. I won't just be like "this goes here, I don't care what you think." Later I'll explain why I feel that way, and hopefully they agree with it.

Sakari: Do you think that's how you were raised in kitchens?

Charlie: Not all of them, but the ones that taught me the most, that was my first lesson and from there I was able to survive. My first job here, I learned that the hard way very quickly and I never had to learn that lesson again. After you learn that lesson, you can survive in any kitchen in the world, any workplace in the world. Once you realize that nothing is up to you, life's easier.

Sakari: You mean having humility?

Charlie: I call it just doing your job. A lot of people want to come to work and they're like "this doesn't work for me." It's like, you don't matter. Seriously. That's especially for Black people, we can go on for hours about this, but it's like, you can't wear your do-rag in my kitchen, even if I'm a Black chef. I don't care what hairstyle you have. That's not my problem.

That's genuinely weird. If you were a bank teller, would you see a bank teller in a do-rag? No. So why are you in a do-rag in my kitchen?

It's all of it, right? "Oh, I have bad handwriting." I don't care—the rules here are that every label needs to be legible. If you can't write legibly, then you can't work here. It's very black and white.

Sakari: But when I walked through, there was admiration from the cooks, the way you talked to everyone.

Charlie: I still respect them as people. I don't really need you to like me. I need you to do your job and value what you learned in this restaurant. You may feel friction like "I don't like him, he's so hard on us, I don't like the management style." Okay cool. But if you survive a year, when you move on I want you to look back and be like "damn, I see what they were talking about." Wax on, wax off.

It's like your mom, right? "Damn mom, you was right about that ten years ago. I didn't listen." That's what you should want as a leader and boss. If they like you, that's a bonus. If they learn to love you, that's great—that's when you get into mentorship.

I had a cook at Claro—Leo. He quit because he felt like he sucked. But he made it a whole year. He went to The Modern and was like "yo, thank you. I'm on hotline in less than six months because you taught me how to use my brain and think and be present." He's going to be a sous chef in less than two years. He's 23.

Sakari: What's "giving it to him" look like?

Charlie: One night I kicked him off the station. I made him watch us work service and told him to stand there until I said he could leave. I made him stand there until we were done breaking down. So he stood there for like four hours. The whole restaurant watched it and nobody stopped it.

But it was to prove a point—it's not us, it's you. This works. The system works. You're mad at the system and trying to make the system work for you, but it works. You just got to get out your own way and realize you can. And if I thought you couldn't, I wouldn't push you to do it.

Sakari: Everyone can't be managed the same.

Charlie: Everybody's different. Everyone wants different things. Some people don't want to be a chef—I don't hire those kind of people. They don't even get in the atmosphere. But if they don't at least love food and love what they're doing, then it's too hard to manage them. I need them to clean the mushrooms.

It's different when a cook knows they want to do right but they're in fight or flight mode.

I can coach that—you're making bad decisions, we can coach that. But a lack of care? You don't belong in a restaurant that's two, three Michelin stars.

Sakari: What's your patience level for mistakes?

Charlie: It depends. You have to understand that person and what the guest can experience—that's how you should rate how you respond. Is it affecting the guest or not?

I'll pick my spots. This is a problem but it's never going to make it to the guest—I'll address it one way. But a smaller problem that's going to make it to the guest, I may be way more dramatic about it because I'm trying to prove a point about what makes it to the guest.

It also depends, are they a good employee or not? You can be a great cook but a bad employee. And that's not okay. You can be a

bad cook but a great employee, and I'll deal with that. The environment is the most important.

If you show up on time, you're professional, you always call back, you're honest, "Hey chef, I messed this up, how do I fix it?" I can deal with that. But if you're the best cook in the kitchen but showing up late, leaving early, not wiping down, thinking because you're the best cook you can be mean to other cooks—no room for that either. It's toxic, it spreads.

Sakari: When you were a young cook wanting to be the best, what would you say to someone on that same trajectory?

Charlie: You need to define what being the best is to you. What does that mean? No one is the best, it's a very subjective industry. There's room for all of us. There was a time when Daniel Humm was at the top of his game while Grant Achatz was too, Ferran Adrià was still running the world and Thomas Keller was still the man with three stars. They're all extremely different from each other.

I just wanted to be respected by my peers and the guests.

Being the best cook and being the best chef aren't always the same thing. Being the best cook is one thing, but being the best chef—can you be a leader? Can you get people to buy into a vision? Do you understand business? Can you operate the numbers? Can you inspire people?

Sakari: What's your secret sauce for that?

Charlie: I don't have a secret sauce. I'm still learning. You learn from your mistakes. After I make a mistake, I'm like "damn, how could I have done that differently? What am I really frustrated about? What am I really fighting for?"

I think the hardest part about this industry is navigating it—trying to get opportunities, get chef jobs, maybe tour around the world, get into the business side. It's very hard to know how to push forward, and know who to trust. The experience can be loaded, but nobody shows up if there's no food. When you're running a business, there's so much that goes into that plate to get to that guest. The cooks worry about the meat, the fish on that plate. The *garde manger* worries about the sauce. The sous chef worries about the process. But I got to figure out—how does this even exist? Why does it exist? What's the story? How was it treated? Where's the food coming from? The philosophy, the vision, the intentionality, the story behind the plate.

In order to reach the highest level, you need to really start to understand human beings and how to move people emotionally. That's what you're really searching for.

Sakari: Something I always respected about you, you've always been authentically. For me as a Black person, it was so hard to navigate being myself in professional environments. But you were just so comfortable in your own skin.

Charlie: I have this whole thing about how identity is a crutch. Identity is a hindrance. Believing in identity does a disservice. Identity isn't real. We're just humans. But just saying that means you're buying into identity. It takes work though. Early in my career it came from confidence, a little bit of "I think I belong here" and "I only know one way to be." So it came from a little bit of ignorance. Then after that it takes work.

If you can release that, then you can just be yourself. But none of us can be ourselves because you've been told since you were two that you should feel uncomfortable around a White person. You can't get it out of you because you've been told that since you were crazy young. It takes work to get it out.

I don't care where I'm from, I can cook whatever I want. I don't care what skin color, I can do whatever I want. A Black person can't tell me I talk *White* because I'm like "Who taught you that? Where'd you get that from? That's not even your thought. Somebody taught you that."

Both sides are wrong. They're both learned behaviors that you're just not thinking deeply enough. Once you can start to navigate that, you can strip away all these things you've learned and be like "now who do I want to be? What do I like to eat? Do I want to eat this on Thanksgiving or something different?"

Sakari: Do you feel pigeonholed as a Black chef versus just a chef?

Charlie: I think other people pigeonhole identity. But you're fighting for a sense of belonging, which is why we're fighting for acceptance, constantly fighting for a voice in this country. You need to just let that go. You're never going to be accepted. There's never a voice for you. You're punching a wall.

We're busy trying to get White people to accept us and they're not even responding to those punches. They don't give a fuck. You're only wasting your own time and energy.

I think the whole Black chef thing is great. I don't stray away from it. I am very proud to be a representative of anyone—my family, Detroit, my community. But I'll still get more comments from my community than I get from other people outside my race if I'm serving food they think I shouldn't serve. It's not fair to anyone. It's not helping you. In order for you to grow, you have to be okay with being a little bit uncomfortable.

Sakari: What's your style of cooking if it's not soul food?

Charlie: It changes, and the most important thing is to allow yourself to change. Ten years ago I thought my food would be very classic French—that's what I fell in love with. Then my diet changed, I eat more seafood. I cook the way I think people should eat, slash the way I want to eat. I'm very in tune with how I want the person to feel or think. I want to cook seafood because it's more sustainable, vegetables as well. It matters where they come from. It's our job as chefs to educate guests. I didn't eat a beet until I was a chef, but it's our job to educate them on what you can do with these beets. I'm a cook at my core. I like to cook. I'm not into too much manipulation. Ingredients should be treated as they are, with respect and very intentional. They should be identifiable.

Sakari: Do you wish you could change how you grew up eating?

Charlie: No, I wouldn't change nothing. The way I ate influenced me to get into restaurants and taught me about how I don't want to eat. I was a fat kid and had resentment with my family because I was like "y'all just made me overeat." Americans just overeat and I have a hard stance on that.

People are like "it's not enough food" and I'm like "yes it is." The American portion size is fucked up. You don't eat to feel stuffed. Food is fuel, nutrients. It's not meant to make you feel like you got a stomach ache.

Soul food is packed with sodium, pork, sugar—it's heavy. But eating like that and then learning to cook fine dining, I realized the disconnect. There's no balance, it's not multiple flavors. You have no idea what's in this food. You really think that chicken in the grocery store is the same chicken I'm serving? If I wouldn't have grown up eating like that, I wouldn't have so much value in showing people that it is different. If I would have grew up eating fine dining food, I probably would just be pretentious. But I have value in "hey, your experience with food can be different. You don't need to feel like you need to take a nap as soon as you eat."

Sakari: Do you have a mantra? For me it's "noble promise"—my name means noble promise. Do you have something you connect to on a day-to-day basis?

Charlie: Multiple. For family like, I have a certain responsibility and obligation within my family which affects my drive for my career. I left where I was from to create a new trajectory for my family, my household, my name.

"Cooking is fun" is more of a reference to cooking, that's the joy of the restaurant, but the restaurant industry sucks. The cooking is the fun part and all the rest comes as a consequence of wanting to cook for people.

Later in my life: "waste no time, waste no talent." Sometimes you don't realize it. Sometimes you don't think you're talented or you think you have so much time. The reality is we don't. Time is one thing you actually have the most control over, although you're sold that you have no control over your time.

Even more later: "one day never comes." We're all just like "one day, one day, one day." It's like, do it now. That doesn't exist. Tomorrow's not promised. Your next birthday is not promised. Take advantage of the time now, what's in front of you right now.

There's so many people who don't have it. Me being from Detroit, I know people who just don't have it. So for me to waste it, half-ass it, not give it my all, that would be a disservice and irresponsible.

I didn't ask to be the first Black chef in New York City to get a Michelin star, but it just kind of happened. I didn't ask for all those people to be looking up to me. But when it happened, I was like "who am I not to embrace it?" To not be available if I can be, to not drop gems if I can, to not give as many opportunities as possible if I can.

This responsibility landed on my desk. That means it's meant for me and I need to figure out how to live up to it, own up to it. It's God's plan. If you don't, you're messing up the script. This is what you're supposed to be doing.

Sakari: What's the importance of mentorship to the next generation?

Charlie: I wasn't raised to believe in mentorship. I still don't. But I said about James—one regret I had was that I didn't value mentorship when I was younger and probably should have. But I still think I'm right about it.

I was raised very religious, you don't fear the flesh, you don't idolize the flesh. I don't give a fuck how many Grammys Jay-Z got, I don't know what he does behind closed doors. How can he be my idol? I don't even know him. How can you mentor me? You might mentor me about being a chef, but what if you're a bad person? Bad with money? Don't treat your wife well? Bad parent? So for me it's about learning to listen. Be okay with listening. Don't be stubborn, have an open mind. If somebody is better than you at something, respect that and be your own worst critic.

I was running Claro Hill and was like "I don't know what I'm doing. I can cook and yell at these kids and pick fancy plates, but I don't really know what I'm doing. How do you become a New York City chef?" It humbled me enough to have vulnerable conversations with people who had accomplished what I wanted to accomplish.

Will I mentor my cooks? Absolutely. But for the ones who want to open that door. The way you do anything is the way you do everything. I know your room's dirty because your station's dirty. Chefs need to train themselves like athletes mentally and physically. Your diet matters. How much sleep you get matters. If you had a good weekend or bad weekend matters. If you're in a toxic relationship, that matters. If you have daddy issues, that matters. If you have childhood trauma, that matters. All of those things affect the way you show up here.

I'm not perfect. I got my own shit. But it is important and you got to learn how to listen. Especially for young men—our ego grows faster than our maturity grows. Men don't want to listen. We're right, we want to compete with every person put in front of us.

Kobe became Kobe because he respected what Michael Jordan built and just wanted to be like him. The mamba mentality thing was after it was branded. That's not really what it was. He was like "How can I be Michael Jordan?" He monitored everything he did wanting to be Michael Jordan. That birthed Kobe Bryant.

I don't know if it's mentorship for me, but it is learning how to have discernment and listen to the right people. Take gems from those people. If somebody's smart about money, talk to them about money. Doesn't mean they're smart about how to raise a family.

You got to be vulnerable. You got to be hungry enough where you're like "shit, I got to get to where I'm trying to go. If this question is between me and where I'm trying to go, I need to ask this question."

I want to do it all. I want to learn. I want to be in the real estate deal meeting, the profit meeting, the meeting about the food. I don't know shit about commercial real estate. So what do I do? I get a book. I read about it. Stay open-minded.

Earlier in my career I would have learned to be more vulnerable, ask more questions, be more willing to take on advice and not be motivated by fear or trying to prove people wrong—that's our ego. It got me very far, but it won't get me to the top of the mountain. It won't get you championships. The chef journey is solo, but restaurants are a team sport. I'm relying on him to put the right salt and lemon juice in that pan every pick while I'm 10 feet away. The more he dislikes me, the less likely he is to put lemon juice on every pick. But the more he respects my viewpoint and I inspire him and he truly understands what he's doing, he's more likely to do it.

You can't do it all by yourself. Life is a team sport—family, community, friends, whatever else you're into.

Sakari: Last thing—failure seems important to your philosophy.

Charlie: Failure is a part of success. If you're afraid of failure, don't try to be successful. You're just wasting your time. People who do should never listen to people who don't do. Broke people are always going to tell you how to spend your money. People out of business are going to tell you what they would do. People who are afraid to try anything will always try to talk you out of trying something.

Part of Jordan was missing shots. LeBron took a lot of Ls. He's still going. Can't be afraid to fail or you won't reach success. Just got to go for it. I started therapy last year. He was like "how does that feel? Being Black and successful?" I was like "boy, we don't got enough time for that. We have to spread that one out over the course of the year." Look at the Drake and Kendrick shit. These dudes are huge, and we still have this tension within the culture about one success being more valuable than another success. That whole thing was a great example of how hard it is. Damned if you do, damned if you don't.

CHEF OMAR TATE: ON FINDING PURPOSE THROUGH HARDSHIP, BUILDING COMMUNITY, AND COOKING AS POETRY

"Find hardship. Don't find something that makes you comfortable. Find a challenge. Get the fuck off the screen, read a book, and find a challenge.

Dedicate yourself to it and stay there for a year and hate it. If you hate it, hate it. If you love it, great. But if you hate it, stay there for a year. Find hardship. Find a challenge."

I was naive when I first met Omar.

Fresh out of Eleven Madison Park, I thought chefs were supposed to look a certain way—clean-shaved, crisp whites, polished shoes. Omar had a huge beard, a worn apron, dirty Crocs. He was a sous chef working under JJ at the time, grinding it out, but already talking about this dream called Honeysuckle.

I didn't understand then. Now I know that's what the real work looks like. That's what dedication looks like.

Omar Tate is a lot of things. Esquire's Chef of the Year 2020. TIME100 Next honoree in 2021. James Beard Foundation Semi-Finalist 2024. The chef-owner of Honeysuckle in Philadelphia. But titles don't capture what makes him different.

He's a poet who happens to cook. An artist who uses food as his medium. A historian excavating stories that have been buried or stolen. When he talks about his food, he'll tell you: "I don't think it's a rendition. If I just made that dish and never told you what it was, if it didn't have this context and story, it would just be a good dish. But when you assign meaning to something, then people begin to define the senses they're experiencing through that thing through the meaning of your assignment. That's storytelling."

Omar put me under his wing early. He taught me about Black food history, about researching dishes, about creating cuisine, what he calls Black Heritage cooking. He challenged everything I thought I knew about being a chef. Made me feel dumb as hell when I proudly told him I don't like reading books. That's what good mentors do—they push you past your comfort zone.

This interview is Omar unfiltered. No polish, no PR spin. Just the real story of how a broke drug dealer who got fired from hotel jobs became one of the most important chef-artists working today. You'll hear about the Muslim driver during Ramadan who got him to a life-changing interview. The 14-year-old kid on the news in New Orleans who redirected his entire purpose. The dish called Clorindy that uses cuttlefish ink to represent Blackface and protest the human condition.

What I've Learned:

- Your origin story doesn't have to be inspiring—it just has to be honest
- Poetry isn't just words on a page; it's a way of seeing and communicating
- Building a team means giving people titles they've never held and trusting them to grow into them
- Partnership means your wife isn't behind you—she's right there beside you, equal
- Purpose isn't found in comfort; it's found in hardship

Sakari: For people reading this, I want to help young cooks on their journey. You speak about how cooking was a chore for you at first. How did that shift?

Omar: I don't think I ever really thought about the shift. In hindsight, I recall how much I actually did enjoy cooking, and then made intentional choices to make food that I wanted to make when I was a teenager.

The chore part was my mom asking me to take a chicken out the fridge and roast it, learn how to boil beans. Then I started to have fun with food. I love cheesesteaks—I wanted to learn cheesesteaks. I started buying my own meat, watching people make them, trying to emulate that in the house. I got really into making BLTs. Philly's a big sandwich city, so hoagies. I cared not just about making them, but how they looked in the end, the type of vinegars I was using. I would spend my own money from whatever jobs I had to make sure I had the ingredients I wanted.

That was the first time I can remember giving a fuck about food. But the word "chef" just wasn't part of my vocabulary. The food I made was so good that people would always ask me to make them cheesesteaks. But I never had any intention of taking it beyond that step.

Sakari: When was the shift? When did you know this is what you wanted to do?

Omar: Bro, I'm trying to tell you—it wasn't like that. I started cooking, but I was selling drugs. I was in the street, trying to get out of jail most of the time and talk to girls. I didn't care about cooking at all. I didn't give a fuck about cooking.

From age 17, I was a dishwasher, a porter at a hotel. I was an overnight dishwasher, and sometimes set up for banquets. But even still, in the way you and I understand kitchen as a place to do this job, it was just a fucking job to me. I clocked in, shot the shit with people I fucked with, listened to rap, hid out in the break room talking to girls on the internet, got my check, and tried to duck out from as much work as possible. I was just like a normal nigga—nothing special going on.

I would eat this food and be like, "Yo, it's bland. It has no seasoning whatsoever." I was completely turned off from commercial dining. But they would have stocks going overnight, and everything they were doing was French—I didn't know that then because I didn't care, but the stocks would smell so good. I fucked around so badly. I was stealing shit, would clock in, leave, go fuck with shorties in the middle of the night, come back at 3 a.m., hurry up and do my job and go home. I got fired for that shit. Then I went full-time street—hustling, selling drugs.

I was always looking for work though. I worked at the Gap, BJs Wholesale—I had all these jobs while selling drugs. I was a broke hustler. I got fired from another hotel job, and I was looking in the paper for work. This golf club was hiring for a prep cook or something like that. I'm like, "Well, fuck it. I worked in kitchens, let me see if they'll hire me." It was two and a half hours outside Philadelphia. The way I got there was by calling the manager from the hotel job I was just fired from. The only reason they fired me was because I was late every day, 30 minutes late every day because I had to take this regional train and I'm not a morning person. But the manager was like, "Listen, I like you, but you gotta go. If you ever need anything, call me."

So I needed a ride to this interview. I thought it was gonna be a taxi, but they called me a luxury car. I only had $25 in my pocket. The car hits $25—we're not even halfway there. It's Ramadan, so I'm fasting. My driver's Muslim, he's fasting. I'm like, "Yo brother, listen, I don't have enough money to get to this place. I have $25. I'll give you every dollar in my pocket right now if you just get me to this interview because I need this job." He said, "Look man, you know what? Ramadan. I'll get blessings. Keep your money. Good luck. Get the job. I'm gonna drop you off, but you gotta find your way back home." They wanted to hire me on the spot. I said I can't start today because there's no public transportation to get me out here and I don't have my car. So I leave, and as I'm walking out, there's this bus coming down the road—a city bus. I get on, and the sign says it's going back towards Philadelphia. I'm like, "Yo, I thought there was no public transportation to get out here." The driver's like, "Today's the first day of this route."

I had a way to work. I took that as a sign, this is what I'm supposed to do. That's what I'm trying to tell you. There was no "I love cooking." I didn't care. All I wanted was to have a job. The only reason I started looking for cook jobs was because I'd worked in kitchens, the next step above what I was doing was cook, and I wanted to design a life where I wasn't at the whim of someone else's negotiation on my pay. It was all about pay.

At this interview, they asked me to julienne a shallot. I didn't know what either one of those words meant. I never heard of a shallot, never heard of leeks, never heard of scallions. I never heard of food, bro—except the food I grew up with. When they hired me, they said, "You don't know what you're doing. We'll make you a dishwasher again. We're gonna pay you minimum wage. You're gonna work 14 hours a day, we're only gonna pay you for eight. But look at this like school, we're paying you to go to school to hone the craft."

I took that to heart. These people are taking a chance on me. I'm taking a chance on myself.

Sakari: Talk about your time in the South. How did you know you wanted to go down South?

Omar: I don't think I ever leave with the thought of "I'm kind of good at anything." I know what I'm capable of and what I can do, but maybe to my own detriment, I never think I'm good enough. I only ended up going down South because I felt like, more important than being good at something, I had a charge—I had something to say. There's a void that I was seeking to fill for my own self that I thought was necessary to share with people.

Sakari: About food? Or just more about you?

Omar: I thought it was about me, and I thought it was about food, and I quickly learned that it was not about food. That perspective that I cannot help but have, I think that's what makes my food my food.

I always had this sense of missing home and this nostalgia for a time period when I didn't exist, where I didn't exist. Never felt fully American. Never felt like I had a country. Didn't know where my family was from, didn't know my family story.

In 2017, I was becoming exhausted from just working for people, not getting what I wanted out of the experience in terms of creative output. I realized I wasn't doing as good of a job as I possibly could as a leader in the kitchen because of the disillusionment I had with my role and the way I wanted to express myself. So I decided to demote myself. I was a CDC at this point. I left that job, became a line cook at a Black restaurant called Peaches in Brooklyn. I didn't make much money. Then I started studying—not just Black food. I started with food. And as soon as I started reading about food, if you read anything Black from the early 20th century, you realize almost all these things are encoded autobiographies. From that moment on, it became about food and the people together.

As a chef, the only boxes I could check in terms of Black creativity were Southern food or soul food. I didn't grow up with soul food because I was Muslim, so we didn't eat pork. My mom made a lot of

Middle Eastern dishes. We were vegetarian for years. We ate very Philadelphian meals.

My family left Charleston in 1929, the same year I learned my family was from Charleston. So I'm three generations removed from the American South with no connection to that land, no connection to that heritage other than conversations and a little bit of dishes like fried fish, succotash, lima beans and buttered corn. But even that food still wasn't enough because it felt very much on-the-nose Southern, and I'm not fucking Southern. So I'm like, "What is Northern Black?" That was the first thing I tried to create.

But there were three books that changed all of that and directed me towards the South: Edna Lewis's *The Taste of Country Cooking*, Dr. Jessica B. Harris's *High on the Hog*, and *The Gray Album* by the poet Kevin Young. Reading these books sent me to the South. I thought, "Okay, this is the path—learn about my family, then I'll learn about food, then geography, and then I'll have home. A home for my soul." But for some reason, I didn't go to Charleston first. I went to New Orleans. That very first day, I go to this bar, I'm talking to these ladies, they give me red beans and rice. We're having a fine time. The news is on—the local news—and I watch this 14-year-old kid on the news because he shot two people in the French Quarter.

I'm like, "Well, that's really fucked up." But I also just left Philly and left Brooklyn where this also happens. This is a young Black boy. I don't know if I mentioned to you previously that I was shot when I was 19. Someone right next to me was murdered, and several other murders happened after that.

That moment—if there was ever one of those very clear redirecting, reorienting moments—that was it.

I'm sitting here in this kid's city almost with the leisure and luxury of curiosity. What were the conditions that created this human being? The conditions that created this human being are the same conditions that created slavery, the same conditions that perpetuate systems and cycles of violence, the same conditions that cause hunger, why there're single moms and dads in prison.

My food needed to be about that, because our lives are about that, and the food only exists within the context of our lives.

Sakari: Walk us through Clorindy or any dish. When you're coming up with a dish, what's your process?

Omar: Clorindy came about because I was reading *The Gray Album*, and I was reading about Paul Laurence Dunbar. The poet Kevin Young was describing the play called *Clorindy* and the way it was conceptualized.

These folks who were either formerly enslaved or had a direct relationship to slavery are now in entertainment. Entertainment was largely a vaudeville expression—White people in Blackface pretending to be Black people and humiliating them for profit. Then Black people trying to do the same thing but be themselves, and having to wear Blackface like White people do and humiliate themselves. That's the most absurd thing.

Clorindy was a satire written by William Cook and Dunbar. People didn't think it would do well, and it became a smash hit. The highest grossing box office film would also star Bert Williams, a very popular vaudeville minstrel actor who was Black and exceeded all expectations. He broke this glass ceiling, demonstrated possibility for Black folks in the entertainment industry, all while using language and mocking White oppression through this dance called the cakewalk.

In *The Gray Album*, it mentioned that the play was conceptualized between Cook and Dunbar over a meal of raw beef, bell pepper, onions, and beer. When I read that, I'm like, "So they ate fucking tartare."

I wanted the dish to have Blackface. I'm like, "How can I make this dish have Blackface?" Surf and turf makes sense, the cuttlefish ink becomes the surf, the beef is obviously the turf. From there, I'm like, "What makes a tartare taste good while utilizing what they actually had?" Raw beef, bell pepper and onion is Holy Trinity—I pickled that. Almost all tartares have acid, all tartares have fat. Hence the reason why I pickled the Holy Trinity in the first place, then Blackfaced it by adding cuttlefish ink.

To represent the ceiling, I created these puffed Black rice crackers and put that over top of the dish. When you see Clorindy, it looks like this Black mess. If you've ever seen how people put Blackface on, the way they used to do it was to burn a cork—like a wine cork—and muddle it into a paste and mess their face. The dish had to emulate that.

Sakari: So you're inspired by reading, you get inspired by this story, and then you create your own rendition.

Omar: I don't think it's a rendition. If I just made that dish and never told you what it was, if it didn't have this context and story, it would just be a good dish. But when you assign meaning to something, then people begin to define the senses they're experiencing through that thing through the meaning of your assignment. That's storytelling.

I think it's beyond storytelling. For me, I characterize a sense. You begin to—just like a good book, a good movie, a good song—you begin to feel the note. That, to me, is the big difference.

Sakari: You combine poetry with your food. How do you combine the two? Do you look at it all as one art form?

Omar: I look at every single thing that I do, every discipline that I practice, as a form of poetry—whether it's cooking, painting, writing, or object making.

Poetry is the most honest form of conveyance.

It's about language, about human communication. It abstractifies our actual conditional living and can make things sometimes very plain, very clear without the notion of dogma. It's not dogmatic, not prescriptive, not like a divine prescription. It's completely unbounded. It's the most brave, spineless language. Through poetry, I'm able to find bravery and freedom of expression in complete totality. Poetry is the most malleable and bendable artistic substance as a material that we actually have. I can collect different types of materials and utilize them as forms of language that have nothing to do with letters and everything to do with the fact that we're both human, that we can and do experience the same sensations.

Sakari: How were you able to make the shift from being an artist to also being a businessman?

Omar: I told you at the beginning of this story—I just wanted a job. I need money. I've always had an entrepreneurial spirit. I never liked listening to anybody. I never liked authority. I just don't. I think most people are full of shit.

When I was in high school, I would paint T-shirts and sell them. It was just in me. And I come from a place where I was doing my own books basically when I was selling weed and crack. I told you again—I was not a good drug dealer. This is not some story where I'm like, "Yo, I was making bread." No. I had a job and I sold drugs because I was bad at both of them. I couldn't capitalize on either one because I didn't care enough.

Sakari: When did you care about cooking?

Omar: The second I realized I was going to be able to—when I got hired at the golf club, they said "We're going to give you a job." I'm like, "I want to take this as far as I can." I didn't even care my first week. I cared about self-determination. I didn't care about cooking. If I had the opportunity to work at an architecture firm, you'd probably be interviewing an architect right now. But thankfully, that's not what happened.

I fucking love being a chef. As a chef, I'm actually able to do all the things that when I first took on this job that I cared about so much—I looked at cooking as a sport. Being on the line is like a sport. But it also piqued my curiosity. I've been able to explore the world, not even in a physical sense but in a metaphorical sense, through food. I didn't even know what a fucking scallion was. I learned so much just by being around food and around people who care about food.

Then there's the artistry part. All these things are wrapped up in being a chef, plus more. Chefs take care of people. Chefs have a responsibility to nature, a responsibility to the community because they hire people. Things I didn't even know I cared about, it brought it out of me. I'm very thankful for that. I don't know if I would be the person I am without it.

Sakari: How important has your wife been in this journey?

Omar: I want to go back to that statement "behind every strong man is an even stronger woman." I hate that fucking phrase because my wife's not behind me. It's very important to know—my wife is not behind me. She's not holding my back up, she's not propping me up. So I can be incredible, while she's also incredible.

TO ME, A PARTNERSHIP IS ABOUT RESPECT AND ACKNOWLEDGING WHEN THAT RESPECT IS NOT BEING TREATED WITH THE KIND OF TRUTH AND CARE THAT IT DESERVES.

At the end of the day, if I were to fucking drop dead right now, this place wouldn't fail because *we* are this place. I don't want to be king made. I'm no king maker, and I don't want to be looked at as a king. I revel in the fact that I do have this partnership. That statement only shows up when the dynamic is a man and a woman. To give her the kind of respect that will be afforded you is to say that she is Cybille. Period. That's it.

Sakari: Has it been hard?

Omar: Yeah. Every partnership is hard. We don't see eye to eye. We have a family dynamic. We have all kinds of things. We have our own ways and visions of how we see the world and how we see business. All these things, it's always challenging.

Sakari: Advice for someone going through a difficult partnership?

Omar: Just be honest. That's the easiest thing to do and the hardest thing to do. It's the easiest thing because it should be on the tip of your tongue because it's the reality—I don't like X, or I am he, or whatever. But people have fear. So we craft new narratives for comfortability. And what lives in that space of comfortability, you're trapping the possibility for evolution. It's caged in comfortability. I don't think that's a very comfortable place to be.

Sakari: What's your non-negotiables? Your boundaries?

Omar: Respect, first and foremost. Honesty. I think they go hand in hand. Everything else falls in if you have those two things. You're good. You remove the air for toxicity. It's easy to spot a liar in a house of truth. I think it makes everything else more clear—not necessarily easy. I don't care about easy. I care about clarity. Transparency. That's all very important.

And be curious. Don't come to me with bullshit run-of-the-mill trend-setting views of anything because I don't care. Egos—that's not to say I don't have an ego or pride or whatever, but in a detrimental way where it crosses the boundaries of respect, I don't care for it.

Sakari: How do you keep your ego in check?

Omar: I don't. You saw what just happened? Chelsea came in here making—that was my check. I bought that chicken today. I got a bunch of love—I love my fucking restaurant, bro. I love my people. I just got good people around.

Sakari: Talk about your leadership style. Your relationship with your staff.

Omar: You came into this restaurant and you encountered a primarily Black staff. You encountered, whether you know it or not, I think primarily a queer staff, woman-led staff in the back and in front. Mixed ages, age ranges, skill sets, all this stuff. And you saw with your own eyes how customers were in awe.

Earlier, when you asked me about the food here and all that, the first thing I said to you was I think our service is the best thing we have going for us. That is because we all are here in an upliftment. I think we all feel a sense of self-determination, a sense of camaraderie. You saw that one of my employees was here having fucking dinner. The girl with the colorful hair? I was like, "Thank you for coming to work." She didn't work today. She just likes being here. I think that's culture and environment and all that stuff.

Chelsea the manager, it's October 2025. March of 2024, she was a counter person at a soul food takeout restaurant in West Philadelphia. She did not work at Honeysuckle. She became a barista at Honeysuckle. Turns out she's a Drexel grad, studies Black political theory, super smart, great writer, orator, all the stuff. She's managing this restaurant. She's never run a restaurant before. One of the smartest people I fucking know.

Jamar, Director of Fermentation—met him five years ago. When I met him, he told me he likes to ferment. I was like, "Alright, you're a fermenter. Come work on Honeysuckle. You gonna be our—I don't give a fuck what you call yourself. You're gonna call yourself Director of Fermentation? I don't give a fuck. Ferment shit." Now he just came back from Japan. We helped him learn about *sakari*, we helped him get there, we paid for that. He went out there, he's making *sakari*. Hamza? He's a photographer. Never bartended before in his life. Fucking bartender now. Tyra, she worked 13 hours today. She graduated from a 10-week culinary program through Philabundance, which is a free food program, right out of high school. She's been with us since she was 17. Now she's leading the prep team. She's like 19 or 20 now.

NO ONE HERE, INCLUDING MYSELF, HAS EVER OCCUPIED THE POSITION THEY OCCUPY HERE EVER IN THEIR LIVES.

People don't know what success means. I find success every day when I look at these people doing what they do because they weren't doing it before.

Sakari: That takes so much trust to be able to do that.

Omar: You know how hard it is to get fired from here? You would have to piss on my face to get fired from here. That's how hard it is.

Sakari: What does savoring your journey mean to you?

Omar: On a personal, selfish note, my favorite part is that I do get to have full reign over all of my ways and needs to express myself. I very often feel like a vessel. Altruistically, I feel like because I am that person, I do need to support that. The most beautiful thing that I have in this journey, whether this restaurant is a success or a failure, is that my wife is a fucking business owner. Tyra is a CDC of one of the renowned restaurants in the country right now. Chelsea, Jamar, Hamza, Sherlock—who was a fucking high school student—is now—that. I want more of that. That's why I want to grow this company. I want to see—we have 30-something employees right now. I would be happy to have 100 employees that can find self-fulfillment through this place. I didn't even mention our farmer, Teddy, who we've been working with since Juneteenth. He's on our payroll, farming, educating people. Half the restaurant just had a whole farm day. I wasn't even there. They had a whole farm day this past Tuesday. They organized themselves on their own dime—they weren't like, "Yo, I'm not doing this unless we get paid." They just fucking did it.

Sakari: Last question. What advice would you give to a young cook?

Omar: Get the fuck off TikTok. Go find a job that's really hard, that pays you a little money, but has really, really, really high integrity, and don't waste your money and focus your attention on getting better. That's it. That's my only advice.

That's how you find purpose. Find hardship. Don't find something that makes you comfortable. Find a challenge.

Get the fuck off the screen, read a book, and find a challenge. Dedicate yourself to it and stay there for a year and hate it. If you hate it, hate it. If you love it, great. But if you hate it, stay there for a year. Find something to hate for a year. Shit sucks. Find hardship. Find a challenge.

Sakari: You should look around and be proud. You have people that support the vision—not even just you, people that support Honeysuckle.

Omar: The one thing that I do know that I and very specifically me and Honeysuckle and me as Honeysuckle has impacted on not just the restaurant scene but very specifically the Black restaurant or chef perspective is the need to be a storyteller to be a viable concept or person in the mainstream.

[Kitchen manager Taylor enters. They review tomorrow's prep: burger counts, truffle inventory, tamale sales. Omar knows they sell more tamales on lower cover counts. They coordinate protein counts, crab portions, fish, chicken, lobster, pasta. They discuss morning prep timing, when staff will arrive, and delegate responsibilities. This real-time moment shows the constant mental chess game of running a restaurant—always thinking ahead, managing inventory, coordinating staff, while still being present.]

COMPARISON IS THE THIEF OF JOY.

CHEF BJ DENNIS: PRESERVING GULLAH GEECHEE FOODWAYS

"Don't get caught up on what everybody else is doing in the popular thing. Do what makes you happy and is going to take care of yourself."

I met BJ through Chef Omar and Chef JJ. We were working, moving, doing the thing. One day I made him coconut stewed collard greens. He appreciated my young hustle and left his door open. That was years ago.

I kept knocking. I kept working. And now I'm stepping through with this interview.

Here's the thing about BJ—he didn't invent Gullah Geechee cuisine. That's not his claim. But he's the one who brought it to the forefront and the masses. When everyone was sleeping on it, when chefs from other places were coming to Charleston and repackaging the food without giving credit, BJ said no. He decided to be the one telling the story.

He came up from the dishpit at Hyman's Seafood in Charleston. That job convinced him to switch to culinary arts. He worked every position—line cook at Anson's, Carolinas, Hank's Seafood, 82 Queen. He went to Trident Technical College, not the CIA. He didn't get handed anything.

Then he spent almost five years in St. Thomas. Not vacationing. Working. Learning. Understanding the Caribbean foodways that connect directly to the Gullah Geechee of the Lowcountry. That's not a resume line. That's commitment.

He discovered hill rice in Trinidad in 2016—rice that was thought to be extinct. He was on Netflix's *High on the Hog* and *Taste the Nation with Padma Lakshmi*. But that's not why he matters.

What's wild about BJ is that he turned down the easy path. He's not rushing a restaurant. He's working as a private chef and caterer because that gives him control. He's writing a book on his own terms. He's hosting pop-ups that educate people about what Gullah Geechee actually is—not heavy, not fried, but intentional, seasonal, connected to the land and the ancestors.

He matters because he's the voice saying: this is our food. This is our culture. And I'm not letting you erase it.

He came up in the gutter. Dishpit to line cook to respected chef. Then he chose to take everything he learned and point it back toward his roots, toward his people. That's not a business strategy. That's purpose.

What You'll Discover:

- How he went from flunking out of college to bringing Gullah Geechee to the masses
- Why he chooses catering over the restaurant trap
- What real mentorship looks like—and when you stop forcing it
- Why foundation is about science, not geography or tradition
- How traveling changed his understanding of his own heritage
- What he saw happening to Gullah Geechee food and why he decided to speak up
- The difference between appropriating culture and honoring it
- How faith carried him through when nothing else made sense

Sakari: How important is mentorship for you? Can you speak to some of your mentors or people that you mentor?

BJ: That's a deep question because mentorship is so different on so many levels. Coming up, I started as a dishwasher, so I got a different perspective. My mentorship was from the OG line cooks in the seafood houses down here—a lot of brothers, you know what I'm saying? I didn't see that as mentorship in the classical way we think of the industry. It was just older heads and line cooks at these restaurants. Some people call them tourist traps now, but they were OG seafood houses in Charleston.

Then I went to culinary school at Trident Technical College. I was lucky to work with some chefs who had established restaurants locally. That was in my favor because I went to culinary school mainly with retirees and housewives—only a few of us were really into it.

Most everybody else who could afford it went to Johnson & Wales, but I couldn't afford that.

Sakari: Did you know that's what you wanted to do when you were going through that?

BJ: Nah. I went to College of Charleston for a year and literally didn't do nothing, man. My parents were pissed. They had to come out of pocket and education was big for them. So when I came home and pretty much flunked out, my parents were like, "You're not going to live here for free. You gonna work. You gonna pay us some money to stay in this house. We'll still help you pay for school because you got to go to school." That was big for them.

I had to get a job. Charleston was really limited back then. Most of my childhood friends left—Atlanta, DC, New York. But the culture was always heavy. I started working restaurants and kind of fell into it. But looking back, I'm the middle child, the only boy. I was the only one used to ask my mama questions, particularly about cooking stuff. High school, I wanted to be a video game designer. But the school I wanted to go to, my parents couldn't afford to send me out of state and I didn't have the grades for a scholarship.

So same night as graduation, everybody's partying and I'm taking two courses to get into college. Next morning after graduating high school, I'm back in class. That was a sign, man. Then I went to college, partied, didn't do nothing. Parents were pissed. When I chose CIA because everybody was like "that's the best school," I didn't even know that's what I wanted to do. I was just trying to make my family happy. My family's from Jamaica—they were super about education. When I went up there, that's when it really fell in my lap and I started to fall in love with it.

Sakari: Do you think doing every position—bus boy, dish pit, everything—gave you a foundation for where you're at now?

BJ: Oh yeah. Dishwasher is the main person I want everybody to respect. I've been in kitchens where they throw stuff at the dishwasher, and I've been in kitchens where that was not tolerated. Everybody's important. I washed dishes for maybe the first three years on and off—Red Lobster at one point, bro. Then bus boy, food runner, and when I started as a fry cook, one of my teachers was like, "You're more than a stick man. Don't let them put you in a box. You can do what you want."

One of the best kitchens I worked in was Hank's Seafood under Chef Frank McMahon. He worked at places like Bucco and Republique. His skill set was through the roof. He ran a really high-end seafood restaurant—different from what I came up with. But in his kitchen, when you first got hired as a cook, you had to work one weekend in the dish pit. Just so you could understand. I think that sticks with me. You gotta be able to put yourself in everybody's shoes. That gives you a totally different perspective.

Sakari: How do you look at teaching younger cooks now?

BJ: Social media has made it really different. I got a couple young cats who get it. There's this one young sister from Charleston working in a kitchen. I gave her advice—"Don't work for this property, you're young, living with your parents, they not moving you up on the line." I could get you into other kitchens. She didn't listen and I didn't hear from her for months. That's the difference in the generation.

I reached out and she texted back, "I'm waiting to hear from you." And I'm like, you waiting on me? I'm the one chasing you trying to get where I'm at. She was joking but nah—y'all got so much access to us now. I didn't have access to these chefs. I had to go to the back doors of restaurants, knock and say, "Hey, y'all hiring? I'll wash dishes. I'll start from the bottom." That was after five, six years working in the business already.

Now random cooks are hitting me up saying, "Chef, I'd love to do an event with you." And I'm like, you? Who are you? No disrespect, it's just different. You have access to people now. I look at this kid's page like, you don't even know how to cook really. So mentorship is different but the same.

When I first came out, I tried to really reach out to everybody. I realized that those who are hungry are gonna reach out to you. I know these people know me—I own platforms, whatever. But I'm thinking in my mind like, if I had access to chefs like me and these other chefs back in the day, I'd be breaking my neck to reach out. Now I wait for young chefs who are hungry to reach out to me. Because everybody I reached out to, they're not really hungry. They don't want it. You gotta want to help yourself.

Sakari: How important is the foundation of technique? I know a lot of people think French technique is the foundation, but I think it's science that's the foundation.

BJ: Yeah, science. You can look at food and it might look so simple, but the earth did so much flavor to that vegetable. The farmer did so much already to put love into that soil. These vegetables got a flavor and nuance you don't even understand. Little techniques bring that out without masking it. That comes with time and being intentional.

But you're telling me down here during okra season or collard green season, you're still buying frozen stuff from Restaurant Depot that's coming from Mexico when the farmers got it right here? You want it pre-bagged and chopped but that don't have no flavor. The coffee from that farmer is different.

Fundamentals—I always wanted to work in two or three star Michelin restaurants. I didn't get the opportunity but I worked with chefs who worked at those establishments. You learn the kitchen structure, the discipline, the nuance stuff. But 75% of that is mental, man. Yeah, 100%. The food is the other thing. I've eaten at really great restaurants and sometimes I'm like, you know what? It's just food. Flavor and a little bit of technique—that'll take you far.

As long as you can follow directions, that's foundation to me. As long as you understand the why. If I tell you to fry an egg and I don't want any browning, you need to understand heat control, conduction. If I have too much fat in the pan, fat expedites browning. That's not about French versus African. It's not about culture. It's about the foundation of food science. You can learn any type of cuisine as long as you have the foundation of food science, heat control, ingredient functionality. Why does pear go well with fig? Why does kimchi go with whatever? You gotta understand the science and then you can adapt it to any cuisine.

Sakari: Do you have a food memory—a specific moment understanding the importance of where your food comes from?

BJ: Coming up with two parents who grew up living off the land because that was the only way they could survive. My mom still had a little garden in the backyard. I remember going to my granddad's house as a kid. We had to weed the okra plant. My granddad was showing me and my cousins the difference between the baby plant and the weeds. Then eating that same okra grown in my granddad's yard, cooked by my grandmother with the shrimp that he caught. Those memories, man. Being in the field, all of that.

Sakari: How important has traveling been on your journey? I know you spent almost five years in St. Thomas.

BJ: I would tell any young cook—travel. When I do events at these big hotel resorts, I see everybody coming in on owner visas. People really want to work. They're working in these spaces. I just came back from the Cayman Islands doing an event at a resort. I see different beautiful cultures, just meeting people from Nicaragua who you'd think are from Jamaica because they're from the Caribbean coast. They still have a similar accent. Meeting people from India, Yemen. Traveling helps not only your cooking but your growth.

Almost five years in St. Thomas really impacted me by meeting other people. Being able to travel like I have has been a blessing. You meet lifelong friends. For me getting up and going to Africa now is nothing. I can just make a call like, "Yo, I'm coming, can you help set me up?" and all I gotta do is afford that plane ticket.

You gotta go with an open spirit and leave that Americanized mindset to the side. Just be in the moment, learn and understand where you're at. Learn the culture. Meet people and you'll see the connection, especially when you go to Africa. You'll feel those little nuance connections of why we do certain things a certain way.

Sakari: What made you decide to cook Gullah Geechee food specifically?

BJ: I got tired of everybody bigging up Charleston and not any chefs talking about the story. You can say it's their fault or not but it's not their duty to tell our history. If you're cooking some type of cultural food, you need to respect where things come from. But it's our duty to uplift our stories.

When I came back to Charleston in 2008, I was reading about these chefs in Charleston in Food Arts magazine. I saw this chef I worked with—Jeremiah Bacon—who I consider a really great mentor for professionalism and technique. He was opening up with Team Per Se. That inspired me.

But then I was like, okay, they're talking about Carolina Gold rice and Sea Island red peas like it's new. But the hot John still tastes better from my grandma's house using Uncle Ben's from the grocery store. One specific chef said that hot John wasn't good until they brought the Carolina Gold rice and the Sea Island red peas back. But you never ate in anybody's house on a Sea Island. Your perspective's coming from another lens. I'm talking about the source—the actual tradition.

So I was like, all this talk about bringing things back, but y'all not talking about the roots of the food and culture. Y'all not mentioning anything about it.

Sakari: How would you describe Gullah Geechee?

BJ: It's very seasonal. Very seafood-focused, very seasonal. I look at Black food culture and I look at it in disdain because we're so disconnected from our roots. That's why the food looks heavy, you know? From my mom's spot. You see oxtail. I don't care if it's Southern food culture, soul food that migrated out the South, or Caribbean food—everybody labels it as heavy and fried. I just disagree. I think we're just so disconnected from our agricultural heritage and roots.

Sakari: What's something you'd want people to know about Gullah Geechee?

BJ: Words. "Cracking teeth"—that's a Gullah Geechee word. *Kumbaya*—that's also a Gullah Geechee word. The Southern US, the eastern part—it's the westernmost part of the Caribbean. Just happen to be in the US. You see these same words. Jamaicans say "nam," we say "nam." Growing up I was like, "Man, what y'all naming on?" I never put that together until we studied the histories.

Gullah Geechee is a distinct American culture, but when I say

American, people tend to forget that America is not just the United States. The Americas—that's the Caribbean, Central, South America. It's a culture of the new Americas. One thing I want people to know is that we're not a dying culture. We might be getting gentrified, but we're still here. America makes you lose your cultural identity after generations. That's what we're fighting right now. But the people are still here.

Sakari: One thing we speak about in the book is that your journey is the treasure. What piece of advice would you say or the best advice you ever received?

BJ: When you don't think people are watching, they're watching and they appreciate you more than you think. But sometimes you're not always gonna hear it. And that's okay. It's always gonna be the ones who don't hit that like button or make that comment who are the ones watching the most and got a blessing coming for you.

Sakari: How important has faith been on your journey?

BJ: Very strong. I was living in an efficiency apartment in kind of the hood still. Guy's still hustling and I'm in *T Magazine*. People think, "Oh, you see me on this and I already have been made." But magazines and TV shows don't put food on my table. I'm still a chef trying to compete with other caterers and personal chefs in a big food town. There were nights I sat up all night like, "Damn, what am I doing?" I cried. But I stayed the course because I knew this was my journey.

Every time you're ready to take it to the next level, there's always gonna be a hurdle to make sure you're ready for that level. You can't get to that level if you're not able to get through these hurdles. Sometimes your blessings just ain't gonna be given to you. You gotta fight for it.

Sakari: Any lasting advice for young cooks or anyone reading?

BJ: Don't follow what everybody's doing. Every cultural work is deeper than just food. You gotta have a passion for history, passion for other things. There's so many different lanes in the industry. You could be a great cook and chef for somebody's restaurant group. Nothing wrong with that. You could go into corporate—there's money. You could be anything. Don't get caught up on what

everybody else is doing in the popular thing. Do what makes you happy and is gonna take care of yourself.

But also remember—this industry can make you overconsume and not consume enough for yourself. Take care of yourself. Do what makes you happy, because everybody wishes they had a restaurant or had this or that. But what about what I love? What about the happiness I have to spend time with my family? Do what makes you happy.

Sakari: What's on your excitement list right now?

BJ: My book, man. It's been a five year project. I had to find the right writer I wanted from the get-go. The original writer and I had to go separate ways to get some business stuff back in line. But I locked in the photographer. Hopefully top of next year we'll start writing, and by spring of '27 the book drops.

I'm also looking for potential partner investors to get my own event space. Commissary kitchen, event space—so I can host events. When your book drops, I can bring somebody like you down for a book signing somewhere I can host and cater. Catering has always been good to me. It's given me a life outside of being in the kitchen. People want to come and they want cultural events. That's what I'm working on.

I'm right outside Charleston now, closer to Savannah. But I'm looking at moving back home to Charleston to do this. Trying to talk to my family about our family property and doing it out there. We'll see.

HIDDEN GEMS: ADAPTION, CHANGES AND TRANSITIONS

Chef Nyesha Arrington,
Chef Thijs Meliefste
Chef Camari Mick
Chef Alex Belew

CHEF NYESHA ARRINGTON: MASTERING EXCELLENCE THROUGH BALANCE

"Instant gratification is not something that should be prized. Things that are worth having generally take a little bit longer and generally tend to have more value."

Those words capture the essence of Chef Nyesha Arrington's approach to both cooking and life. When it comes to focus, execution, and relentlessness, I think of Chef Nyesha. She's someone who has mastered the art of sustained excellence while maintaining her authentic self in an industry that often demands everything you have to give.

I first came across Chef Nyesha when I saw her competing in a culinary competition for the Bocuse d'Or. As someone who values competitions deeply—they've been crucial markers in my own journey—seeing one of the only African American women going head-to-head with everyone else and laying it all out there was astounding. Watching her career progress from TV to restaurants, I realized she's an epitome of what people strive for in their own way.

What struck me wasn't just her technical skill, but how she made excellence look effortless. I think it's so much harder to be an Black woman in this industry, but she does it with such grace and determination that it appears easy from the outside. Nyesha represents something unique in our industry, she's figured out how to maintain peak performance without burning out. While many of us in the culinary world glorify the lifestyle of late nights, little sleep, and constant grinding, Nyesha discovered the power of taking care of yourself. She's living proof that prioritizing your health, body, sleep, and fitness allows you to perform and execute better and longer. Her journey from working at Michelin-starred restaurants to becoming a media personality alongside Gordon Ramsay shows what's possible when you combine technical excellence with authentic storytelling and strategic career moves.

In this conversation, Nyesha breaks down why instant gratification is the enemy of lasting success, how to embrace your cultural heritage while mastering classical techniques, and why your personal care routine might be the most important ingredient in your professional recipe. You'll discover her insights on transitioning from behind-the-stove work to media, the importance of building community outside of kitchens, and how to approach mentorship both as someone receiving guidance and giving it.

Whether you're a cook burning out from the traditional grind, an entrepreneur trying to scale without losing yourself, or anyone looking to build sustainable excellence, Nyesha's approach to balancing authenticity with ambition provides a blueprint for long-term success. Her philosophy extends far beyond food: life is meant to be lived fully, not just survived. That perspective has shaped everything she's built, and it can reshape how you approach your own journey.

Sakari: Can you speak about some times in your process where you thought something was going to go one way and then it went another way, but it ended up working out for the best?

Nyesha: I mean there's been multiple scenarios of that. I think that's definitely part of the lived human experience—not living in a future unless you're really creating what you want. I think there's always a learning opportunity.

Sakari: What advice do you have for a young cook or chef to embrace their culture and heritage while still learning classical techniques?

Nyesha: I think it's important to have a foundation and a base. Once you know the guidelines and how to identify product and what knife cuts are and what cooking methods are, then the next layer of creation is adding in your heritage, your storytelling.

I mentioned this in my TED talk—as pillars on this planet, we all have an individual responsibility to carry the message of our ancestors, and luckily we have been able to find that message through food. I think that's extremely powerful because it lives on this axis of mother nature. We take from the earth what she gives us. We add creativity, cooking skill, technique, heritage, storytelling, and it becomes a periodical of time. It really bridges us as a people. I think it's important to first know the fundamentals. A lot of times we get caught up in the moment—we want to be a head chef right out of culinary school or do these fun things, but it's so important to focus on the basics and the simple things because if you can do those things well, then over time you can draw off the lines a little bit. Once you understand what the lines are, that's where you can then blur them. I think that's really important in craft and art, any right-brain driven endeavor. You want to understand the fundamentals and then create your own style.

Sakari: Talk about some of those moments that maybe broke you down, but also helped build you back up.

Nyesha: I remember working at this beach club. It was my first professional kitchen job, and they put a case of bell peppers on my station—a case. And I was like, "Sick." They're like, "Okay, well, you're going to *brunoise* this entire case. Perfect brunoise."

I remember being like, "Okay, up for the task." But then three-quarters of the way through the case, my fingers hurt so bad every time I would go to cut down onto the cutting board. I had to work through the pain. I finished that case, and the chef tells me, "Wow, this is the most beautiful brunoise I ever saw. Here's another case."

It literally broke me. Tears came to my eyes and I walked into the hallway and said to myself, "Nyesha, this is what you signed up for. If you walk away now, what are you doing for your future?" I was ready to leave. It was beyond painful. I walked right back in that kitchen and did three more cases of brunoise—it got me so much respect in that kitchen. I'll never forget that. That was a formative instance in the crafting of my staying power.

Sakari: What advice do you have for a young cook living the life-style—not getting sleep, going out, maybe drinking—to operate at a higher level?

Nyesha: I really have done a lot of work. I think in the beginning stages of our lives in our twenties and thirties, we're still learning, still collecting data. We're not fully developed humans. Being the baddest ass chef out here was all I cared about. When you have that sort of vision, a lot of other things aren't prioritized. So like for me coming up, sleep deprivation, my health, being out too late, it was a lifestyle. These days I really value my personal care routine because I can operate the same amount of output but then equip myself better. It's been invaluable.

For me, finding weightlifting has impacted my chef's life immensely. It's all about the micro movements in weightlifting. They are a similar expression as the micro movements in cooking, and so it trains my brain to just move like a freaking ninja. That's why I literally do it. I've trained with Gordon, and he's a beast in the kitchen. He didn't know I'd be lifting like I do. It's imperative and you see it with any successful person. They really understand the value of that. Any actor, like Kevin Hart, like Mark Wahlberg, they're very much killing it in the gym before they even do the thing. I also think it's important for perspective to have community outside of the kitchen because it's all-encompassing.

Sakari: Can you speak about your restaurant journey, the highs, the lows, lessons you learned?

Nyesha: I learned so much in those two restaurants. I always wanted to learn the business side and valued it and was killing it on my food costs always. I always kind of had trouble with labor.

Mainly what I want to say is I'm handling and managing people and communication so much better than I used to. I came up under hot-tempered chefs, and I did lead that way in the early stages of my leadership style, but always with loving energy, very direct, very militant, very results-driven.

These days, my leadership style is a little bit different. I have more capacity to meet the person where they're at. My goal always is to work with the deficit and then very much champion where they're strong. That has exponentially helped me because in the previous two restaurants it was hard. I didn't have those tools. I was just running as a single owner-operator with partners. I didn't know what I was doing, looking back to be honest. My restaurants were killing it. Both were top 100 in LA, but me and my brain and how I'm wired, I like to do everything perfectly. I'm letting some of that go and finding humility around being a student. I'm a constant student of life.

I think ultimately when the concept is true to what the chef wants to express, that resonates in the soul of the diner immensely. That's the kind of shit that people come back for and what makes a restaurant successful.

Sakari: How important has traveling been throughout your journey?

Nyesha: There was this guest, Mark—whatever his last name is, Flanigan or something. He was from Ireland. He would come sit at my bar and was a director, just this amazing salty earth human. He had such an impact on me.

I came up from a blue-collar family and was the first of so many things in my family. He was the person who would sit at my bar and tell me about his travels. He said, "If anything, just get your passport." Every time I saw him he would say, "Did you get your passport yet?" I finally got it, and when the opportunity came to travel, I haven't really looked back. It's actually the thing I connect with the most and highly encourage. I think it's imperative for people and young cooks to travel because we get an amazing perspective on global cuisine.

For who I am as a chef, I connect with people through their food and through their storytelling as much as my own. I want people to taste my heritage, but I also want to experience theirs. That's what you get when you travel, that firsthand experience.

Like making bread with the matriarchs in Morocco off of a clay stove they built with their own two hands. That's what I'm here for. I think that's what makes us real, especially coming up in fine dining. There's so many different ways to be in food these days. You're a foodie, a food person, a content creator. Before it was just the white coat, the write-up in the New York Times, and people patronizing your restaurant. That was the recipe. Now there's so many facets.

Sakari: What lessons have you learned transitioning into media and working with Gordon?

Nyesha: Gordon became my north star. He's killing it authentically in restaurants at the highest level. He's killing it in media. I've learned so much from him.

I was working in this two-star Michelin restaurant and wanted to quit every single day. I was running a station, basically a junior sous at that station, making all the sauces, cooking every bird, breaking every animal down, running a set of three *commis*. This was 2006, 2007 maybe. I remember scrubbing down one night and thinking, "I'm willing to do this for however long it takes me to be successful." It was one of those pillar moments similar to the bell pepper where I was like, "Fuck, this is crazy." To be able to work next to him now on Next Level Chef—we treat that set like a kitchen. We have morning meetings, we talk about the challenges, we think about it as chefs and cooks. That's why I love it so much.

I think it's important to approach this media stuff similar to how you would set up your station. It's this similar expression. What is the guest experiencing? What am I doing? When you're on the line, every moment, every second is thought about before you execute it. I think it's a similar mindset.

Sakari: Talk to us about mentorship—how important that is, how do you view it?

Nyesha: I wouldn't be where I am without great mentorship. I would say mentorship, it's not just providing opportunity. I think it's also about letting people know when they're not doing something correctly. I think knowledge is meant to be shared, and it really strengthens the entire landscape and dialogue of who we are as a collective. The idea of mentorship is really just about being able to share the knowledge. Who are we to just garner all this skill set and then not share it? But people have to have an innate passion and want and drive and grit and resilience and these character traits that make a mentor want to take on a mentee, because they can see that the information will not be forsaken. That's really where it starts—in the individual. They have to want it first, and the mentor is always going to see that because they've been there.

Sakari: How would you describe your cooking philosophy?

Nyesha: My cooking philosophy is very globally inspired. I very much cook through the seasons and I think that food simultaneously has the ability to be a gateway to the future and a bridge to the past. For me, cooking is not just about the art of the technique or whatever that fine dining mindset approach is. It's a lot deeper and rooted for me. I think it has the ability to celebrate the seasons. I think it has the ability to continue to build on culture.

We can look at this as far back as the spice trade and ingredients and how they moved around our planet, that's already a documentation of food philosophy in itself. Where we are, we're just adding to that pot as we go. Food is ever-evolving, which I love. It's really good for my brain and how I love to be a student of life. I literally have a tattoo of CHEF on the inside of my fingers on my right hand. I'm the type of person that's definitely married to the game. I am a chef. There's nothing else on this planet that would have suited me better.

I've lived it in the most interesting, gnarly rockstar times. And also on this other side of post-MeToo movement, post-toxic inclusion, post-reckoning in the industry of drug abuse, alcohol, losing great chefs. I'm in this one foot old school, one foot new school thing. I'm so grateful that I found my passion at a young age because my food philosophy is something that has come naturally to share with the world, and it's cool to see people listening. It's scary but it's super cool.

Sakari: What would you say your life philosophy is?

Nyesha: For me, life, as cliché as it sounds, is really meant to be lived truly. I happen to be a chef, but I live like a wanderlust. I love to understand and roam this planet and I get to do it through the eyes of an explorer. I think it's important to experience different cultures. For me it's a tandem, life and also being a chef, but I'm not too far in the world of chef that I cannot also experience life. I think family is number one and so important to be connected to your spirit. That's very important. They inspire one another. If you're happy and spending time with your family, I think that just gives you the fuel or energy to want to create a dish or want to do something career-driven.

Sakari: Where are you on your journey as far as what's next?

Nyesha: That's a great question because it's literally pertinent to the questions I'm asking myself currently. I've just been in this data-collecting age of experiencing life, working through fine dining, working in a café, working overseas, traveling, just figuring it out. Now I have all this lived experience and I'm like, "Okay cool, what do I want to do with this?"

I hope people don't think, "Oh, she made it." For me, this is a chapter in my life. I'm grateful that I get to work next to someone so amazing, but it's not that I think I'm done and I'm going to hang up my hat. When I think about it, a lot of my sentiments right now are like, how do I give back on a larger scale? That is something I've been really thinking about for my future. I've always felt myself doing something great for people, not even for personal gains or legacy and notoriety, but just true human interest. That's really where my mind's at. How do I continue to give back, and to sort of hone in what is my cooking perspective?

Sakari: What would be one piece of advice you would give to a young cook or chef?

Nyesha: I think instant gratification is not something that should be prized. Things that are worth having generally take a little bit longer and generally tend to have a bit more value. I would say not to try to appeal too much to mass, but just stay authentic. I think that's so important on the journey and not to have these fleeting interactions or fleeting moments. Really be intentional. Really be intentional and not get too downtrodden when things don't work out. I'm saying that even to my younger self. I've been there where I thought, "Oh, I closed the restaurant. Where am I? What am I? Oh, I lost that Top Chef episode." Marcus would be like, "Dude, do you know how many restaurants I've closed? You're fine." But it's like your entire world crumbles. I say that now looking back thinking, "Wow, how much more equipped I am because I went through and came on the other side." I'm sure there'll be many more times where I have areas of opportunity and growth in my life. I hope I do. What a blessing.

For other people coming up, just stay authentic and true to yourself. Don't spend too much time overthinking it. You can find inspiration in so many things. Being around family and a good community of friends can inspire your work even outside of the kitchen. You might get the best idea of your life walking down the street having ice cream.

I think it's important to not get too far away from family values because I didn't always value that coming up. I missed some holidays. I always think things happen for us, not to us, and they help us.

CHEF THIJS MELIEFSTE: ON TRANSITIONS, PERSISTENCE, AND KNOWING WHEN TO CLOSE THE DOOR

"Never give up. Keep pushing. Even if life gets hard, eventually it will be better. There's no elevator to the top. You need to take the stairs. No shortcuts."

Those words from Chef Thijs Meliefste capture a philosophy forged through decades in professional kitchens, starting when he was just thirteen years old. When I had the chance to visit my old stomping grounds in the Netherlands, I knew I had to reconnect with Thijs—the chef who welcomed me into his restaurant Meliefste when I was learning my craft, and who was there when the restaurant earned its first Michelin star.

I first came to work with Thijs through a recommendation from another Dutch chef who told me, "You'll learn more working with Thijs in a few months than you would working at a three-star restaurant all year." He was right. While larger operations might make you "one part of a machine, putting herbs on plates all day," working with Thijs meant being right there alongside him, learning not just technique but leadership, persistence, and the Dutch approach to hospitality.

What made the experience special wasn't just the Michelin-starred food, it was the culture Thijs created. We'd blast music until service started at 5:00 PM sharp, creating an atmosphere where hard work and joy coexisted. He taught me that excellence doesn't require suffering, and that the best kitchens are places where people actually want to be.

The relationship between the Netherlands and New York runs deeper than most realize. New Amsterdam, founded by Dutch colonists in 1624, became the foundation of modern New York City. The Dutch brought not just their language and customs, but their approach to food—emphasizing fresh, seasonal ingredients from both land and sea. The Netherlands' mastery of seafood, particularly from regions like Zeeland where Thijs worked, influenced early New York's culinary landscape. Even today, New York's emphasis on quality ingredients and innovative preparation techniques echoes the Dutch culinary philosophy that Thijs represents.

When I visited him recently, Thijs was in the middle of a major life transition, closing Meliefste after eleven years to pursue a new chapter with Tomorrowland, the world's largest music festival. This wasn't failure; it was a conscious choice to prioritize family, explore new challenges, and break the traditional cycle of restaurant ownership that can trap chefs for decades. His story represents something profound about sustainable success: knowing when to close one door to open another, understanding that career pivots can be strategic rather than reactive, and maintaining the persistence to keep building even when it means starting over.

In this conversation, Thijs shares insights about building team culture, the importance of "doorzettingsvermogen" (Dutch persistence), and why he believes the restaurant industry needs more fluid, concept-driven approaches rather than the traditional "buy a building and stay for 35 years" model. You'll discover how he maintained quality while fostering joy, why he's choosing family time over expansion, and what it really takes to earn a Michelin star in a small Dutch village.

Thijs's approach to combining excellence with sustainability offers a blueprint for success that doesn't require sacrificing everything else that matters. His philosophy extends beyond cooking: every journey is unique, but they're all special in their own way. Whether this represents a chapter closing or beginning, there's wisdom in his simplicity and approach that can guide anyone building something meaningful.

Sakari: I'm here at Restaurant Meliefste in the Netherlands. This restaurant is closing at the end of the month. How do you feel about that?

Thijs: A bit of mixed feelings, but I'm okay. I'm happy to close it down also, but it's also been my life for so many years. My daughter is almost as tall as you are now, she's going to high school within a few weeks. My wife is okay, but she's been sick, and she's also happy that we're closing down. More time to spend at home. Family time is so important. She needs to not work as much as I do. For her it's better to work less. Last few years have been quite hectic. Right now it's full for lunch and dinner every day for months.

Sakari: How long have you been here?

Thijs: Almost eleven years. I've been in kitchens since I was thirteen. Sixteen I started full-time and never left. So this is all I know. I can't do anything else. This is my life. I'm also a little bit scared of leaving, but it's part of the journey. In October I'm starting my new job—executive head chef of Tomorrowland, the festival. It's the biggest festival in the world. I've been doing it already for several years, and we do around 500,000 people, two weekends. We do everything from street food like burgers and fries to fine dining, all on a very high level.

I've been running the restaurant there since 2019, and we do like a thousand covers a day. The festival is one of the main jobs, but the brand Tomorrowland is expanding rapidly. That's why I'm coming to Vegas also—we're hosting events from the end of August until October. We're opening a very big venue in Dubai next year, and there's already a big Tomorrowland in Brazil.

Sakari: Looking back at your journey, what advice would you give to your younger self?

Thijs: Never give up. Never give up. Keep pushing. Even if life gets hard, eventually it will be better. There's no elevator to the top. You need to take the stairs. No shortcuts. That goes for every profession, not only ours. If you want to be the best baseball player or basketball player, you need to train your ass off. Nobody's born with talent alone. Talent is one thing, but you need to hone it and grow it. You need to be consistent. In Dutch we say "doorzettingsvermogen"—perseverance.

Sakari: What do you think your superpower has been throughout your career?

Thijs: Just not giving up. Even when everything is falling apart, keep your head up and go through it. That helps a lot.

I also become friends with people that work with me. Not with everybody, but when I like you a lot, I would go to the moon and back for you, but you need to have the same connection also. As a boss, I don't feel like being a boss. I also clean toilets. I really don't mind. There's not a job within my profession which I think I'm above. I do it all, and sometimes I don't like it, but it needs to be done.

You need to work hard, but you also need to laugh a lot and have fun in life in general. Sometimes when operations look too heavy, I bring a bottle of Jäger and then everyone's laughing again.

You can't work when you're drunk, but just having fun, having a laugh, I think it's very important to laugh every day.

Sakari: I remember the culture here was special. We'd listen to music until service started at 5:00.

Thijs: I think it's very important. We have our main room here, the front of house plays their own music, and we have a third room now for bread production. When it comes to music during prep, everybody's rocking, talking to each other. As soon as five o'clock comes—boom—it's service time.

Sakari: Can you tell me about the Michelin star experience?

Thijs: I still remember it because we were full already, and then two regulars came in who come here every week. Then all of a sudden I said, "Venrooy is in the house"—that's his name, Venrooy Loun. He's the guy who was the boss of the whole Belgium, Netherlands, Luxembourg region.

I still remember because you were usually on the pass, but I said, "No, fuck that. I'm going to go on every station." I was touching every single piece of food, tasting every single piece of everything. But we pulled it off.

Now I know the guy pretty well because we have this love-hate relationship with Michelin. I used to work for Roger Vandamme—he's very popular in Asia and has restaurants. He was world famous for his desserts, but he also had a normal restaurant. I was head chef of the normal restaurant. It was always full every day, only open for lunch, but it was hectic. Every day was a queue outside waiting to come in.

Sakari: What's the food culture difference between Belgium and the Netherlands?

Thijs: Belgians are crazy when it comes to food. Here, everybody brings their sandwich to work, but there everybody goes to restaurants. In the Netherlands, everybody lives cheap. Act normal, feet on the ground. You bring your sandwich. Maybe in Amsterdam you go to a restaurant, but here you don't go for lunch on a daily basis. But in Belgium, it's normal. Every day they do business, wine, everything. In the Netherlands, it's the other way around—business first, and then when it goes well, we drink and chill. Belgians just go for the wine, which I like more.

Sakari: Why are you choosing to close rather than continue building?

Thijs: We're at a crossroads of buying the whole complete building, but it's an investment of millions. We can afford it, but it's not the right time. Something happened after COVID within the culture and within the minds of people—they don't have the same mindset that I have anymore.

Building and maintaining a team is even harder than it was before. We're now debating with staff members that come in one minute to nine, and when I say they're late, they say, "Well, I think I've worked enough for this week." That's the attitude. If this is going to be the attitude for the whole year, then I'm not sure if I want this for the future. If I'm buying the building and investing 3.5 million in total, this is for the upcoming twenty years. I want to have fun also and not be dealing with staff problems for the next twenty years.

Sakari: What's your philosophy about restaurant ownership?

Thijs: We still live in a culture where you need to buy the building where you have your restaurant—this is the way of life, you do this for the upcoming thirty-five or forty years. I want to break that cycle.

Why does it need to be for the next thirty-five years? I've done it for between ten and eleven years. Maybe create concepts which have an expiring date, we do this for five years, this is what we strive for. We invest this amount of money and try to gain that amount, and that's it. Up to the next—create different concepts, different experiences. Trends are coming and going. Be a little bit more fluid. I think you'll learn a lot and see much more, and you'll be happier and have fun. Then whenever you feel like the right time to do whatever the next thing is, you'll feel it.

I've been in kitchens for more than twenty-five years. Time to go out.

Sakari: How has the food scene changed?

Thijs: It's shifting. Everybody wants it to be quicker. They need to have a choice instead of the endless tasting menu where you're sitting at a table for four hours, which is very normal here.

The trend now is more bistro style, very approachable food with good wine lists, not the craziest but solid. It's packed, everything is full. Good energy. A few of them are super hot spots right now, almost impossible to get in.

Sakari: What's your approach to training young cooks?

Thijs: If I have a guy in my team that tells me he'd love to learn bread because he's interested, I tell him, "You need to give me one year. I cannot teach you in two or three months. If you want to own the profession, give me one year of your life and I'll give you the rest." It takes around four months until you really get into it, and then after that you start to polish your own profession. Within one year, you're rocking and rolling.

But at smaller places like this, if you're in the line, you need to follow because I'll push you through. You're right there learning, being able to see how I operate and how I treat people and how hard I work.

Sakari: Any final thoughts for young chefs?

Thijs: If you want to reach something, it doesn't matter what in life, you need to own it. Go for it. The younger generation thinks, "Oh, I'm doing Instagram so I'll be a millionaire," but it doesn't work like that. You also need to work your ass off in all aspects—create content, edit, everything. It's a whole job, a whole process.

But whatever is meant to happen is going to happen. I want to break the traditional cycle and create different concepts, different experiences. Travel, learn about different cultures, different cuisines, different kitchens. Just learn and absorb, and hopefully within a few years we can do something in the countryside or go for a bigger city. Whatever life brings.

CHEF CAMARI MICK: BUILDING HER OWN WAY

"Accolades don't really mean much. You need to dine at the place, really see if you blend into their ethos, and see if your morals align."

When I was putting together voices for this book, Camari was one of the first names that came to mind. She's an emerging chef doing really, really great work. But more than that—she speaks to something that needs to be heard right now.

If you're a young Black or Brown chef in this industry, if you're a woman navigating kitchens that weren't built for you, if you're trying to figure out if you're crazy or if the space around you is—Camari's voice matters. She's lived it. She's still living it.

She's worked at Michelin-starred restaurants—Daniel Boulud, Eleven Madison Park, Lilia. She's done stages. She's learned from some of the most respected kitchens in the world. But here's the thing: she saw the game and decided to build her own instead of playing someone else's.

During the pandemic when everything shut down, she was selling donuts. Biking around New York City, building traction on Instagram, making more money than she'd made in years at fine dining. Not because she was getting rich, but because she was finally in control.

She's young but she's been doing this since she was seven—Easy Bake oven, then KitchenAid at twelve. She knew early.

What's special about Camari is that she doesn't just cook. She thinks about representation. She thinks about why certain ingredients are looked down on. She thinks about how her mom made oatmeal with evaporated milk because of the African diaspora and what that means when she brings it to a fine dining kitchen. She thinks about the fact that Black people would make the best restaurant critics because we never get consistent service.

She's honest. She'll tell you that accolades don't mean shit if the environment is racist. She'll tell you to dine at a place before you work there. She'll tell you that your culture matters and to demand respect —real respect, not the "Oh, you're a celebrity chef now" kind of respect.

She sings in a choir. She does yoga. She knows the industry will chew you up if you let it, so she's building something different. She's building something intentional.

What You'll Discover:

- What it's really like being a Black woman chef in fine dining
- Why she walked away from prestigious kitchens to sell donuts

- The difference between accolades and actual integrity
- How to weave your culture into your cooking intentionally
- What representation actually means in a kitchen
- How to take care of yourself in an industry designed to break you
- Why mentorship and community matter more than the next big title

Sakari: I want to talk about the time where you were really hustling—selling donuts, biking around. Can you speak about that time and what it taught you?

Camari: That's not the only time I was really hustling. I've been in Michelin star kitchens working for the past decade. But when I first started, I didn't get to see my family. I moved to New York to be closer to my sister when she got pregnant, but I was working so much I still couldn't see them. That's when I was working for Daniel Boulud as pastry sous chef. No weekends off. Every holiday worked because it was part of a hotel. Same thing at every restaurant—when I was pastry *chef de partie* at Lilia, same hustle. Only work. Only hustle.

It wasn't until the pandemic that I got the opportunity to do the black entrepreneurial series at Maison Yaki. When I started the black entrepreneurial pop-up, I saw a boom on Instagram. I was like, how do I keep this traction? I didn't have a job. I wasn't working anywhere. So that's when I started selling donuts. That's when a bunch of micro bakeries popped up in New York City, and I was part of that wave.

I had nothing else to do, but I was making more money than I was during the pandemic than I'd made in my whole career. At that point, we were all bringing home like $1,200 a week. But this wasn't really for the money. This was really just to keep the traction going. I started biking around selling donuts and delivering. That's what got me to the job at Musket Room. From there we built Rafts together, then opened Cafe Zaffri. Now I'm still taking that same idea—that hustle of biking around—and starting to build L'Atelier Ébène, an Afro-Caribbean brasserie.

Sakari: So the hustle has always been in you. You went to Daniel

Boulud, Thomas Keller restaurants—those are hard kitchens to get into. What made you make those decisions?

Camari: I knew cooking was my thing since I was seven. My parents bought me an Easy Bake oven when I was seven and I got really attached to it. Then they bought me a KitchenAid when I was twelve. I still have it too. There's something about kids who get appliances when they're younger—they grow up connected to that thing.

When I was deciding which kitchens to go into, I started in Philadelphia at Zahav. That was one of the best restaurants in the city—it's still highly regarded. It started that whole Middle Eastern wave. I knew I wanted to be in fine dining, so why not go to the core of fine dining? After Nantucket—which was grungy, like working in a basement, hot, dirty, like the beginning of Anthony Bourdain's book—I really wanted structure. I wanted to know what it's like to work in a brigade system, a brigade-style kitchen. If you're going to work in food, might as well be New York.

Before I decided which job to take, I shopped around. I vibed most with DB Bistro. It was a really great introduction to New York kitchens because they're built differently in how the kitchen is structured. It's not Daniel directly, but it's one of his restaurants—it has the structure but it's not super intense. It was a good stepping stone. A lot of people don't know this either—I worked at Eleven Madison Park after Daniel Boulud, and I was like, "I don't like this." So after that I went to Lilia.

Sakari: How important was staging for your journey? Would you recommend it?

Camari: It's very important. Here's the thing about *stages*—a lot of restaurants in the 2000s and '90s built their whole financial structure on free labor. *Stages*. Trails. That's not sustainable. You can't build that into your labor model. That's just dumb.

But here's the full circle: there's a new wave of everybody needs to be paid to *stage*, which I disagree with. I think it's a job interview. You're spending four hours there—four hours of your time. It's important for you to see if you like the kitchen, how they're running it, if you fit the vibe. You get to learn something new for a day. Just because you did it one way at one restaurant or in school doesn't mean that's how you'll do it at this place or in the real world. You get to learn a new technique, meet new people, taste food. It's a win-win for both sides.

I disagree with labor models having *stages* as free labor, but I think you get way more out of a *stage* for a night than just a paycheck. When people ask, "Oh, is it paid?" it rubs me the wrong way. We've had to cut our teeth in kitchens. I've trailed and learned so many things. Did I take that job? No. But I learned a cool technique that I use now. Even if you're happy in your job, still go stage around.

We live in a world with direct access to everybody's final dish. But what's it like to actually shadow a chef and see how their brain actually works rather than just seeing the finished product on social media? With that said, don't expect to be paid for *stages*.

Sakari: During your time at these restaurants, was there a lesson that stands out to you?

Camari: Accolades don't really mean much. The people giving out these accolades are not there day-to-day. They're not seeing how people are being treated. They're not seeing how clean the kitchen is. They're not seeing the SOPs, the tracking order, the microaggressions. Accolades don't mean shit. While they may give you a direction to look in or make decisions, you as a person starting to find your voice and figure out who you want to be as a chef need to dine at the place.

How many times have we worked somewhere and never even tasted the food as a patron? Dine at the place. Really see if you blend into their ethos. See if your morals align. If they don't reach your morals, why are you working there? Why are you sacrificing yourself to be part of a World's 50 Best?

Sakari: When you're thinking about building your own kitchen and team, what makes a kitchen feel safe to you?

Camari: It's definitely a collaborative effort. You want to be heard no matter where you are in your career. Your point of view and the things you see may be different from what I'm seeing. If you're plating the same thing over and over every night and have the station set up a certain way and you say, "Chef, I think we should switch this"—you're the one doing it a thousand times a night. Who am I to say no? It's very important to me to make a collaborative effort and to be cognizant of each other's opinions.

I will admit I was a very sensitive cook. I couldn't take any criticism. I would cry. I'm the last child, so I think that attributes to it. Getting a tough skin is definitely needed because everybody's a fucking critic. You look at social media now—everybody's a critic. It's about weeding out and knowing your audience, continuing to cook for yourself and your audience.

Sakari: You spoke about representation being really important. How did you get through those moments when you were the only Black cook or the only woman in the kitchen?

Camari: It's hard not to think about it when you look around. Even in simple things like conversation about ingredients. Let's say you took four people from four different ethnicities and all talked about how to make a bowl of oatmeal. There's going to be four different ways. For me, my mom used to make it with evaporated milk. Come to find out, evaporated milk is definitely something from the African diaspora because we never really had full access to fresh produce and fresh dairy. So we used evaporated milk more often than fresh milk.

When I say I make oatmeal with evaporated milk, brown sugar, and butter, everybody looks at me like, why the fuck are you using evaporated milk? That's a cultural thing. Or if I'm talking about making ham hock or putting turkey neck into beans—cultural differences that maybe get frowned upon because these ingredients aren't necessarily seen as good or fresh. Especially when farm-to-table became trendy, nobody's using canned anything.

It's really important for the representation of our food to continue in a way that's healthy and seen as equal, not as lesser than. That's why representation matters in the kitchen and overall in having spaces.

How many times have you gotten subpar service because you're Black? There are prime instances where, especially dining in New

York, halfway through the meal they find out who I am and the whole service lights up. It literally just happened the other day.

Somebody recognized me in the kitchen and I was already having a bad time. It took 15 minutes for them to drop menus, 10 minutes for them to get my drink. And then somebody from the back came out and said, "Oh yeah, this is Camari. She's a pretty big deal." And the whole service flipped. They dropped extras, gave me glasses of wine, picked up pace.

And it drives me insane. Because I just want normal service as a normal human being. I shouldn't have to be a celebrity chef to get proper service. This is why I think Black people would be the best restaurant critics because we never get consistent service.

Sakari: You spent about a month in Paris. How important is traveling?

Camari: Traveling is extremely important, especially now. The things we're being fed through our news media—we need to dissolve that facade. We need to experience things and educate ourselves outside of the US. It's truly imperative, especially traveling to Africa. I was in Côte d'Ivoire earlier this year for a solo trip for my birthday. My friend owns a hotel there, so I stayed at his property and was treated like a princess. It was enlightening.

The food is just so much better outside of the US. The stuff they're pumping into our food here is bad. Things just taste 10 times better outside of the US.

Sakari: You're working on L'Atelier Ébène, and you were a partner at Ralph's Croissants. Can you describe a perfect croissant?

Camari: The perfect croissant is about time. You need to make sure your temperatures are good, age your dough, make sure you have the right product from the start—proper flour, proper butter, milk. Good products give good results. With croissants, you make the dough one day, freeze it, pull it the next day, let it thaw, and when you hit the right temperature, you start laminating. The butter needs to be the same temperature—pliable, malleable. Then you're doing your book folds and finding exactly what you're looking for.

There are different laminating styles, but essentially you're going for that spiral and honeycomb look. It's time, patience, and strength. Truly.

Sakari: You took something classic like a croissant and weaved in your cultural references—beef patty croissants, jerk ice cream. How do you think about your culture when creating something classic or a new menu item?

Camari: Sometimes it's literal. Beef patty croissant—flaky dough, meat, flaky dough, meat. It just makes sense. Am I the first to do it? I don't know. Is anything original anymore? But it's one of my favorite things to make. It's so good. I figured out what spices to put in the dough to get that vibrant yellow color. Then I figured out how to fold it to incorporate enough meat.

Sometimes it's not as literal. Sometimes there are Easter eggs in the way I make things. The jerk ice cream is a prime example. To get that smoky flavor without actually smoking the ice cream, I took the jerk seasoning and made a burnt caramel the way you'd make browning. I put the jerk into the caramel, and as it started to smoke, I covered it, turned off the heat, and let it smoke onto itself. Then I made ice cream.

That's exactly how the Maroons would do it in the islands so they wouldn't be discovered by slave catchers. Up in the mountains, they'd dig a pit, put wood, put meat, put banana leaves, cover it so the smoke wouldn't escape and give away their location. It's similarities that only the person making it would know.

Sakari: What's your number one piece of advice for someone your age or younger?

Camari: Have patience with yourself. This didn't just happen in one year. I'm young but I've been doing this since I was even younger. So having patience with yourself. Knowing that times are changing and there are more Afro restaurants, more AfroCaribbean restaurants, more of our heritage restaurants.

Give the same respect that you would give to Daniel or Eric Ripert to these same chefs. Yes, we look like you, and we are your cousins. We want to love you and bring you into the kitchen, but do give us that same respect.

You know how many times somebody's walked into the kitchen and just called me by my first name? I don't know you. Respect is important. Give chefs respect.

Sakari: What's the best advice you've ever received?

Camari: Just keep pushing through. Keep your head down and keep pushing through. But that was also some of the worst advice I received in the same breath because it's twofold. Keep your head down, don't make any waves, be a mouse, be silent. And then also just push through it. Keep it on your resume, get in, get out. I get it because that was an institution. I was never going to make any structural change coming in. I'm not going to change their ingrained racism overnight. So it's kind of like use them just as much as they're going to use you. Take it how you want to take it.

Sakari: I remember seeing you at a yoga studio. How important is self-care in this industry?

Camari: You need to take care of yourself. Self comes first. Our industry just recently went through a mental health crisis. We are seen as necessary artists. We've been put on a pedestal at times for our creativity, and then you're only seeing the creative, not the person. With all the accolades come a ton of criticism, comments, accessibility, social media—and that's mentally tolling. That's something we're all going through together.

Take care of yourself. Do what you need to do. Have hobbies outside the kitchen. Cooking is a hobby for a lot of people, but it's also our job. How do you separate the two and still keep your love for your job and hobby?

Having something to do outside the job helps. I have yoga. I sing in a choir. And maintaining relationships—a lot of people in the kitchen are socially awkward sometimes. That's why some people are in the back of the house instead of the front. Definitely maintain relationships and participate in community.

You can't have a community without inconvenience. If you have to wake up two hours early to be a good friend to somebody and then work a double, sometimes that's the sacrifice. In order to keep the community, you should sacrifice certain things.

CHEF ALEX BELEW: THE RIVAL WHO BECAME A FRIEND

"My view of success is simply waking up and being appreciative of what you get to do and what you have. Success doesn't come with a number or monetary value. It's about finding joy in what I get to do every single day."

When I started Hell's Kitchen, Season 21, I didn't like Alex. We were competing. We were going at it. Two different approaches, two different mentalities. I was the young buck. He was the older gentleman with wisdom. Somewhere between the signature dishes and the finals, something shifted.

We became real friends.

Here's what makes Alex special in this book: on paper, he looks like what everyone thinks success is. He won Hell's Kitchen. He's been cooking for a very long time. He's had his own restaurant. He's talented as hell. But that's not why I wanted him in here.

I wanted him in here because he's going through something right now that a lot of people are afraid to go through. And he's being honest about it.

Alex has always had two loves. Music was his first love. From the time he was seven years old in church choir, touring the country, then, life happened. He got married, needed money and went to culinary school. He built a restaurant. He worked his ass off. And somewhere along the way, music went to the back burner.

Then Hell's Kitchen happened. Then he formed his band. Then he wrote 60 songs. And suddenly he's facing a choice that most people never allow themselves to make.

This is the thing about Alex, he's not bullshitting. He'll tell you about the $90,000 a management team took from him after Hell's Kitchen. He'll tell you about the restaurant he lost during COVID. He'll tell you about his dad telling him he was a fool for going to culinary school. He'll tell you about winning the biggest competition of his life and feeling like it didn't fix anything because it wasn't what he actually wanted.

He's 44 years old, with a wife, two kids, and soccer games six nights a week. He's releasing music with his band. He's asking himself hard questions about where his joy actually is.

And he's decided that if music could be his career, he'd leave cooking without a second thought. That's clarity. That's honesty.

What's magical about this conversation is that it's happening while

Alex is in transition. Not looking back. Not stuck. Just figuring it out. Just like everyone else is.

If you've ever felt like you're supposed to want something you don't actually want. If you've got a hidden talent that everyone told you to ignore. If you feel pulled between two things and don't know which way to go. If you've ever won something big and realized it wasn't what you needed. This interview is for you.

What You'll Discover:

- How two competing visions of success can coexist
- Why losing everything can be the best thing that happens to you
- How perspective changes when you've been through real struggle
- Why mentorship matters more than accolades
- What it actually takes to build something real (and why it takes longer than you think)
- The difference between a fan and a friend
- How to not let fear control your decisions
- Why being present matters more than being productive

This is for anyone brave enough to admit they don't have it figured out. For people with competing passions. For anyone who's failed publicly and has to keep going anyway. For people who won and realized winning wasn't the point. Alex represents something real. Not the Instagram version of success. The actual messy, complicated, beautiful journey.

Sakari: How did you end up in this life? You didn't start out wanting to be a chef.

Alex: No, man. I was a server and a bartender. I was always more of a people person. The back of the house seemed like a bunch of misfits—chain-smoking raga muffins who looked rough and gnarly. Where I grew up, we didn't have any chef-driven restaurants. It was all Logan's, Chili's, Applebee's, Outback. Just chain stuff.

Music was always my first love. Since I was seven, I was in church choir. We toured the country—Alabama, Georgia, Mississippi, Florida. I played saxophone in fifth through eighth grade, piano. In high school we had the Riverdale Singers—an audition-only choir. I was one of only two freshmen to make it. We were the fourth ranked choir in the United States. We got to go to London and sing at Westminster Abbey and St. Paul's Cathedral. My junior year we sang at Carnegie Hall. Those were huge things.

I got vocal scholarships to college but didn't want to take them because they wanted me to sing opera. I love classical music but I have no desire to sing in that style. I'm blues and rock. That's what I wanted to do.

Sakari: So what fueled you to make that shift?

Alex: I worked in restaurants because it was easy money, quick money. Everybody had fun working. You'd get off work and hang out together. I was in bands, in college, trying to do both. I didn't even start cooking professionally until I was about twenty-two. But I was bartending at J Alexander's in downtown Nashville and one of my regulars asked me to do a dinner party at her house. I'd never cooked for anybody before. I just said yeah and ripped off other restaurants. I had no clue what I was doing. There was no formal training at that point. I didn't go to culinary school until four years later.

Sakari: When did cooking become the priority?

Alex: I got married, needed money. That's when I decided I wanted to go to culinary school in 2004. Started in 2006, graduated in '08, and immediately wanted to quit. I was going to school twelve hours a day then going straight to a restaurant and working from six p.m. to midnight. That was two years of eighteen-hour days all in food. By the time I graduated, I was burned out.

I started catering just to pay off my student loans. I got a twelve percent interest private loan. By the time I paid those off, I'd paid $142,000 to go to culinary school for two years. It's absurd.

Sakari: That's a lot of debt to carry.

Alex: It was brutal. But I think perspective comes with age. I think I mean, discipline—you're never motivated. I'm never motivated to go to the gym. I wake up like, "Shit, my back. Alright, I'm going." But most things in life are team efforts. A marriage is a team effort. Raising children is a team effort. Running a business is a team effort.

Sakari: You've talked about mentorship being really important. Can you speak to that?

Alex: A thousand percent important. It takes a village to raise a child and that's 100% true. I didn't really have any chefs as mentors coming up. I didn't work for my first real chef until 2008 and I'd been in the industry for ten years by then. I literally just sent Gavin DM on Instagram. He worked for Daniel, he's worked with Thomas, he's the president of the American Bocuse d'Or team. I wasn't expecting anything. Now I can FaceTime him and he'd be like, "What's up, brother?" He's a rare gem of a human.

Mentorship isn't just about learning techniques while you're in that building. It's developing relationships that carry on. I can send Gavin a text right now and ask for honest feedback. That's invaluable—to have people that will speak to you truthfully, hold you accountable, not worry about hurting your feelings. If you can step outside of your emotions and go, "Okay, I'm wrong." If you can muster those words without getting defensive. That's how you get better.

Sakari: What about teaching others? You taught culinary arts for three years.

Alex: Safety and sanitation, knife skills, the danger zone, how to cool and reheat food properly, how to season correctly, time management, and being proactive. I remember walking through a kitchen and there was a dirty towel on the floor. I walked over it and thought, would a James Beard or Michelin-starred chef walk over a towel? They'd pick it up and put it in the dirty bin.

Being proactive and fixing problems you see, even if they're not your problem—that's the right mentality. It's a team effort.

I posted on Threads about holding a knife properly and people came at me saying I'm not welcoming to newcomers. But if you hold your knife improperly and you're showing people how to cook, you're doing a disservice. You're teaching them dangerous information. It's not rude to critique someone and tell them when they're wrong. It's actually the opposite. You're helping that person.

Sakari: You were on *Hell's Kitchen*. What was that experience like for you?

Alex: *Hell's Kitchen* was interesting because of perspective. I'd spent two years running a restaurant through COVID. The punishments they gave us—peeling carrots, shaving garlic cloves—I was just thinking, "I spent two years doing this through a pandemic. This is eighteen days max." You think about it through that lens, how bad can it really be?

The first night Zeus couldn't nail the carbonara. I was stepping in making his carbonara and Gordon was like, "Let him do it." I was like, "Shit, man, I'm just trying to get the food out." It's not me versus Zeus. It's us versus them and I need us to perform well. That's the way it should work. It's a team effort.

Sakari: Did winning change your perspective on success?

Alex: My view of success is simply waking up and being appreciative of what you get to do and what you have. I don't feel the need to have more. We're not wealthy. I have a car payment. Everybody still thinks I got a quarter of a million dollars and it's okay. I just don't have a desire for materialistic things.

I want my boys to be healthy. I want my wife to be happy. I want to wake up and say I *get* to do this, not I *have* to do this. Success doesn't come with a number or monetary value. It's about finding joy in what I get to do every single day.

Sakari: Let me ask you about the music journey.

Alex: I quit making music in 2017 when I opened my restaurant. I didn't have time for both. I wasn't looking to be in a band again or do any of that. I thought I had a trajectory set. Won the show, opportunities kept coming. This threw a wrench in all of that. It's really messed me up honestly.

I brought my guitar to *Hell's Kitchen*. It was in the hotel room with me while we were quarantined. That's just who I am. I was in the Caribbean with Ryan and Robbie cooking for a charity event and got a message from my guitar player asking if I wanted to go to the studio in Phoenix. I hadn't sung in front of people in five or six years. We went in, got two songs done in two days, and they were good. I came home and wrote sixty songs.

Sakari: That's incredible. What happened from there?

Alex: It was all I thought about. We recorded eighteen songs. We're about to hit a million streams on Spotify as an independent band with no PR, no management, no agent, no label. In one year. We've never played a live show because the logistics don't make sense. I'm a chef with a family in Murfreesboro, Tennessee. My guitar players and producers are in Phoenix. One of them tours with Three Days Grace. He's gone for three months, home for three weeks, then leaves again.

But nothing that you want to do is going to be accomplished if you do it halfway. Nothing. You're not going to accomplish anything if you treat it like a part-time hustle. You have to be all in.

Sakari: What would you tell a twenty-year-old trying to break into music?

Alex: Do the hard work. Hustle. Late nights. Sleeping in a van. Playing small gigs. That's the foundation. Most people don't understand that. Benson Boone and Jelly Roll are outliers. They skipped steps. But those aren't normal situations. You have to do the work. You have to grow as your crowd grows. You mature, become a better artist, better performer, and that's what leads you to success.

Performance is a skill. I've been on stage since I was seven. I've done demos for five and six people. I've done cooking classes for twenty people. An event for five hundred. I've catered for a thousand. Then boom. You know how to perform. You know how to articulate your words. I get up in front of two thousand people and cook and demo and talk because I've been doing that my entire life.

Sakari: You mentioned your first video being terrible.

Alex: My first video is terrible. I look like I'm about to bomb a school or something. I look angry. No energy. Tired. It was just crazy. But you can't skip that. You have to go through that to understand you suck. You have to have self-awareness and be self-critical. Dave Chappelle and Chris Rock still tape their comedy specials and listen back so they can analyze the performance. You're always self-editing. *Always.*

There's always time to go, "That didn't work. I said 'um' thirty times. Let's learn how to scratch that from the vocabulary." Because it makes you sound like you don't know what you're talking about. You sound like you're guessing. You need to be confident when you speak.

Sakari: Talk about failure. You tried some products before.

Alex: I asked my grandparents for money and spent it all. I tried the green juice, banana pudding—all these products failed. And I felt like shit about it. You want to make your family proud and you spent all their money and now you're in debt. But in the scope of your life, is a ten thousand dollar lesson that expensive if it taught you something invaluable? In the moment you feel terrible. But you have to hit that wall.

You can't enjoy the peaks without slumming it in the valleys. Everything can't be a win because then winning just feels normal. Hell's Kitchen floored me because it was the first moment of real validation for twenty years of hard work.

My dad told me when I said I was going to culinary school that I was a fool. "Nobody cares about food. People only eat to live." That played in my head every day since 2006.

But that moment was real because of what I'd gone through. It felt so much sweeter because I'd been busting my ass running a restaurant through COVID. Then you get perspective—COVID was the worst thing at the time, but now it's the biggest blessing. That conversation wouldn't be happening without COVID. I lost my restaurant that was named after my grandparents, but it was for a greater good.

Sakari: You mentioned reaching out to chefs you admired. Tell that story.

Alex: I sent Curtis Duffy an Instagram message after we ate at Grace in 2016. He responded and I went to Chicago and sat with him one-on-one for three hours. Then I was in the kitchen during prep, family meal, and a bit of service. I'd never done that before. I'm just an idiot from Middle Tennessee but I asked hard questions. Some people say no. Some people leave you on read. Some people aren't going to read it at all. But that can't stop you from asking.

Rejection is normal. You write a hundred songs to get one or two good ones. You knock on a bunch of doors to get one to finally open. The reason most people aren't entrepreneurs and leaders is because they're too stubborn or too scared to push through rejection.

I read something on the wall at a high school football locker room in 2012: "The difference between successful people and unsuccessful people is that successful people are willing to do the things the unsuccessful aren't." It's so easy to quit. The hard part is waking up every day and going, "Fuck, here we go again."

All the opportunities I've had, came from my asking questions that most people are scared to ask.

Sakari: Let's talk about the social media thing.

Alex: I've been burned out with social media for like four years. Making cooking videos, ten or fifteen a month. It's exhausting. It's expensive. It's lonely. Cooking food is for people. It's not for a camera and a ring light. It's sucking the joy out of it for me.

Do you know how many songs are uploaded to Spotify every day? 141,000. Every single day. And do you know what percentage of those songs get more than 5,000 streams? Twenty percent. Eighty percent of songs never get more than 5,000 streams. We're an independent band, self-funded, no PR, no management, no agent, no label, and in one year we're about to hit a million streams. We've never even played a live show. That's insane.

I was in California for four days and I took one picture the whole time. I'm just so much more used to not using my phone anymore. Being present. But then it bites you because we went through an entire football season and I realized I never took a single picture of my kid playing football. So now I don't have memories. But I was there at every practice, at every game, actively participating. That's better than filming content and not being present.

When you're doing that, filming content is not a priority because you're actually living life. You're not watching someone else live your life. There's more enjoyment in being present.

Sakari: What about expectations from your actual friends versus strangers?

Alex: Total strangers are supporting this band more than my friends. I have 128,000 followers on Instagram and I've asked multiple times for people to go like my band's page. Nobody will do it. I can't get people on board because people put you in a box. They see you living in this box and if you go outside of it they're like, "What the fuck is he doing?"

But here's the thing—I guarantee most of the people I truly know have never even listened to a full song. And it's fine. It's just weird. People tend to think about themselves more than they think about you. That person didn't respond to your text. You don't know what's going on. Maybe something happened. I leave people on read all the time. I'm not trying to be rude. I just get busy.

When you're younger you take everything personally. Maturing is realizing it's not all about you. Did I say something wrong? Did I offend that person? No, man. Just people are people. You never know what they're going through.

Sakari: But there are people you can count on.

Alex: Yeah, there are. I want to see my friends win. I want them to be successful. A lot of people don't have that mindset. But that's understanding the difference between a fan and a friend. I could call Robbie Felice and ask him for anything except to go like my band page. That's just the way it works. People I've hung out with versus people I don't know at all—there's a vast difference.

It just comes down to distance and proximity. If I saw you every day at the gym, we'd talk every day. But I've got a wife and two kids and I don't know what I'm doing day to day. We've got four soccer games this weekend. I'm just hanging on, man.

Sakari: You mentioned something that resonated with me—nobody really thinks about you as much as you think they do.

Alex: Nobody gives a fuck about you. They have their own shit. At the restaurant, they're worried about their floor being dirty. They're not thinking about your problems. When you remove that notion that nobody really gives a fuck, you can move with such carefreeness and less fear. If this book fails, did it really fail? You were willing to do something most people aren't. That's not a failure to me.

Sakari: What's your advice for people reading this?

Alex: Surround yourself with people that inspire you and that you respect. Work at places that are creating the food you want to create. But also work at places doing something completely off-the-wall and new to you because you learn new techniques, new skills, new flavors. All that knowledge becomes a rolodex in your mind. You only know what you've been exposed to. If you've not been exposed to many things, your depth of knowledge is going to be shallow. But if you go out there into the world, meet new people, get a mentor that is trustworthy and honest, there's nothing you can't do.

But you have to be proactive enough to go out and get it. You can't expect it to come and knock on your door. Ask hard questions. Keep pushing through the awkward, the hard, the rejection. Be willing to do the things most people aren't willing to do.

And honestly? If music could be my career, I'd leave cooking without a second thought. I'd never think about it again. I know what I love. I know what's true in my heart. That's what matters.

HIDDEN GEMS: THE PATH FORWARD AND THE COME UP

Chef Marc Anthony Bynum
Chef Kwame Onwuachi
Chef Joseph "JJ" Johnson

CHEF MARC ANTHONY BYNUM: THE ART OF RESILIENCE AND REAL HOSPITALITY

"My superpower is my resilience. I will not stop. I will go berserker. I will scorch earth. I might take time off and relax for a little bit, but I will come back stronger than before."

Those words capture everything you need to know about Chef Marc Anthony Bynum, one of my first mentors, three-time Chopped champion, and the chef whose signature ribs graced the cover of O Magazine. Beyond the accolades, Marc taught me something more valuable: what it means to never quit.

I first encountered Marc not in a kitchen, but as a customer on what turned out to be a very bad date. The food, however, was incredible—watermelon with feta, familiar flavors elevated in ways I'd never experienced. Marc came over to our table, touched base, and showed that I was seen. That simple gesture of hospitality made me feel warm in a way I'd never experienced in a restaurant. That same week, I left my job at a catering hall and walked into his restaurant asking to work for free. The entire kitchen went quiet, Josh stopped chopping, everyone stared. Who was this kid walking into their space? Marc gave me a shot, and that shot led me to the James Beard House, where I met Carla Hall, Alexander Smalls, and JJ Johnson at an age when most people are still figuring out what they want to do with their lives.

Marc was one of the first African-American chefs I'd seen operating at a high level, someone who looked like me, came from where I came from, and was doing something extraordinary. But more than representation, Marc embodied something rare: he was both chef and entrepreneur, leading by example rather than just giving orders. His signature wasn't just on dishes, but on building a brand, creating opportunities, and understanding that hospitality is about more than food, it's about service.

I've seen Marc through the ups and downs of his journey, and the one thing that never changes is his refusal to quit. There's something I've always admired about his resilience. We didn't always agree on everything, but he took me in like I was his own.

In this conversation, Marc breaks down the difference between wanting to be famous and wanting to serve people. He shares why he calls himself "a Hall of Fame G-League player" and what that means for building others up. You'll discover his philosophy on mentorship, why success doesn't make you a mentor but experience does, and how

SAVOR YOUR JOURNEY

he's learned to balance demanding excellence with creating an environment where people actually want to work. Marc's insights on relationships, communication, and the importance of "real food and real hospitality" apply whether you're running a kitchen or building any business. This isn't just about cooking—it's about legacy, resilience, and understanding that we're all in the business of service.

As Marc says, "If they never know your name, they should know your service." That philosophy has guided everything he's built, and it can guide you too.

Sakari: What do you think your legacy is right now, at this very moment?

Marc: I don't think it's there yet. It's still being written. I don't think a person can really speak of legacy until it's done because of what I see—just from you—I don't see my legacy as I'm living because people are affected by things that I'm doing now, affected by things that I've done in the past that they're learning about me.

I don't speak on my legacy. I just work on it every day because I'm not going to say I'm the greatest. I'm not going to say I'm one of the greatest. That's for people to say. All I can do is put in my work and that's all I'm doing.

As far as legacy, I just work on it. It's still a work in progress.

Sakari: What drives you through the ups and downs of your career?

Marc: Just wanting to be better. The driving force to me is the legacy piece, but I don't think about it because I'm "too busy" putting in the work. Since I moved, it's shown me everything that I've done for the first 45 years of my life was for a reason.

Now the driving force is to prove myself worthy of the badges that I wear—whether it be Marc Concepts, husband, dad, every title that I have. The driving force is my kids and the legacy that we leave behind. But we don't know what we leave behind until it's behind us. Right now my legacy is how I can make my mac and cheese better than it was. The driving force is I want my 60 acres with my compound and a business that when I'm gone and even while I'm living takes care of my kids. A kid came and worked for me the other day and he called his mom and was like, "Yo, mom, I'm feeling so inspired." She said, "I'm happy you found this guy because I was praying for you and I was praying that you'd find somebody." As much as my legacy is food, it's more about the community of people and the world that I create. Just being good to people. That's what hospitality really is. We've lost hospitality in our lives just because of life, and it shouldn't be. Hospitality is life. It's given me life and it's given my kids life.

Sakari: People ask would you change anything about your journey. You say no. What advice would you give to the next generation about enjoying that process?

Marc: Live life like you're going to make mistakes, but everything that we've done has been purposeful. We grew up in a certain area, and had certain parents. For us it was different. We didn't have what everybody else had. I think about the equipment—one of the reasons why I moved was so I could have backing, so I could have better equipment, so I could be better. We didn't have that. We had to go overseas or work for somebody else that really didn't look like us to understand those things.

Sakari: How can young cooks enjoy the grind when they want instant gratification?

Marc: They just have to do that. Enjoy the grind. Nobody wants to own so fast. You don't have to be the lead so fast. Everybody wants to show what they've learned instead of learning. I had a cook come in earlier. I was just with a chef, and I'm 31 years in and I still have an ear to hear. I still listen to what people say. I'm still learning. For the kid that's learning right now, keep learning. You don't got to be the lead to be the guy. Just because your name is on the coat, that don't mean you the guy in the coat. Just go and learn. Go and stag. Learn different cuisines.

Me, I didn't have a chef to look up to on the line. So I had to become that chef. I had to learn how to make pizza because nobody was going to teach us. I had to eat a whole bunch of ramen because when I went to the guys and asked them to teach me ramen, they said no.

But the kids that are coming up really need to know what hospitality is, know what you're getting into—not the fame, not Top Chef, not all of these shows. But what cooking really means and the essence of it. We're serving people. Yes, it's our food. Yes, it's our creation. But we're in the business of service. If they never know your name, they should know your service. They should know your brand.

There's cats that walk into any kitchen that I'm in and they'll smell whether it be the burnt butter for the cornbread or the ribs coming out of the oven and they'll be like "yeah this is Chef Bynum's kitchen." That's all you really want. Your name doesn't even have to be there, your product does. The only way you get a better product is by working on it, and the only way you are going to work on it is with somebody else's money.

Everybody wants to be the chef, but you don't know nothing about food cost straight out of school. So you going to be getting your ass kicked by ownership because you want to be a chef instead of just going and working *garde manger* for six months and perfecting your dressings and perfecting your knife cuts.

Nobody wants to be perfect anymore. Why? Because that doesn't get the highlights. The industry now is mixtapes instead of the NBA. Mixtapes. No fundamentals.

Make me a *beurre blanc*. "What's that?" You need chicken stock. "What's that?" One of the five mother sauces. "What's that?" But yeah, you got 10,000 followers on social media and you think that you are going to open up the next restaurant. Go sit your ass down somewhere. Go learn, bro. Go learn. Be quiet.

Sakari: I remember coming into your restaurant asking to work for free. What did you see in me? What do you look for in a young chef?

Marc: One, if you look like me, I'm going to give you a shot. Your spirit was kindred. You grew up in Farmingdale. There were so many parallels and I knew what it was like to be exactly where you were and not have anybody that looked like me to look up to and say, "Okay, I could do this shit."

For me, that's everything. A kid has to prove that he doesn't want it. Sometimes you prove that you want it. Sometimes you're just like "I don't know if I want it." They got to prove that they want it. You proved it. I look for kids to prove it. Kids don't prove it no more. People use the word mentor not even knowing what it means. A mentor is somebody that doesn't push you in a certain way. They just give you instructions based on their life experience.

Success doesn't make you a mentor. Experience does. It's the scars that are showing you to stay away from the fire. I've been burned a few times. Stay away from that fire. Every mentor is different and every mentor helps you in a different part of your journey. For me, I'm the best G-League player in the world. I'm a Hall of Fame G-League. I know that my Sakaris and my Byrons—I was the first chef that they had. Byron was my first chef. Did you know that?

For me, I just want to be the best person as a mentor to help them get to the next level. I'm like the PAL coach, but I'm proud when I see my guys in the NFL because I'm like, "yo, I gave them that. I helped build that foundation." I like good foundations because you could build anywhere on a good foundation.

Sakari: How important have relationships been in your career?

Marc: It is priceless. I've always been a boss or looking to be the boss. So I know the value of real relationships now because now I have real friendships and relationships. That's only because for the most part I was at a point that I was so high and I fell, and all the people who I thought were my friends really weren't my friends. They were just there for checks.

Now I really understand the importance of relationships and building real relationships and taking time to cultivate them. The relationship that you and I have is a real one. It doesn't have to be where we speak every day. When I get on the phone with you, we pick right back up. That's a real relationship.

The pricelessness of a relationship and not an employee-employer type of transaction, businesses go in and out, empires fall because you don't have the right relationships. It's really about communicating and not being fake. Communication is just as important.

Sakari: What would some of your advice be to your younger self?

Marc: One thing I would tell my younger self would be it's okay to trust. That's where it came from—not trusting people, not trusting myself and trusting good judgment that I'm choosing the right people.

You think that as a chef, "oh, I finally got a good employee. I finally picked a good person." It's just like, nope, this shit did not work. So sometimes you second-guess your thought process, and then in second-guessing it you're like "no I'm not going to trust this person" and then you lose out. I would say it's easier to trust certain people and fail fast, which is what I've learned over the years, and not to be so emotional in it. It's okay to fail. I'd rather fail fast than take eight years to fail knowing it was failing for six and just keeping it going. There's so much to be said about communication. If you really say how you feel, people will accept it or they won't. But then it's on you because you said it.

Sakari: How has your leadership style changed?

Marc: There's a balance to everything. I didn't have to be so hard. I'm not as hard as I used to be. I deal with people better than I would before. Before I would just rip people's heads off. Instead, I just walk away and I try to teach. If I can't teach them, then I move them out. Before, if you weren't good, I would just keep you around and punish you to either get better or get out. But that was me thinking that I'm going to raise you like my mom raised us, which was hard. And that's not the way to raise. Some people don't need to be raised. You're not there to be a father figure to people. You're there to be an employer. So if they don't work out for you, just get them out.

It was a plantation mentality for a while because it was just like an ego trip. It's not about ego. I'm trying to build an ecosystem and a community. I want people to be happy to come to work. Not like, "Fuck, I got to go work for chef." It used to be where people walked into the restaurant, they'd be like, "Oh, chef's here." That's not the way to live. That's not the way to run a business. And then eventually it's going to fall.

I could have done things better. But I also know things run smoother through fear than they do now just being with people because we are less aggressive. We deal with mediocrity because we have to deal with lawsuits and this or that. But it's taken away from hospitality. It's taken away from being perfect. If I can't yell at you for messing up eight dishes in a row and I still got to pay you, there's only so much that I can try and hold in. Now instead of doing things the way I want, I try to simplify the dish where it works for everybody. The flavor is still there. The aesthetics are there.

Does that help me? No. But it helps everybody stay sane because then I won't be able to have employees. There has to be a balance. But there's also a person in the back of my head saying I want to do the food, but then that's when I just do a private event and I do the food the way I want to do it because it's for 18 people instead of 800 people.

You just got to find that balance. Finding the sacrifices that you want to make, choosing your battles.

Sakari: You've always been an entrepreneur along with being a chef. What's your secret sauce?

Marc: I just think I'm like Wolverine in the fact that I have great healing power regardless of what comes. That to me is my resilience.

I remember I was doing a party right when I was closing up The Pie Hole and a lady was asking me, "So what are you going to do now?" I was like, "Well, we still got the truck. We got this. We got the catering. We got the commissary. The brand is always going to be." She was like, "You're never going to—" I said, "No, I'm never going to stop."

Me and my wife sit—I'll sit across the table from a billionaire and he'll be like, "You're going to work for me?" I'm like, "I'll work with you, bro. I don't work for nobody because they're never going to pay me enough to live next to them." So I just got to work for it. And even if I don't, my kids will. I want my kids to not worry like their kids don't worry. I want my kids to be able to fuck up the way their kids fuck up. I want them to have the opportunity to be everything.

My superpower is my resilience. I will not stop. I will go berserker. I will scorch earth. I might take time off and relax for a little bit, but I will come back stronger than before. Some people don't have that, and that's why they become salesmen. I want it. I

want to be on TV. I want the books. I want to do motivational speaking. I want it all, bro. Why? Because I put in the work. It's not like I'm saying I want it and I'm just sitting on my hands. No, I get up every day. I bust my hump. I learn.

Before I was just like, actually believing what people were saying: "No, you want too much. You want too much." And after a while when people tell you that you want too much because they see you getting a lot, you believe it. Like maybe I'm asking for too much. Maybe I need to pump the brakes. No. They wanted me to pump the brakes so I wouldn't pass them. Fuck you. I'm passing your ass. All gas. No brake, bro. That guy that you met years ago that asked me what do you want to do and it was world domination—I want my world domination again because why not? Everybody else is trying to do it and they're not that nice. When I say they're not that nice, I'm not talking about their food. They're not nice people, bro.

Sakari: What do you want the next generation to know about food and about you?

Marc: I want real food to always be real food. I want cooks to strive to be chefs. I want cooks who want to strive to be chefs to go through the process and understand the process. They might be burning books and they might be burning history, but they do not burn the history of hospitality. If you think about hospitality, hospitality was started from the people who served, and the people who served these motherfuckers were us.

In everything that we do, I want people to understand not just my legacy of being a chef, but my legacy of being a servant and what that means to serve. I fought it so much when I was a kid. We would serve in church. I'm like, "I hate serving. Let me just cook."

Bro, to have a church, to have a brick and mortar, to serve people and give them your fellowship is everything. That has to be kept sacred. Above all else, hospitality has to always be hospitality because if not, we're animals.

Be of service.

CHEF KWAME ONWUACHI: ON CRAFT, AUTHENTICITY, AND WHY YOUR BRAND IS ONLY AS STRONG AS YOUR SKILL

"Focus on your craft. Focus on your craft, the rest will follow. The only reason why Michael Jordan got one of the best deals in Nike history is

because he was one of the best players that ever played the game. Your brand is only supported by your craft."

Those words from Chef Kwame Onwuachi cut through all the noise about personal branding, social media presence, and building a following. A James Beard Award winner, acclaimed author of *Notes from a Young Black Chef,* and the culinary force behind Tatiana at Lincoln Center, Kwame has built his reputation on one simple principle: be exceptionally good at what you do, and everything else will follow.

When I met Kwame, he was just coming up in DC and had just taken the helm of Kith/Kin. I was just a young, hungry cook that wanted to prove that I could. Kwame was one of the first people to see something in me that I didn't see in myself by offering me that sous chef position.

Kwame is intentional with his time as he continues to build what he wants his legacy to become. I admired that, seeing Kwame killed out here—his courage to write his book, his thoughtful leadership, and introducing food that is so reminiscent of how I grew up, and it was all at the forefront for the world to see.

This interview was special. It came after I just saw him at the US Open—and not just any appearance. He walked in wearing a durag, walking swiftly but cool, unapologetically himself in a space where people like us often feel the pressure to code-switch, or conform. Kwame represents: authenticity over optics, craft over clout.

When I called him for this interview, he was in the middle of opening his new restaurant in Las Vegas, "SAHARA"—a concept celebrating Maroon culture and the impact on displaced Africans to global cuisine. This was an opportunity to honor his Jamaican heritage, right in the heart of Vegas. Throughout our entire conversation, you'll hear him making doubles, setting timers, directing his team on pizza oven temperatures, and checking on green goddess dressing. He never asked to reschedule. He never said "let me call you back when I'm not busy." I appreciated that. For Kwame, this *is* the work. The craft doesn't stop for interviews or photo shoots or brand-building exercises. And that's exactly the point.

His award-winning restaurant Tatiana at Lincoln Center exploded onto the scene. It earned critical acclaim for celebrating the Afro-Caribbean diaspora and the parts of New York that don't usually get celebrated in spaces like Lincoln Center. But as Kwame says, "The goal is never the accolade. The goal is to look good in the mirror." Beyond the James Beard Award and the bestselling memoir, Kwame is committed to creating real opportunities for the next generation. He provides full-ride scholarships to the Culinary Institute of America—complete with his phone number, regular check-ins, and real mentorship about where to extern and who to work for.

In this conversation, Kwame breaks down why food is actually the easy part (it's the storytelling and experience that's hard), how he thinks about opening restaurants in real-time, and why he believes every day should be treated like day one. You'll discover his mantra of "caring" as his secret sauce, why authenticity is easier than being fake, and how he learned to lead with humanity after experiencing James Kent's leadership style at Eleven Madison Park.

As Kwame says: "We only have such a short period of time on this earth. I'd rather spend the majority of it being the best version of myself, but also the most authentic version of myself and not worrying about people's perception of me and just focusing on my craft at the end of the day."

Kwame does a lot of things behind the scenes to help kids and the next generation. And so it felt very aligned to have him be featured in this book. His final advice? "Read this book."

Let's just dig right into it.

Sakari: I appreciate you taking the time, man. I know you're super busy.

Kwame: Of course, man. Recipe testing right now for one of my new restaurants.

Sakari: If you had to describe your entire culinary journey in just three words, what would they be?

Kwame: Just three words. My entire culinary journey.

[Long pause]

Um...fucking exhausting.

[Laughs]

What I would say—probably **intentional, fulfilling, and rewarding**.

I've been able to do so much because of the food industry. I've been able to meet so many people, impact so many lives, create jobs. I've brought people together. I've witnessed first dates and weddings, people that had their first dates at my restaurants and then got married because of that first date.

Sakari: Did you ever think it would turn out to be where you're at right now?

Kwame: I fucking hope so. I put in enough work. Hell yeah. That was part of the plan—to grow and be afforded the opportunity to do what I love in various places.

Sakari: A lot of times people have superpowers that don't get shine if you're working in fine dining where everything has to be super precise. You speak a lot about how every dish needs a story. How would you define your own secret sauce?

Kwame: Just **caring**. That's what it all boils down to. I think my "secret sauce" is caring. Sometimes it's out of fault, but it's just about caring about all the fine details, about caring about people that are on my team. Caring about what message am I getting across.

Sakari: Do you have a mantra you live by?

Kwame: The mantra is always "every day is day one." To have that same enthusiasm you had the first day about things. It keeps you in perspective that we're given this gift of life every single day.

Sakari: When you think about Tatiana, did it live up to what you wanted it to be?

Kwame: Yeah. Tatiana exploded for sure. But I don't think you shouldn't be doing anything without the desire to win. So, it was always like, this could be incredible.

The goal is never the accolade. The goal is to look good in the mirror. When you look at yourself, you're proud of what it is. And if someone says, "Hey, you look good today," that's just an added bonus. The goal was to create a restaurant that was intentional and

meaningful and celebrated the part of New York that doesn't get a chance to be celebrated at Lincoln Center.

Sakari: You're doing R&D for your new restaurant in Vegas. What usually comes first—the story, the flavor?

Kwame: It's a little bit of everything, but the story always comes first. The story guides the menu. It guides the design. It guides the uniforms. It guides the logo. Once you have a story, things kind of fall into place.

You're not just picking a perfect season, right? Same thing for a business—you are doing it for something. You're trying to tell somebody something at the very least. That's why it resonates with people because it means something.

Sakari: How do you think young chefs can create food that doesn't just taste good but that next level—that resonates?

Kwame: I think once you understand that the food is the easy part and to just let the food sing, focus on giving people the best version of whatever you create. I don't care if you're making cheesesteaks—make sure it's the best cheesesteak that you can possibly be. That's the easy part.

Telling the story and getting your point across, now, that's where some effort comes into.

You know, I'm making doubles while on the phone with you. I'm just trying to get the dough right. We've been making it for three days and it was good day one, but that's the easy part. How are we putting this restaurant together where it resonates with people and people feel like this is actually a special experience? Because food is food. Yeah, I'm going to make good doubles, but you could probably get better doubles in Trinidad for 30 cents. But what am I offering, and what am I bringing to the table that's different besides the food?

Sakari: A lot of times as chefs we don't think about all the other hard stuff—business, food cost, or even building your personal brand. Was that part of the plan?

Kwame: Focus on your craft. Focus on your craft, the rest will follow.

The only reason why Michael Jordan got one of the best deals in Nike history is because he was one of the best players that ever played the game. He wasn't like, "Let me focus on my brand." I think people get it twisted. Your brand is important. You have to protect your brand. But just focusing on your brand—I don't think any good company just was like "let's focus on our brand." Like what the fuck does that even mean?

Your brand is you, right? You have to focus on your craft most importantly. I don't care. That applies to everything. If you're a reporter, you got to be a great reporter and then yeah, you can have a brand around that. But your brand is only supported by your craft.

Sakari: Are you taking that approach with the restaurant in Vegas?

Kwame: Well, it's the name of the restaurant so it's going to be very heavily influenced by Maroon culture design-wise, food-wise, everything. That's what the story is rooted in. It's telling the story of a people that should have more recognition for their contributions to the food industry, but also the plight of Black people, of Africans escaping slavery.

Kwame: *[To staff]* Pop it in the pizza oven. Wait till it gets to like 500 and I want to get at least to 600 degrees. And then pop it in. Spray first.

[Back to interview]

Sakari: That's literally an example of you putting your craft first.

Kwame: Yeah. It's important. It's so important. And I think it gets forgotten a lot. Obviously, there's going to be a huge dirt pit in the restaurant. That's going to be a big part of the menu. But my job also is to make delicious food. So that's a really big part of it, making sure that the food is good and use that as a vessel to tell the story.

Sakari: I remember you stepped away from the industry a little bit, moved to LA, wanted to do acting. What's your advice for the next generation that looks at food as a vehicle to do other things?

Kwame: Be good at cooking first. Pharrell is one of the greatest music producers to ever live. That's it.

I'm not gonna lie—when I started my career professionally I was acting, I was doing music, and I was cooking and then cooking took off but I just focused on it. I just had a TV show, played myself in a scripted TV show—that's cool. I have more opportunities like that. But at the end of the day, none of that comes without being good at your craft.

The reason why Pharrell's opportunity was given these opportunities—he is a legend in his own right. So then that comes with opportunities. The reason why LeBron has a movie is because he's one of the greatest basketball players to ever play the game.

SO YES, THOSE OPPORTUNITIES WILL COME, BUT I DON'T THINK THAT SHOULD BE A FOCAL POINT. THE JOURNEY IS THE REWARD AND FOCUSING ON YOUR CRAFT IS THE MOST IMPORTANT THING YOU CAN DO.

I've been cooking since I was 5 years old. Once I found out that cooking for me didn't feel like work, then I just focused on that. I think it's important to not let people put you in a box, you know, and not label you. But you can't forget to be great. You can't forget to be a student of the path.

[Kitchen interruption]

Kwame: Great. Look at these flowing. So, I'm gonna steam them in here and then I'm gonna recook them in like two hours.

Kwame: *[To phone]* Hey Siri, set a timer for two hours.

Sakari: How important has mentorship been for you? Alexander Smalls said he doesn't believe in mentorship—he believes in relationships.

Kwame: Yeah, I mean, life is different for everybody. I didn't really have many culinary mentors growing up. I didn't have a lot of chefs that looked like me. So there wasn't many people to turn to. We're all essentially fighting for a spot. There was only a place for one of us at every event.

I think now it's a lot different. There are a lot of chefs of color doing really amazing things. I had some slight mentorship along the way. But I had to figure out a lot of stuff on my own. I think mentorship is great though. Fuck. If you can find it, why not get lessons from people that will help you skip steps? I have mentees. I have a scholarship in my name at the CIA that I send someone on a full ride to every single year. And it comes with my number and it comes with me checking in on them and it comes with me telling them where the fuck they should go on externship and who they should work for. I think that's incredible. I wish I had that.

I THINK THAT'S WHERE WE FIND ULTRA SUCCESSFUL PEOPLE AT YOUNG AGES MOST OF THE TIME IS BECAUSE THEY'VE HAD MENTORSHIP.

Sakari: Can you speak about your relationship with Martell Stone?

Kwame: Yeah. It's about giving people opportunities that normally wouldn't have them. Seeing something in someone that not everybody sees and teaching by example. It's going through the ups and downs with them to ensure their success.

I remember at Per Se they'd be like, "We don't fail." Every day—we will get to service. You may get yelled at, but someone is going to help you get to where you need to be because we have diners coming in and they have to eat.

Take that philosophy and put it into actual development of somebody's career. We're going to go through tough times, but you're going to get to this destination whether you like it or not. That's what mentorship allows.

Sakari: One thing I've realized with you is you're very authentic. Two years ago at the US Open, you came through in a do-rag. You were unapologetically you. When I was a young cook, I used to think I had to speak a certain way, maybe I couldn't show off my tattoos. But you're always unapologetically yourself. How important is it to be authentic?

Kwame: I guess for me it's harder to be inauthentic than it is to be authentic. So I choose the easier route. If I am feeling social then I act social. If I'm feeling reserved then I act reserved. I'm a human being going through emotions and I'm not worried about my brand. I'm worried about my brand in terms of I'm not trying to fuck shit up.

But I don't need to be this larger than life character. Even if that's what people assume of me—because I didn't put that. That's someone else's perception. That has nothing to do with me. It's also like if they're talking shit about me, that has nothing to do with me. So I don't care.

WHY NOT BE YOURSELF? WE ONLY HAVE SUCH A SHORT PERIOD OF TIME ON THIS EARTH. I'D RATHER SPEND THE MAJORITY OF IT BEING THE BEST VERSION OF MYSELF, BUT ALSO THE MOST AUTHENTIC VERSION OF MYSELF AND NOT WORRYING ABOUT PEOPLE'S PERCEPTION OF ME AND JUST FOCUSING ON MY CRAFT.

Sakari: Comparison is the thief of joy.

Kwame: Yeah. Absolutely. That's a good way to live. Because if you're just worried about what other people are thinking or about your past, then you're not really in the present.

Sakari: I'm a big believer in things happen for you and not to you. Can you name something that to the outside world seemed like a failure but ended up working to your favor?

Kwame: I guess Shaw Bijou. But once again, I opened a restaurant and I closed it. Crazier things have happened in this world. So that's someone else's perception—I don't care at all.

Although I was young, maybe that to other people was a failure, but for me it was like great. I got to learn how to open a restaurant. I did it four months after I won a James Beard award. It was like getting paid to go to school. I got to learn so much about opening a restaurant.

Sakari: *Notes of a Young Black Chef* was super inspirational for me. Do you think cookbooks are still relevant with all this social media?

Kwame: I mean I think all mediums of education and arts are always important. So yeah, definitely important.

Writing a book is a lot of fucking work. I'm writing another one right now. It's just—it's a lot. But it's great when you hold it in your hands and you have this thing that people can reference to and it's something that will live for all of eternity.

THAT'S HOW OUR CIVILIZATION HAS GROWN BECAUSE WE'RE ABLE TO PASS THINGS DOWN FROM GENERATION TO GENERATION, FROM FAMILY TO FAMILY. THAT KNOWLEDGE IS PARAMOUNT TO THE SUCCESS OF CIVILIZATION.

Sakari: For this book, for every book we sell, we will be donating proceeds to food organizations in NYC to provide a nutritious school lunch meal to kids. Growing up, a lot of times our lunch meal was the only thing we would eat. Do you have any experiences with food insecurity in the Bronx?

Kwame: We didn't have a lot of food growing up. We used to eat tuna fish sandwiches for lunch and dinner. Used to go get free lunches in the summertime at the public school. We were very food insecure. The Bronx is very food insecure. I think it's the number one food insecure county in the country or something crazy like that, especially being in the biggest financial hub in the world. Lots of times it was tough. My mom is a chef, she's a caterer, so very seasonal her work and the winters were hard.

Sakari: Has there been anything you've learned from other successful chefs? I remember Daniel Boulud walked into Eleven Madison and said hello to every single cook, every porter, every person. That stood out to me.

Kwame: I would say James Kent. The way that he talked to me during my stages was just something so different than what I was used to in the fine dining industry. When I would make a mistake, the way that he would explain to me, he just treated me like a human being and I felt seen for the first time.

Sakari: Do you take that into how you coach your staff?

Kwame: Yeah, definitely. His leadership style is very indicative of the way that I lead my team. Which is firm for sure but it also comes with understanding and democracy. It's not just what I say goes—it's definitely a joint effort of whoever does it best is right. I learned that from him.

Sakari: You have a lot of different concepts now. How important are systems or trusting your staff?

Kwame: Systems are so important for the success of any business and it keeps things consistent. We have a lot of systems in place. We try to take a lot of the guesswork out of the game for the cooks, so they can just focus on whatever skill they have to nail to get that dish. I think that's why we've been really successful and consistent across the country.

Sakari: What are you most inspired about right now?

Kwame: I'm focused on what's in front of me. The Vegas concept is what I'm most excited about.

Sakari: Any advice for the next generation reading this book?

Kwame: Read this book is my advice.

Sakari: Say that again?

Kwame: I said "Read this BOOK," is my advice!

CHEF JJ JOHNSON: COOKING CULTURE, BUILDING COMMUNITY, AND REDEFINING OWNERSHIP

"I add value to whatever I'm a part of. When I become a part of it, I'm adding value to that. So when those people go into the street and say, 'We're working

with Chef JJ,' you know there's some type of integrity, or values, or morals behind whatever I stand for."

Those words from Chef JJ Johnson encapsulate what makes him one of the most important voices in the food industry. A James Beard Foundation Award winner, Forbes 30 Under 30 honoree, and two-time Nation's Restaurant News Power List member, JJ has built a career on making African diaspora cuisine accessible, while maintaining uncompromising standards of excellence.

I first met JJ at an event in the Hamptons that Chef Marc took me to—Chefs and Champagne. JJ was the host, and this was one of the first times I was able to meet a chef who looked like me, doing food that represented his culture, and the things he was passionate about. That stood out to me because it's easy to blend in within our industry, especially when learning fine dining where we look at French and Italian food as the most well-known.

JJ was able to usher in a new era where he could highlight the culture that he and Alexander Smalls wanted to celebrate. I remember taking my mom and dad to one of JJ's pop-ups, and to this day, it's my mom's favorite meal. There was something very comforting about JJ's cooking, it wasn't overdone, it felt reminiscent. It was one of the first times we were able to have food that connected to us.

Cooking with JJ helped me understand not only being personable and connecting with guests, but also how to embrace flavor—using bird's eye chili, ginger, garlic, and cilantro stems in ways that felt authentic rather than forced.

JJ's accolades speak for themselves: his cookbook *Between Harlem and Heaven* (co-authored with Alexander Smalls) won the 2019 James Beard Foundation Book Award for Best American Cookbook. But beyond awards and media appearances, JJ represents something crucial for the next generation: he's figured out multiple models of restaurant ownership—from investor-funded concepts, to licensed deals, to joint ventures. He's built Fieldtrip into a fast-casual empire with locations across New York, the Bahamas, and Michigan, all while maintaining his commitment to food justice, sustainability, and community impact.

In this conversation, JJ breaks down the difference between being a cook and being a chef, why you can't do media and cooking simultaneously (you have to choose one first), and the importance of understanding ownership structures, from cap tables to license deals and joint ventures. You'll discover his philosophy on rice as "the greatest connector," why he believes Black people deserve credit for rice culture in America, and how he thinks about adding value to every partnership he enters.

JJ says his family has been invested in his culinary journey since he told them at a young age this was his path—even when they didn't want him to pursue it. That sense of accountability to the people who believed in you first, combined with a relentless drive to add value wherever you go, defines his approach to both cooking and life.

Sakari: For a kid that looks like us that wants to cook their flavors but they're learning French or Italian technique, what would you say to encourage them to embrace where they come from?

JJ: I think when you're in culinary school, you are taught to hone your craft. You're honing skills. There's nothing wrong with honing skills, you need to know how to dice and blanch and make stock and poach and roast. Most of the skills you're honing are formulated in a European cooking style.

Then when you get into the industry, those are the restaurants you go to cook in. There wasn't much of a playground for you to say, "Oh, I'm going to go work in a Moroccan restaurant or a Korean restaurant." Back then when I was coming up, there wasn't much of that.

What I consider my generation has been able to do well is take those honed skills, take who we are as a person or culture or ethnicity, and then start to cook the food of who we are and put that on a white tablecloth or in a restaurant. You can grab Kwame Onwuachi in Oklahoma City or Ming Tsai. You've been able to really see that, which gives the future generation a place to work in restaurants that look or feel like them.

Sakari: What was the first moment where you felt like you were cooking your food?

JJ: It took me a long time. The first time I was even able to have a conversation around cooking my food was with Alexander Smalls. Before that it was, "Let me see you do risotto or make pasta with double-zero flour." That was the conversational point.

Most people know I self-published a book, and if you look at the photos or recipes in that book, they look nothing like the food I cook today. Maybe one or two dishes. The documentation of what I thought I should be cooking to what I'm cooking now is very different. I didn't even think you were allowed to cook that food and be successful, or be considered somebody people would talk about.

Sakari: How important was that relationship with Alexander?

JJ: I think relationships are key. I watched my parents' relationships growing up. My dad ran a nonprofit basketball program, and we couldn't afford to go to a lot of tournaments, but he knew those guys and they would discount them or let us come play. That was all based off relationships.

Taking trips to Ghana, having those conversations, feeling like you can cook your food, or research your food, or talk about your grandma's kitchen, that was important for me. I grew up in the Poconos, so I wasn't around culture except in my family's kitchen and when coming to New York City. Being able to have that dialogue definitely gave me the entry point to express myself or cook or be who I wanted to be. Alexander definitely helped me with that, 100%.

Sakari: How important is traveling for the next generation?

JJ: Traveling is important. I used to make these jokes like, "Yo, I don't need to travel. I'm in New York City. I can go get food anywhere." But traveling is a whole cultural movement. You're around different people, you feel the textures, you see the way the streets are, the way the air smells. It's a very different approach than just going to a restaurant in Queens and being like, "Yeah, I'm around all the culture." You are, but you're not as immersed.

Sakari: Can you speak about the importance of ownership and what it really entails?

JJ: When I was at The Cecil, I worked really hard for good people and I used to say, "If I work really hard for these dudes, what happens if I work that hard for myself?" I didn't know how to raise money. I read books, watched YouTube videos, and talked to friends. I educated myself.

Parsons was literally the first investor to Fieldtrip. That's what they say you're supposed to do, ask if you leave a business, ask those guys to invest. And if they really believe in you, they'll write a check.

In this industry right now, there's many ways you can have a restaurant. You can have a restaurant through a license deal, a management deal, or raise your own money and open a restaurant. I think it's important that in your journey, one of those restaurants is yours that you own with investors' money or your money. It shouldn't all be built on a license deal where you only own the intellectual property.

At the end of the day, those guys you operate that restaurant with can close it at any point and then you're done. A prime example is Kanye West with Yeezy's—he owned the intellectual property, but it was a license deal with Adidas. He doesn't physically own the sneaker. He had to go sell the license again to somebody else. It's important to understand how ownership works, how partnerships work, how you sit on the cap table. At Fieldtrip, there's an ownership pool, an investor pool, in a growth model. Then there's other restaurants like Wonder in a joint venture model, and Red Rooster in a license model. I play the arena in many different ways of ownership.

Sakari: What made you go from fine dining to fast-casual?

JJ: There wasn't enough money, reality. I wanted to open a restaurant similar to Momofuku, just rice-focused. The money didn't come together. I never worked in a fast-food restaurant in my life. My parents couldn't write me a large enough check. I met a young investor along the way who believed in me—super young guy, friends of Parsons.

It just worked itself out. That's why it was a fast-casual brand, and I've been learning along the way. That brand is five, six years old. It's really young. We're fortunate we've been able to expand, but there's still a lot of learning.

Sakari: Is there a lifestyle difference?

JJ: There's no lifestyle difference when you're an owner of a business. You're functioning 24 hours a day mentally. You got to make sure payroll gets run, sales tax gets put in, P&Ls get run, things are fixed. Those things don't stop when you're in a business. The mental part of the business still runs. It might close at 9:00 and open at 11:00, but there's still functionality that needs to happen.

Sakari: What do you think about the culture of your business?

JJ: For me, it's all about being a safe space. I came up in an industry where there was a lot of verbal abuse, not hiring people based on how they look or their gender. If you look at who I hire, people say, "Oh man, you got a lot of women." I'm not hiring them because I want to hire women, I'm hiring them because they're the best person for the job.

You worked for me—Samantha, Omar. The kitchen spoke mad different languages, and the front of house had to be reflective of what New York looks like. How can you be in a restaurant and it just looks like one type of person?

What concerns me is I don't get enough White people applying for jobs at Fieldtrip. Why? In a White business, do Black people apply? Look at Sweet Green—they have a lot of Black employees. As an owner, those are things that go through my mind.

Fieldtrip has immigrants, migrants, New Yorkers, people moving, college students, grown people with families. There's a space for everybody. It's a safe space for all. Our retention rate is really high. We have Malik who speaks Wolof—nobody speaks Wolof at Fieldtrip. Sometimes I have to call my ex who translates for him. But he's a good worker. He works hard. We figure it out. That's what the restaurant industry is and what it's supposed to be.

Sakari: What advice do you have for someone wanting to get into media?

JJ: I got really lucky getting into media. Instagram growing, Esquire naming me best new chef, being on a show called The Next Great Burger on Esquire—David Chang was supposed to be on that show and something happened, and I was the next guy up. I'd never done television before. The reason I've been able to get on television and do things is because of the food. I'm also trapped in that era where I'm in between Marcus Samuelsson's era—they're all like 15 years older than me but I click with those guys—and then this new era of Kwame Onwuachi, Eric Adjepong, and Jonelle. My era is smack in between, and I lost four years to COVID.

You got to pick one or the other—either you got to cook and then go into media, or you got to do media and then cook. You can't do both simultaneously. If you want to be a food creator, be a food creator. If you happen to be a chef, you have knowledge other food creators don't have. You can drive that home, then roll into being a chef or back in the restaurant.

Everybody can't be a food creator. Everybody can't be on television. I used to think a lot of my friends were going to be stars, and I was managed by this woman who's big in the food business. She's like, "Everybody don't have the magic when the lights come on." She's right—you could be nice playing street ball, but when you got to get on the basketball court with the lights and the ref, you might be trash.

Sakari: Why rice? Why go all in on rice?

JJ: I just fell in love with rice. Everywhere I went, rice was delicious. People were loving it. The only place nobody likes rice is here in the US.

I wrote a single-subject book. James Beard Awards has a single-subject book award—I didn't even make it to the finals. The person who won it was on pasta. It shows you nobody understands rice in the US, and the perception that somebody writing a rice book should be from the Asian continent. But not understanding where the culture of rice in America comes from—it comes from the American South. It was born by Black people. It is the reason why we all consume that. There's no way around it. There would be no rice in the US except for Black people.

Sakari: Has there been a moment where a door closed but led to something great?

JJ: I call it the yellow brick road. There are points in your career where you have to make a decision on which way to go. I could have become an executive sous chef for Leon Ter ren or gone to Ghana with Alexander. Two doors.

There was a time I could have done a Complex show for $500 an episode. I decided not to. Pamel Watch took it, and that was his first entry point into a long-form series. You're like, "Oh, maybe I should have done that." We opened Fieldtrip uptown at Columbia University. We never knew there would be riots, that Columbia was going to be a mess. That location could have been somewhere else with a guaranteed base. You have these moments where you look back and think "what if," but it just is what it is.

Sakari: What drives you throughout your career?

JJ: Two things. I'm obsessed with food. I don't really see myself doing anything else. And my family is so vested. When I say my family, I mean all my family, they've been invested in me being in food since I told them at a young age, even when they didn't want me to do it.

All the restaurants my uncle Donald took me to, me doing my internship sailing with my grandfather co-signing on my student loan—people were invested in this belief that I told them this is what I want to do and I'm going to be great at it. At the end of the day, I can't let those people down.

Sakari: What's your secret sauce?

JJ: I add value to whatever I'm a part of. I add value to Chef's Club, The Henry, Hollywood, Rock Center, Atlantis. If it's a landlord, if it's a brand, when they go into the street and say, "We're working with Chef JJ," you know there's some type of integrity or values or morals behind whatever I stand for.

Sakari: What's a piece of advice you would give to your younger self?

JJ: Cook in better restaurants. I could have worked at the best restaurant in the Poconos. Even in culinary school, I would have worked in better restaurants to get better skills, more experience. I think that's just important.

HIDDEN GEMS: BUILDING EMPIRES AND TAKING OWNERSHIP

Chef Alexander Smalls
Gary Vaynerchuk
Will Guidara
Chef Josh Capon

ALEXANDER SMALLS: ON OWNERSHIP, LEGACY, AND MAKING PEOPLE FEEL SEEN

"People think the value is in the accolades, not the journey that brought them to that place. My accolades came about as a result of my passion to do the

work that I set out to do. The accolades was icing on the cake, a moment of recognition, but I did not go into doing what I was doing for those accolades.

I met Alexander Smalls at Chefs and Champagne in the Hamptons—the same event where I first met JJ Johnson.

I had no idea who he was. To be honest, he just looked like this welcoming older gentleman with a big, lovable presence. But as I learned about his journey—opening Cafe Beulah in 1993, the first African American fine dining restaurant in New York City, winning a Grammy and Tony Award as an opera singer, authoring five books, mentoring an entire generation of Black chefs—I was instantly locked in.

This is the godfather. This is the OG. And for him to be so willing and open with his time, I was extremely grateful. When Alexander invited me into his home—the legendary red room that's been talked about for ages—he had two rules: put your things down and wash your hands. He got me something to drink, sat down, and took the time to get to know me before we even started the interview. That's hospitality. That's presence.

Alexander Smalls is a James Beard Award-winning chef, restaurateur, and author. His restaurant Cafe Beulah opened in 1993 on Park Avenue and 19th Street and changed the conversation about Black food in America. Before that, he was an acclaimed opera singer who performed for presidents, governors, and nobility across Europe. His books—*Grace the Table*, *Between Harlem and Heaven* (co-authored with JJ Johnson), and others—have defined a new genre of culinary storytelling. Beyond the accolades, Alexander represents something crucial: **ownership**. He understood early that he couldn't own an opera house, but he could own a restaurant. And ownership became his path to freedom and self-determination.

What I've Learned:

- The accolades mean nothing if you're chasing them instead of doing the work

- Ownership is the only way to do what you want on your own terms
- Your ancestors and their sacrifices demand that you do something meaningful with your life
- Being present is everything—people remember how you make them feel
- Mentorship isn't manufactured; it grows from genuine relationships

Sakari: You've won a Grammy, Tony, James Beard Award, all these accolades. But I think there's a much deeper story. People hear "I've done this" but don't understand what really goes into it. Take me back to 1993, Cafe Beulah—the first African American fine dining restaurant in New York City. How did you have the foresight to do that?

Alexander: It was a mission. But you said something a moment ago that resonated with me—people wanting accolades but not understanding what really goes into it, not understanding the journey. That's the problem.

People think the value is in the accolades, not the journey that brought them to that place.

My accolades came about as a result of my passion to do the work that I set out to do. The accolades were icing on the cake, a moment of recognition, but I did not go into doing what I was doing for those accolades. And this is where a lot of young people get confused. They want the accolades more than they want the accolades to be the result of the extraordinary work that they have created. That point is so often missed. It's like people want to be famous, people want to be rich, because they associate that condition or state of being as being exceptional. But you're either exceptional or you're not, no matter those things. We all know a lot of people who inherit wealth, who are a fucking mess. They have no sense of what that journey was.

You must be committed to do the work. You must be committed

to feel not only honored, but that you have been chosen to do something important, and that something has to be the motivation and the force behind your achievement.

Sakari: What was it for you?

Alexander: As an opera singer, I traveled the world. I'd been the guest of presidents and governors and ambassadors and nobility, counts and countesses. I was somewhat of an enigma because I was this Black male opera singer that so many people, whether it was in America or in Europe, had not seen. Black women were at the time exotic, and there were more of them. Black men—they didn't make a seat for us at the table.

I was always the first Black to do this, first Black to do that. Growing up, I integrated my schools. I integrated my high school. I integrated the college I went to. Two years ago, they gave me a doctorate, and I gave the commencement speech to a school that had less than 10 Blacks when I went. Now it looks like the Bronx. Conservative White all boys school, now co-ed. In my career, there were a whole lot of firsts, and there was a whole lot of breaking the barriers and the standards. But I often found myself in places where I knew I was on borrowed time, where no one really created a space for me to be in that place, and yet I was there. I was either tolerated or I was seen as change, or I was exotic. It really didn't matter. I understood that was part of my mission.

One of the things as a young opera singer—food was already important for me. As a child, I saw the world through the lens of culinary arts and music. I was an artist first, and those were my two languages. When music took center stage, food and cooking was my comfort and my go-to when I needed a break from music. I made a pledge to myself in the surroundings of understanding that we as Black people did not have a seat in the bigger conversation of the culinary arts. Our food was an afterthought. It was essentially an indulgence. It was considered good but bad for you. It was demonized and looked down upon by those who held up culinary as their expression and belonging to them. I sought to change that. There was no way you were going to convince me that the French grandma's heavy cream and butter sauce was better for you than my grandmother's brown pan gravy that basically had natural chicken stock, some flour and some drippings from the chicken. That somehow was inferior to all that butter and heavy cream.

I said to myself, as a young opera singer experiencing the culinary excellence of everybody but people who look like me, if ever I'm able to change that conversation, that's exactly what I'm going to do.

Sakari: What was the turning point?

Alexander: Well, as fate would have it, trying to integrate an elevated discipline of the highest regard—opera, which belonged to the wealthy and the upper class—I hit the glass ceiling so many times.

The last time I hit it, it was my second audition at the Metropolitan Opera House. I was represented by the best classical management talent in the world, CAMI, Columbia Artists. Normally you go and you do an audition, you sing an aria, you start the second, and then they stop you and tell you what they're going to do with you.

I sang two arias and started the third. They stopped me at one point and simply said, "Oh, you've grown so much as an artist. Your voice sounds incredible. We're doing a production of Porgy and Bess here at the Met next year. We would love for you to be a part of that. There are a number of character roles that we feel that you could do."

There was a pregnant pause, and I absolutely was stunned. I looked at my agent, who was sitting there waiting for me to have a reaction. And it was like I heard somebody say—because it was an out of body experience to me—"I would not be interested in that."

The room, the air—I could hear it, feel it—it just left. The air left the room. People were stunned. This is the Metropolitan Opera, and this little Black boy is standing up there talking about he's not interested in what they're offering him.

I got the courage to move a leg or two, and I left that stage. Finally somebody broke out in applause. I took my coat from where my manager was. She comes running behind me. She says, "What are you doing? This is the Met. Sometimes you have to come in the back door." I said, "Listen, back door, front door, side door, flying through the skylights—I seem to be the only person in this room that understands I've just been insulted by the Metropolitan Opera. They're offering me bit parts in an opera I already have a Grammy and Tony for and sang the lead." I went home, I drank that bottle of red wine I had smuggled from Paris. I woke up the next day with a plan to open the first fine dining restaurant.

THAT WAS THE SIGN. THAT WAS THE SIGN THAT IT WAS TIME FOR PLAN B.

18 months later, I was building that restaurant in the most expensive neighborhood in New York City—19th and Park. Union Square was two blocks away. Gramercy was one block away. It was the pillar of food. And there I was, little Black boy, Park Avenue and 19th.

Sakari: Do you really think it was your Plan B, or was it your Plan A? Like, was it your calling?

Alexander: The singing and the food was always Plan A and B. I vacillated between them like it was two languages. I'm speaking French one day, the next minute I'm speaking Italian. It was my calling more than Plan A and B. It was the fulfillment of something that I could control. What I recognized is that I could not own an opera house, but I could own a restaurant.

OWNERSHIP BECAME IMPORTANT BECAUSE IT WAS THE ONLY WAY I WAS GOING TO DO WHAT I WANTED TO DO.

I wasn't the first chef that could have created Cafe Beulah or that kind of restaurant, and I couldn't be the first one who thought it was a good idea. But my advantage was I owned it. I owned my advantage.

Everyone thought I'd lost my mind. Black folks—Black on Black crime. They'll go to a White-owned restaurant and eat all that stuff and not make one complaint. "Oh, thank you so much. Thank you for having us." But they come to your place? Oh, they got so much to tell you. "Oh, this isn't how my mama makes it. Oh, you need to have my mama—" I'm not your mama. I'm not your mom. And if you want your mama's food, you should have gone to her house. I'm here to give you an experience like you've never had before.

I went through it all. I had to defend being Black. People would attack me—"How can you call this Black food? I don't care what kind of plate you put it on." It was interesting how we really ate each other up.

Sakari: You spoke about self-awareness, understanding this was your calling. How can the next generation know what their moment is?

Alexander: What I was doing that night with the bottle of wine was saying goodbye. I was having a private grieving session of closing one chapter and getting ready for another. That's what I understood.

Sakari: How do you know when to fight versus when to let go?

Alexander: It wasn't the first time a door slammed. My whole life—doors slammed. Whether it was going to an all White school, whether it was trying to join a particular club, whatever it was. I'm no stranger to doors slamming. It's sort of like an actor who understands that no, that door is going to slam off you and you're going to kiss a whole lot of frogs before you get where you need to go. What made this time different is the culmination of times when I started to write another story for me. I had decided this is the last time you are going to knock me down. I'm not a glutton for punishment.

I had seen so many Black men, some twice my age, still trying to make it in a field that didn't want them. What I understood is that me becoming an opera singer had nothing to do with my talent as much as it did whether they were going to give me permission, whether they were going to allow me in, whether they were going to basically allow my talent and ability to be showcased.

I watched so many Black men be held hostage, be kept away from their dreams and not know how to move beyond the chains that bind them. I simply took them into my own hands, and it was like I understood that destiny was calling me to do something big, and either I was going to be held hostage or I was going to get out of the Volkswagen I was in and get in a Lamborghini.

Sakari: Where did you get that courage from?

Alexander: Let me let you in on a secret. This is what my mother used to say about me all the time from a child: "I worry about that boy. He doesn't have a sense to know what he doesn't know."

I was fearless. You couldn't tell me I couldn't do something. It just motivated me. When I was a young opera singer, my voice teacher—this White man—said to me one day, "I'm almost embarrassed taking your money because you'll never make it in opera. You'll never. Look at me. I can sing my ass off, and I didn't make it. What makes you think you can?" I told my parents. They didn't let him come back to the house. But I said I want to work with him because I'm learning from him. My father wasn't gonna let that cracker back up in that house, so I started having my lessons at the Conservatory in town.

But the point is, it just fuels me. A door slams, I'm told no, I figure it out. I keep going.

What I understand is my destiny, my destination—not all the shit in the middle of the road, not the hurdles and the ditches and the distractions. You have to know what you want and be focused and determined. Otherwise, what's living worth? If every time you get knocked down, you settle in the place that you got knocked down, what are you doing? What are you really achieving?

You have to be fearless about the things that are absolutely important to you.

If somebody had told me 10 years ago that I would be sitting here now having opened five critically acclaimed restaurants in New York City, having authored five books and seen as an authority on a subject, I would not have been able to understand it really, because that was not my destination.

My destination was excellence. All of that happened because my destination was excellence.

YOU CAN'T WANT THE ACCOLADES. THEY HAVE TO WANT YOU, OR YOU HAVE TO MEET THEM AT SOME POINT LIKE A LONG LOST FRIEND. BUT IF YOU ARE WORKING FOR THOSE THINGS, THEN YOU ARE MISGUIDED.

That's extremely important for people, young people, to understand. We are in an instant gratification society. We have survived the Paris Hiltons and the Kardashians and all of these people who basically fed us, fed a generation or two on the idea of immediate gratification and being famous for being famous—not really having any talent per se, except marketing ability, able to clown out on YouTube or whatever else to garner all of this attention. But where's the worth and the value that supports all of that? Therein lies the rub.

Sakari: You spoke about ownership. Did you always know? Were you taught about ownership?

Alexander: I learned about ownership from not owning. It was just the reverse. I understood that people can't throw you out of your own house when it's your house. People can't throw you out of your job when it's your company. Basically, people can't tell you what to do if it's you who's creating the standard of what that company is doing. So I learned about ownership by default. Yes, I had parents who owned things, so I knew that ownership was—just like education. My parents basically felt like the only way our lives were going to be changed for the better was that we had extraordinary educations, which is why they raised us a certain way. My parents' greatest fear, their greatest wish, was their greatest fear when it came to me. Because essentially, I turned out to be everything they had hoped I would be—equal to all the White folk in that one horse, racist, segregated town I came from. And it scared the shit out of them.

My father came to me one day when I was in high school. I was the most popular kid in high school because I could sing and I could do everything. Everybody just loved me. My father said, "Son, I'm not trying to tell you what you should do, but it's important that you understand that every time you go away from here and spend the night with your rich White friends in their rich White houses in their communities, your mother doesn't sleep."

And even now it slaps me.

He says, "I'm not telling you to change anything, but listen to your conscience. Your mother and I grew up in a very different time. We don't have the luxury of trust in White folks that you have. And you're her only son, and she needs you to come home in one piece."

Sakari: Wow. That's empathy.

Alexander: So guess what I did? I invited the White folks home with me. My mother was like, "Oh Lord, the Klan is gonna burn down this house your father and I worked so hard to build."

I share that story with you so you can understand the culture and the foundation of where I come from. Those people on that wall—they informed me of how important being alive, being given a talent and the will to exercise that, it's almost sacred. It's a blessing. It was a blessing and a gift.

AND IF YOU DIDN'T DO SOMETHING WITH YOUR LIFE, IT WAS LIKE YOU BETRAYED ALL THOSE PEOPLE. YOU BETRAYED ALL THE ANCESTORS, ALL THOSE PEOPLE WHO MADE ALL THOSE SACRIFICES FOR YOU.

That's why they call it a gift, because it's given to you.

Too often, because I have my generation one behind me to thank, you know, raising so many Black and brown kids without a consciousness of their history, without understanding how hard won the privileges that they have, the choices that they have are.

There are some people who argue that integration was the worst thing that happened to Black and brown people because it created a sense of equalness, a sense of entitlement that we don't have in our society.

Sakari: The word that pops in my mind is gratitude. You're grateful for the gift you've been given from your ancestors.

Alexander: Gratitude. Know where you come from, knowing

where you come from, your roots. It's so important. So many young people spend so much time running from where they come from or trying to establish an identity beyond what they come from. There was a family unit that was important, and for many of us—myself first and foremost—I sought to create a family beyond my own family to maintain a kind of cultural expression that was important to me. So many of these photos are of friends of mine. They're my family. I've recreated the family on that wall here, the notion that I belong to something, somebody, a culture that is powerful.

That's what young people lose. That's what they don't hold on to, because they have grown up in a disposable environment. Everything is disposable. They sometimes throw out what is most valuable. There's so much truth in the expression "standing on the shoulders of those who came before." That also plays into the concept of mentorship—the need to essentially establish ties and relationships with those who have gone before you.

Sakari: Why do you feel mentorship is important?

Alexander: I don't create mentorships. I create relationships, and relationships evolve, and many times, mentorships.

It's always curious when people approach me and ask me to be their mentor. Sometimes I don't realize I'm somebody's mentor until I hear it come out of their mouth, and I may have known them, three, four years. The other day, I was being introduced, and this wonderful friend—an extraordinarily talented chef at a very important restaurant—jumped up and said, "I'd like you to meet my mentor, Alexander Smalls." First time I heard it. I was like, okay.

MENTORSHIPS ARE BORN. THEY CAN'T BE FABRICATED OR DIRECTED.

For the longest time, I thought I didn't have mentors because I didn't understand what the word meant. Then once I understood, all of a sudden I went, oh my God, I have this mentor and that mentor. Sometimes we lose the fabric of those relationships when we don't see them as relationships, but we use terms like mentorship that really speaks to someone who is instructing you. It's a relationship.

My aunt and uncle moved from Harlem, from the Harlem Renaissance. She was a classical pianist, he was a chef. Those two had the most profound effect on my life and who I became—mirrored who they were. She was a classical musician, he was a chef and creative artist. He taught me the language and conversation of culinary expression. She taught me the classics—Bach, Beethoven, Mozart and Shakespeare.

If you can imagine, in a one horse town in South Carolina which was still segregated, little Black boy, 10 years old, in his mother's rose garden reciting Shakespeare, that's who I was. Those influences shaped you. But it was also quote unquote mentorship. Somebody saw something, somebody saw your talent and shined a light on it. It can be a moment or a lifetime.

LIFE IS A RECIPE. YOU'VE GOT TO PUT TOGETHER THE RECIPE OF YOUR LIFE, AND IT WILL MAKE SENSE. YOU GOTTA GET THE INGREDIENTS, THE BEST POSSIBLE INGREDIENTS, AND CREATE THAT RECIPE FOR YOUR LIFE.

Sakari: You're known for these amazing dinner parties. Can you talk about that? How did you turn your passion into your career?

Alexander: My mother thought I was lazy. She said, "The boy won't work. He just won't work." She would go out and try to find me jobs, and something would happen. I remember once she made me get on a peach truck with my friends, all the boys would go pick peaches in the summer, like migrant workers. By the time we got to the place, about two hours, I had successfully developed an allergy. I was throwing up under the tree. They just made me sit there until they took me home and told my mother I could not come back. She was just sad as hell.

But I said that to say, the greatest advice she gave me was: If you love what you do, you will never have a job.

I was always constantly looking for doing the things that I love that somehow took care of me. When I opened my restaurants, I wasn't looking to make a whole lot of money. I just wanted to be able to live comfortably so I could do what I love, open that restaurant every night and carry on. It was my living room.

I remember my parents coming to visit, and my mother would say, "He ain't working. He's socializing. Look at him over there. Everybody else in here is working. These people are picking up plates and doing stuff. He's just talking." But she did say to me before she died, "You made it work. You made just carrying on the way you like to carry on work for you, and I'm proud of you." That means the world to me every day.

Sakari: What are your rules for hosting?

Alexander: So many people are absent in the parties they give. Being present is everything.

People think that just putting out food and drink and getting dressed in a nice outfit and acting like they're the guests, because that's what people do. They throw parties and they act like they're the guests. They're not hosting, they're not mixing people, they're not introducing people unless it's convenient for them.

They have no sense of how to welcome and receive people into their home or into their restaurant. I turned all my restaurants into my home. It was an extension of my living room.

When I opened Cafe Beulah, there was this young Black couple that showed up one night. When the host was taking them to sit them, they said, "We read about the owner here—he walks around and says hi to people. Is he going to come over and say hi to us?" It was such an odd question for the host because that seemed as important as ordering food. When I got there, they told me: "Table 45, this young couple, first thing he wanted to know whether or not you would come to their table, so please don't miss that."

I looked at the corner of my eye—they followed me around the room for about 30 minutes. I didn't go over immediately. I let them, you know. I time it depending on where they are in their meal. When they least expected, that's when I popped up. It meant the world to these people to be noticed and for everybody else to see that they were being noticed. They asked me if I'd take a photo with them.

My major rule in any social gathering is to understand that you're the maestro, you're the conductor, you're the reason that they've come. You're the reason that they will have a good time or not. You're the reason that they will feel integrated and involved in this group of people. I have always created an assortment of energy and characters —anybody from the CEO of a major Fortune 500 company to the pizza boy around the corner who delivers my pizza, who smiles at me and who makes me feel special. There were always layers of different people.

Sakari: Talk to me about how you met JJ Johnson.

Alexander: When I first met JJ and pulled him into the fold, he was working at JP Morgan or something. He had had a series of jobs that didn't work out. He was on Rocco DiSpirito's television show, and he looked like my father.

He also made the dish, the only dish my father made in my family, which was smothered shrimp over grits. JJ made that dish and won the competition. I was immediately attracted to the dish, the way he carried himself, and how much he looked like my dad. Then I started researching, found him online, sent him an email.

He reluctantly came to visit me, to meet me at a restaurant on Amsterdam. I told him about what I was building—The Cecil and Minton's and all of that. He had never met a Black man that was building anything like that. But more importantly, he couldn't believe that I had any interest in him, and it was very hard for him. He wrestled with it.

Then I invited him into my home, and he would come in here because I wanted him to understand who I was, the kind of food I created, and also who I was in the culinary hospitality space from a personal place. Because if you could understand who I was, then it wasn't a leap to go into a restaurant with me. He was too young. He had missed my first three restaurants basically. He could have possibly come to Grand Central Station, but I'm sure he made no association that was Black owned, because it was way before its time—opening the first Black owned restaurant in Grand Central Station 25 years ago was unheard of.

So he came in and he saw, and he was like a low plant in the corner, and then slowly got his legs under him. Then I took him to Africa because I wanted him to understand what Africa was, what it meant to him, and how it fueled who I was. Africa was essentially, at that point, I had had three restaurants based on Lowcountry cooking from Charleston and the Gullah Islands. The Cecil was about to become my global culinary expression. I spent 10 years traveling throughout Africa, South America, essentially traveling the slave routes all the way through the Indian Ocean and Asia to understand how through slavery Africa changed the global culinary conversation.

So I took him on that journey. We went to Ghana. I had been invited to create my culinary expression at a resort there, and that was how we foundationally started to work together.

But it was important that he understood who I was as a man and how food was a conversation and a lifestyle for me.

Sakari: I want to end on this. My mom just sold her house and is moving to North Carolina. I speak a lot about people's superpowers. She's moving because she didn't have that many connections here, and I think she'll be able to get that sense of connection there.

I've been doing research on Blue Zones—places where people live a long time. My great grandmother is 100 years old. I think a lot of that has to do with that sense of connection. My mother calls my great grandmother every single day. Having that purpose, that sense of connection. One thing we spoke about this entire time—through every part of your life—has been that importance of connection. Can you speak about that to the next generation?

Alexander: I'm going to sum it up for you in just one simple expression which is extraordinarily powerful, and you've heard it many times, but I really want it to resonate with you after the conversation we've had:

People always remember how you make them feel. Period.

Won't care what you give them to eat. I don't care what you give them to drink or even what you say. But it really is about how you—people come here because they know they're going to leave feeling good. I'm going to give them the best of me. I'm going to make them my most important moment of that time we spend together, and that's what resonates.

That doesn't happen just because I woke up one day and decided it was important, but it comes out of a culture and a legacy and a sense of family that has delivered me. What I love about the restaurant business, what I love about the hospitality industry, what I love about setting the table is feeding the spirit and souls of the people who give me that opportunity, who trust me with that expression.

That's the superpower, because I could have given you something to eat here, but you may have remembered it, you may not have. But you will remember the time we spent together, the quality and how it made you feel, and that will always be there. That's not something that you digest and it's gone. That's not disposable. And it speaks volumes, since we live in such a disposable world, because we shed everything that we take in. What happened to that? What happened? People don't retain, except emotionally.

The emotional bank of people—I try to fill that when people are with me. That's what's key for me.

GARY VAYNERCHUK: ON GIVING WITHOUT EXPECTATION.

"If you say you can't, I'll give you a hundred ways you can. The only limitation is the story you tell yourself."

GARY VAYNERCHUK: ON GIVING WITHOUT EXPECTATION.

I've already shared with you how I met Gary Vaynerchuk—the George Mikan rookie card, the rejections, the reconsidering, and winning the Sorcerer Scholarship. That journey taught me Gary's most important lesson: give with no expectation.

But winning the scholarship was just the beginning. What came next changed how I think about building entirely.

Over the course of several months, I participated in mentorship sessions with Gary alongside four other Sorcerer Scholarship recipients. These weren't polished presentations or staged interviews. These were real working sessions where Gary broke down our strategies, called out our "blind spots", and challenged us to think differently about everything from content creation to partnerships, to what actually matters in life.

The conversations that follow are excerpts from those sessions. I'm sharing them because they contain the kind of wisdom you can't get from watching Gary's content—this is what happens when you get in the room, when you present your actual business problems, when he tells you the truth about your lottery-ticket thinking.

Gary Vaynerchuk is a serial entrepreneur, CEO of VaynerMedia, chairman of VaynerX, and a five-time New York Times bestselling author. Most people know him as a businessman or motivational speaker, but Gary's impact on the food and hospitality industry runs deep.

He's a partner in VCR Group, a restaurant hospitality group with chefs Josh Capon, Conor Hanlon, and David Rodolitz. He founded and sold Resy, the restaurant reservation platform that changed how people book tables. He built and sold Empathy Wines. He started by building Wine Library into a $60 million business and spent five years doing Wine Library TV—900+ episodes of wine reviews before anyone knew his name.

Gary understands the food world from the inside. He knows what it takes to build a hospitality business, what it means to create demand, and how to turn passion into profit. But more than the resume, Gary represents something crucial for anyone building: he plays the long game and controls what he can control.

GARY VAYNERCHUK: ON GIVING WITHOUT EXPECTATION.

Mentorship doesn't always come from formal programs or paying for courses. It comes from giving with no expectation, from showing up consistently, from being someone worth investing in. But when you do get access—when you get in the room—you better be ready to hear the truth. These sessions taught me more about building than any course or book ever could. Not because Gary has all the answers, but because he asked the right questions and called out the bullshit thinking that keeps most people stuck.

What I've Learned:

- 80% of your energy should go to what you can control (content, building), 20% to lottery tickets (big partnerships)
- Giving with no expectation creates karma that comes back in unexpected ways
- Health is the only thing that matters
- Building takes decades—brick by brick, not overnight

Sakari: I brought you banana pudding—my storytelling vehicle. Totally vegan, no processed sugar. People are connecting with it. What's your take?

Gary: I get it. It's exactly like a rapper giving you their mixtape. That's how you share your story. It tastes better than a mixtape though.

Sakari: The biggest takeaway from being here has been observation—taking what's working, what's not, being creative. Like when the mystery box wasn't working, you said "let's do five instead of one." It's like cooking with ingredients.

Gary: It's just how I think about the whole world. The thing that works for me is I'm thinking about four things at the same time. Most people think of one thing at the same time, and that's why I'm getting to unique observations, better operations, more thoughtful decisions.

That comes natural when you're cooking, you're like "what if I add this, what if I take this out?" I don't think that's how people live life or operate businesses enough. They're just in silos. Like, here's the profit margin. But the intuition of taste testing—that's exactly right.

Sakari: I made sure to talk to as many people as possible here, I wanted to get the most out of my journey.

Gary: I like what I'm hearing. This gives me peace of mind that you got a lot out of being here. It's not just branding decisions, I'm religious about how I want our culture to be. I'm incapable of doing anything besides being a businessman. I was willing to die in fourth grade when teachers told me I'd be a garbage man.

Sakari: I'm focused on building demand. We're targeting the school system—partnering with US Foods, Sysco, companies that already supply schools. I want to provide better food to kids. I grew up in public school, we had shit food. I think banana pudding could be a gateway, like how Popeye tricked people into thinking spinach was cool. I'm also thinking about Magnolia Bakery partnerships.

Gary: I think we're in a generation that doesn't understand, I'm talking like every entrepreneur on Earth, getting a deal with Sysco or Magnolia Bakeries is a one in 47,000 thing.

SO YES, YOU SHOULD GO TO THE OTHER 39 THINGS YOU CAN THINK OF AND SEND THEM EMAILS. BUT EVERYONE'S STRATEGY IS LOTTO.

Getting into the school system through Sysco is fucking impossible. I need to make it clear to people because I think people are thinking smart. I just have a pretty good feeling that people don't realize how impossible all these things are.

When I grew up, what you just said was crazy. I think the internet and all this weird shit—like Taylor Swift showing up at your wedding—I think people see a highlight and think it's real. So the answer is yes, BUT make that your "this would be some remarkable shit" while I'm over here doing this. Does that make sense?

Sakari: I'm working on a book. Finding a literary agent, then going to major publishing. I know it's a needle in the haystack, but...

Gary: Book publishers very rarely sign deals based on merit of story. They're in the business of selling books. They look at where you're at and be like, can you sell books? That's okay, because occasionally they're like "this story needs to be told, my business is good this year, I like this kid." We have a relationship. So yes to everything, comma, needle in the haystack, lotto ticket.

THAT'S WHAT I'M STARTING TO FIGURE OUT TODAY. I'VE GOT TO TALK TO PEOPLE ABOUT ALL THE SHIT THAT COMES OUT OF THEIR MOUTH—AS LONG AS THEY UNDERSTAND IT'S A LOTTO. AND THUS IT MUST ONLY REQUIRE THAT LEVEL OF ENERGY.

80% of your energy needs to be content. 20% needs to be fucking Sysco, fucking Magnolia. Most people are doing 100% lotto.

Sakari: How did you learn to not care what people think?

Gary: The reason people are not happy is because they worry about what people think of them. They're trying to floss for everyone else.

They're trying to succeed to stick it to their dad because their dad said you weren't gonna be anything. They want to get the girl or the house. They want to make more money than their sister. It's just always about somebody else.

AND I'M JUST NOT. I'M A HUMAN BEING, BUT MY PERCENTAGES ARE DIFFERENT. LIKE, REAL DIFFERENT. I'M JUST NOT DOING IT FOR ANYBODY ELSE.

It's why I've been able to deal with all the hype. It's why I'm so normal. Somebody said to me in Toronto, "Yo bro, why you being all normal?"

I'm not about that life, and I could be. So I feel like I'm not affected because I don't do it for that either. I do it for me.

Sakari: What's at the top of your hierarchy? What actually matters?

Gary: My family. If everything's clicking and VeeFriends becomes Disney and I buy the Jets, and the next day a child of mine or a parent of mine—health. It's interesting. It eats up the first seven levels of the hierarchy. It's not like it's health and then joy or money. It's like health, and then health, followed by health and health, with health, and then health, and then rallying behind it is health.

Physical health. Me and the people around me being alive and not terminally ill or dead. Binary. That's it. Permanently ill or dead.

Everything about life is perspective. I'm so fascinated by how one human can say one thing and literally change your life.

For me, my perspective is so on point now. Don't get it twisted—there isn't a day where a currency doesn't run through my head about worrying about some dumb shit. It's just that it doesn't stay with me.

The worst of the worst stress that would cripple people gets like a week with me. Normal shit that fucks up my dad for a year is in me for like a minute.

Gary: Everyone listening to this has a fucking cell phone and has context from A to Z. Media is free. Facebook does not charge you to post on it, or Instagram or TikTok.

I'm getting kind of fired up. I think I've hit a tipping point where I'm just not sure I want to allow people to continue to tell me they can't. Because I've got unlimited answers to how you can.

Sakari: When should you pivot versus stay the course when things aren't working?

Gary: Don't dwell. Dwelling is the currency of regret, and there's nothing productive from that. I can't kick myself about missing out on Uber or missing out on a bigger check into Liquid Death. I need to focus on the next decision.

EVERY MINUTE YOU SPEND DWELLING ABOUT WHAT YOU FUCKED UP IS A MINUTE YOU'RE NOT SPENDING ON THE SOLUTION.

Yesterday doesn't matter. The things that didn't work don't matter. What matters is, oh cool, you've now observed that you're ready for it to be slightly different. So now what the fuck are we going to do about it?

Sakari: How do you balance research and execution when there's not enough time?

Gary: By really flowing. VaynerX last year was a pretty bad year. We grew, but we didn't make profit. Like so bad that if it was a public company and I had a board that had say, they could have probably gotten enough momentum to oust me.

But this shit's not gonna stay bad because I'm just adjusting. It didn't depress me. It was challenging, but you understand why. You've made dishes that are better than that, but you're like "yeah, I fucking rushed. I didn't even get to look at the chicken like that."

That's how I think about this—by just not judging yourself. I'm running with the flow. Sometimes I'm really killing it with research, and other times I'm not. There's never a time when everything I'm doing is fully working.

When something's not working enough that I think it's a problem, then I just have to fix it.

FROM A WORK PERSPECTIVE, NONE OF IT FUCKING MATTERS. THE REASON I THINK I'M GOOD AT BUSINESS IS BECAUSE I REALLY DON'T CARE ABOUT IT. IT'S MY PASSION, I'M A WORKAHOLIC, BUT IT'S LIKE THE JETS. IT DOESN'T ACTUALLY MATTER.

If everything burns down, I'll start again. I'll start a blog called From the Ashes. Everyone will shit on me, and then everybody will revere me from building back up.

GARY VAYNERCHUK: ON GIVING WITHOUT EXPECTATION.

Gary: Especially watching my parents' generation—I'm 48, my parents are 68 and 70—watching their friends starting to die, you're really not going to care. No matter how much you want the fame, the recognition, the affirmation, the validation, the financial—you're just not gonna actually care.

The joy of making people happy—that's a big currency. And then underneath that is deep curiosity of how good am I at entrepreneurship. Building Legos, being like a five year old and seeing how big your tower can be. Just the game. Not the money per se. I don't mind living a good life, but if I was analyzed by Financial God—the amount of money my father, my brother, employees—I don't have it. I don't hoard it. I don't have even a good fraction of it. So that's how I know who I am.

When you give, if you start getting mad at people—if they didn't ask for you to give, are you mad at them? That's us manipulating shit. That's me getting joy out of giving and then trying to blame somebody.

Gary: Before Gary V was known, there was fucking decades of actually being a businessman, and then five years of every day doing a wine show before I did a single piece of business content. These things take time.

The VeeFriends thing is a lot of fun for me because I still think I'm in the hole and the concrete. People think it's over because the price is not what it was. I get why, and that's appropriate feelings. But I'm definitely on that journey. I very much know how to do it, but it's gonna take fucking 15, 20 years to get to a place where people really give a fuck.

Gary: You have a much better chance to win the lotto if you play it 50 times than if you play it once. It's still very hard, but the squeaky wheel does get the oil. If you don't annoy people and bother them—whether that's me or Sysco or a literary agent—if you find different ways to ask the same question in a respectful, empathetic way that you understand you're the one asking, then you have a shot.

GARY VAYNERCHUK: ON GIVING WITHOUT EXPECTATION.

FOR ALL OF YOU, WHEN YOU'RE THE ONE ASKING, YOU HAVE TO HAVE EMPATHY FOR THE PERSON YOU'RE ASKING. BUT THAT DOESN'T MEAN YOU SHOULDN'T ASK.

Don't be mad at Sysco—49,000 people ask them to put them in every school today. Don't be mad at HarperCollins—everyone wants to write a fucking book and everybody thinks their story is the best.

But try. And while you're trying, focus on what you can control. You can post on every social and make a video and text everybody. You can make unlimited content of your food. You can cold hit up every VC on Earth.

Gary: Pattern recognition has helped me so much. It's effort and flow. Whether it's health and wellness, whether it's work, whether it's kind candor with your spouse, there's never a time when everything I'm doing is fully working.

I really have a lot of real fires going on right now. But there'll be a point this week, guaranteed, normally on a weekend, where I could take half a breath and be like "okay", And if it all burns down, I'll start again.

You know what I'm starting to understand now? I haven't even started.

People think, you know, someone thinks I can text Messi—which is crazy flattering. I can't. I can text Novak Djokovic right now, but I don't have this one but I do have this one. But I haven't even started—that's how I feel. I feel just like y'all. I just think I'm destined to go there.

I'm not rushing to build. I'm building relationships first. Playing the long game. Brick by brick.

WILL GUIDARA: ON MENTORSHIP, ADVERSITY, AND THE POWER OF RELATIONSHIPS

"Adversity is a terrible thing to waste. We can't always control what life throws at us, but we can choose how we react to those moments, what we decide to learn from them, how we use them to fuel our competitive spirit. If

you talk to any successful person, they will look back at the bad moments with gratitude.

Those words from Will Guidara—author of *Unreasonable Hospitality*, former co-owner of 11 Madison Park, and co-producer of *The Bear*—capture why he's one of the most influential voices in hospitality. Under his leadership, 11 Madison Park became the #1 restaurant in the world, but more importantly, he pioneered a philosophy that transformed how restaurants think about service: not as a transaction, but as relationship-building.

My Connection to Will: I met Will early on in my journey at 11 Madison Park. The restaurant was going through full renovations with a huge amount of new hires coming in. Will's first task was to introduce the culture to everyone. They'd spent the last decade building something special—people caring and supporting one another, striving for excellence—and now they had to get everybody in line.

As I sat down as a young cook, I listened to Will and his grace. The way he explained why he does what he does, why he feels the way he does about culture. He didn't want to call it front of house or back of house. He wanted to call it the kitchen and the dining room. That little difference makes a huge difference in how we all communicate and work together.

He shared the story about his dad: "What would you do if you knew you could not fail?" He handed out a card to every single person in the audience. To this day, I still have that card by my bedside. When I wake up, I glance over at it. What would you do if you could not fail? What would you attempt to do if you could not fail?

A lot of times, fear is what holds us back. On your journey, the possibilities are endless. Imagine you could do anything you wanted if you didn't have to worry about failing, about what he said or she said, about things going awry.

I worked with Will for two years at 11 Madison Park. When I would hear him speak, it took me back to college when our professor, Dr. Brower would count the "umms" in our sentences. There were no "umms" when it came to Will. He would pause quietly and continue to inspire. Whenever it was time for a new menu change, he would leave every single person inspired, which is why he has countless TED Talks and conferences all around.

This interview happened between flights. He was walking through an airport in Vegas, waiting to catch his next flight to go speak. But that's the life of an entrepreneur. I was so grateful he shared his time with me.

I rekindled with Will at VeeCon, one of Gary Vaynerchuk's conferences. After hearing him speak, people that knew my story would come up to me like, "You worked at the same restaurant, didn't you?" On Will's way out, I told him I'd love to get an interview for this book.

One thing he reveals in this conversation: he doesn't remember what I said at VeeCon. He just remembers how he felt after our conversation. And like Maya Angelou says, people won't remember what you said, but people will remember how you made them feel.

What Makes Will Different: Will's father taught him that "you're never too young to be a mentor and you're never too old to have a mentor." That philosophy became the foundation of his approach to hospitality and leadership. His book *Unreasonable Hospitality* became a New York Times bestseller not just in restaurant circles, but across industries—because the lessons about relationships, intentionality, and doing right by others apply everywhere.

What You'll Learn: In this 13-minute conversation, Will breaks down the difference between passion and purpose, why setbacks aren't as extreme as they seem, and how to look back on every moment with gratitude. You'll learn why hospitality is fundamentally about relationships, how to avoid tearing others down to lift yourself up, and why you should never spend too much time talking about how hard something is—what gets talked about gets thought about.

Most importantly, you'll understand the difference between things that are emotionally depleting and things that are physically depleting. Do the physically depleting things. Don't do the emotionally depleting things.

Whether you're just starting your journey or deep into building something meaningful, Will's philosophy on intentionality, grace, and relationship-building provides a framework for not just succeeding, but doing so with integrity and pride.

[Phone rings. Will is walking through an airport in Vegas between flights.]

Sakari: Hello, Will, how are you?

Will: I'm doing well man, how are you? I'm sorry my flight was delayed. You have me walking through an airport to my hotel in Vegas right now.

Sakari: I appreciate you taking the time. You were a big part of my journey. That card you gave me at 11 Madison Park—"What would you do if you knew you could not fail?"—I still have it on my desk. Seeing how you spoke to staff, how you thought about hospitality, not wanting to say front of house or back of house, creating a family. You've been a huge inspiration.

Will: I appreciate that. Thank you so much, dude. That means a lot to me. It actually means more from people that were actually there—that's more impactful.

Dude, I'm so proud of you. So where are you at in the process? how can I help?

Sakari: I'd love to interview you.

Will: I do have time right now. Let's do it.

Sakari: There's never a better time than now.

Sakari: Was there a defining moment in your career that clarified your purpose and passion? A lot of young people don't know how to find their purpose. Saying you want to do hospitality is so weird or strange. How did you know this was what you wanted to do?

Will: I was pretty lucky in that I knew what I wanted to do really early because I grew up in it. My dad was a restaurateur. Because my mom got so sick so early in our lives, he and I out of necessity got really close. He became my hero—also my dad, also my best friend, and also my greatest mentor.

So I was fortunate in that I was born into having a mentor. But over the years I stumbled into more and more relationships like that —whether it was Randy Garutti who was my boss too, or Danny

Meyer, or my time with Drew Nieporent, or lots of people in between.

My dad has a quote that I love: "You're never too young to be a mentor and you're never too old to have a mentor."

Which is relevant because it reinforces the idea that mentorship—on whatever side, whether you're receiving it or providing it—requires intention. It requires seeking out inspiration from the right people.

That means intentionally putting yourself into places where you're surrounded by people that can really teach you but still light a fire of enthusiasm within you.

Sakari: Gary calls it osmosis.

Will: Exactly. Because I don't care how passionate you are as an individual—invariably we need people. We need other people to fan the flames of our passion.

Whether you want to be a YouTuber or a chef or manager or whatever, the only way to be successful is if the fire of your passion is burning as bright and as hot as it can. And the only way for that to happen is to extend invitations to others to push you and to inspire you and to fuel that passion.

Sakari: I think one thing that helped me on my journey has been finding my purpose. I found my passion at a young age—my dad had a restaurant, I loved food, I was just a fat kid. But purpose is so meaningful. What would you say to someone that hasn't found their purpose yet but they're going through their journey and then something bad happens—life happens? Has there been a time like that for you when you were able to learn from it?

Will: Yeah. I think bad things happening can take a couple different forms.

One is that you wake up one day and realize the thing you've been pursuing is not actually the thing you want to pursue. That's hard. You can look at it as "gosh, I've just wasted all this time and now I'm back to square one." Or: "hey, if whatever you're pursuing you pursue with every ounce of your being, you are going to learn things about not only life but about yourself that will help you thrive at whatever you choose to pursue next."

So setbacks when you've chosen the wrong path and you realize it are not as extreme as they might seem in the moment.

Two—bad things happen where you got fired or someone got sick and you had to leave your job or the perfect job ended up being very imperfect.

I'll quote my dad again: adversity is a terrible thing to waste.

We can't always control what life throws at us, but we can choose how we react to those moments, what we decide to learn from them, how we use them to fuel our competitive spirit.

If you talk to any successful person, they will look back at the bad —quote bad—moments with gratitude because they almost always are a part of what got them to where they are.

Now that's not to say that when something bad happens you need to be a cheerleader and be like, "All right, adversity! What are we going to learn from this?" I think that is not a human thing to do.

> WHEN FACED WITH ADVERSITY YOU NEED TO GIVE YOURSELF THE GRACE TO FULLY FEEL THE WEIGHT OF THE DISAPPOINTMENT THAT ACCOMPANIES ADVERSITY FOR A MEASURE OF TIME. AND THEN STAND UP, LOOK DOWN AT YOUR OWN SITUATION, IDENTIFY WHAT YOU CAN GLEAN FROM IT, AND KEEP PUSHING KNOWING THAT ONE DAY YOU'RE GOING TO LOOK BACK ON THAT MOMENT WITH GRATITUDE.

Sakari: 100%. Every time anyone's ever been in a relationship and their person cheated on them, in that moment it feels like the end of the world. But then eventually you find your person and had that person not cheated on you, you might never have found who you were meant to be with. Or you might never have learned the thing you needed to learn about yourself.

It's always easier to say that when you're not experiencing it, but if you can give yourself the perspective and grace—

Will: Yeah. And grace.

Sakari: Your book is incredible. But for someone that hasn't read it—what's one piece of advice from your journey that resonates most with a young chef or young entrepreneur trying to find their path?

Will: *[Long pause while walking through airport]*

Relationships are relationships, and the lessons you learn from those in life can be applied to those in work and vice versa. No matter what phase of your career or life you're in, if you can always push yourself to be creative and intentional in pursuit of all the relationships around you, if you can build up those relationship capital accounts, that will always be the thing that serves you most over the long term.

Sakari: What made you choose that point? Is it really that important?

Will: I mean, hospitality is all about relationships. And I think the biggest mistake I see people make as they're growing through their career is they feel so much ambition that they start tearing others down in order to lift themselves up.

THAT MIGHT WORK IN THE SHORT TERM, BUT IT HARDLY EVER WORKS IN THE LONG TERM. IT ALWAYS COMES BACK ON YOU.

If you can constantly ask yourself "what does right look like" and do that—and by the way, right always looks like doing right by others—not only will you invariably find success, but you can always look back on the journey you've been on with pride, feeling that you've navigated through it with integrity. And no one can ever take that away from you.

Sakari: When you hear the words "Savor your journey," what do you think of?

Will: I mean, you've done a good job with the questions because all the answers circle back to that.

SUCCESS IS NOT A STRAIGHT LINE. THERE'S GOING TO BE UPS AND DOWNS. YOU'RE GOING TO GET A LOT OF THINGS RIGHT. YOU'RE GOING TO GET A LOT OF THINGS WRONG. YOU'RE GOING TO MEET A LOT OF GREAT PEOPLE. YOU'RE GOING TO MEET A LOT OF NOT GREAT PEOPLE. PEOPLE ARE GOING TO CARE FOR YOU. PEOPLE ARE GOING TO HURT YOU. YOU'RE GOING TO CARE FOR PEOPLE. YOU'RE GOING TO HURT PEOPLE.

If you recognize that at every turn there's something to learn, at every turn you have the opportunity to do the right thing, and at every turn you can give a little bit more, you can push a little bit harder, you can be a little bit better—

IF YOU DON'T DELINEATE YOUR CAREER AS BEING FILLED WITH GOOD SEASONS AND BAD SEASONS, BUT RATHER JUST SEASONS, AND YOU ENDEAVOR TO GET THE MOST OUT OF EACH ONE, INCREMENTALLY OVER TIME YOU START TO ACCOMPLISH THINGS YOU NEVER THOUGHT POSSIBLE.

Will: You know the Maya Angelou quote—people will forget what you say, they'll forget what you do, they'll never forget how you made them feel.

I DON'T REMEMBER WHAT WE TALKED ABOUT THAT TIME AT ALL. I DON'T REMEMBER A SINGLE WORD WE EXCHANGED. BUT I REMEMBER THE WAY I FELT AFTER THAT INTERACTION. I WAS IN THAT ROOM JUST GETTING BOMBARDED. BUT FOLLOWING MY TIME WITH YOU, MY GAS TANK WAS JUST A LITTLE BIT MORE FULL.

One of the secrets to success I believe is understanding what your superpowers are, because until you do you have an inability to fully leverage them. And you have a beautiful energy. That's one of your superpowers. And I hope you know that.

Sakari: That means the world, especially coming from someone I've watched close quarters and afar.

Will: Please continue to do the great work. Let me know when this book comes out.

Sakari: I know the book process has been a lot of hard work for you.

Will: Yeah. And fulfillment.

Sakari: 100%.

Will: Dude, nothing is easy if you want to do something great. And it's one of the things with the restaurant business—everyone always talks about how hard it is and how hard it is and how hard it is.

Let me stop doing that. Because what gets talked about is what gets thought about.

If you're doing it, you're doing it for a reason. And if all you want to think about is how hard it is, just do something else.

I loved restaurants because I loved restaurants. And so yeah, they were tiring days, but I didn't think of them as hard days. The book process—I never thought it was hard. It's been tiring at times.

There are things that are emotionally depleting and there are things that are physically depleting. Do the physically depleting things. Don't do the emotionally depleting things.

If you spend too much time talking about how hard something is, it becomes emotionally depleting.

Sakari: I remember someone said your brain doesn't know the difference even if you say something as a joke. You have to be kind to how you speak about yourself. If you speak about how something is hard then it becomes harder. But if you think about it as fulfilling, then it becomes more fulfilling.

Will: Yeah, exactly. The subconscious is real.

Will: You know the Maya Angelou quote—people will forget what you say, they'll forget what you do, they'll never forget how you made them feel?

I don't remember what we talked about that time at all. I don't remember a single word we exchanged. But I remember the way I felt after that interaction. I was in that room just getting bombarded. But following my time with you, my gas tank was just a little bit more full. One of the secrets to success I believe is understanding what your superpowers are, because until you do you have an inability to fully leverage them. And you have a beautiful energy. That's one of your superpowers. And I hope you know that.

CHEF JOSH CAPON: THE KING OF HOSPITALITY

"Life is about relationships, and you gotta nurture them. You gotta respect them, and you gotta support them."

I met Josh at a screening for an NFT artist who sold their work for something crazy—I think it was around 69 million. I don't know. Anyway, I went up and introduced myself. I said, "Hey, I've seen your content. I see you're working with VCR Group." I told him my story and he was intrigued enough that he ended up asking Chef Michael White about me. That was the first time I met Josh.

For most people, Josh's energy is electric. It's very unique.

Throughout this book I've mentioned that I'm a fan of Chef Gary Mehigan. And so anyone that works with Gary must be a special human being, in my opinion. I remember hearing Gary speak about the partnership between Josh Capon, Dave Rodolitz, and Connor Hanlon in VCR Group. And what Gary said was that when he would go to Flyfish Club, Josh Capon brought a special energy on the floor that was unlike anything else. Gary is all about kindness and soft skills. And I think Chef Capon brings that to every work environment he's in.

I was able to see it firsthand opening up Flyfish Club—the world's first NFT restaurant—and working together for the US Open. He bends over backwards for every single person that he meets. He wants to leave a lasting impression with every single person. But he does it because it fuels him. He does it because he loves it.

It's unmatched energy. For some people, it might be too much. But for the right people, it's just enough. It's perfect. It's unlike anything I've ever experienced from a chef. Most chefs are reserved and just focus on the food. But Josh really wants to wow every single person. And then you combine that with 30 years of experience and you have something very special. He has people that work for him for his entire career. That says something.

One of the most special moments for Josh and me was when he let me into his home for his first birthday event. I got to cook for it, got to meet his family, got to meet his friends. We threw a banger. But for me, he's always made me feel like family. That's what's so special about him.

Regardless of skin color or different areas or places, he's always tried to make me feel welcomed. That's very special. It's very hard to find good people like that, and he's taught me that relationships are important. So I forever will want to support him on his journey, along with the VCR Group, as he supported me on mine. This relationship can teach everyone a lot about industry love, about relationships, about everything.

What You'll Discover:

- How he turned a hobby and passion into a skill and profession
- Why traveling became his culinary education and his personal education
- What it means to surround yourself with the right people and right partnerships
- How to bring authentic hospitality to every interaction
- Why confidence matters and how to rebuild it
- How to create lasting impressions and legacy
- Chef Josh Capon: The King of Hospitality

Sakari: For young chefs on their journey who don't know exactly what they want to do—how did you learn this is what you want to do?

Josh: I think if you do something you enjoy doing, you'll never work a day in your life. I found myself at University of Maryland cooking for friends and throwing dinner parties more than I was going to class and performing academically. It was something I was naturally drawn to. My parents saw I wasn't thriving academically and encouraged me to make a change. I made a mature decision at a young age to transfer from University of Maryland to Johnson & Wales. I said, "You know what, I enjoy cooking. I enjoy being around people. I enjoy food. I've always wanted to travel, and I thought that could be a passport to take me around the world."

So I took a hobby and a passion and turned it into a skill and a profession.

Sakari: How important has traveling been on your journey?

Josh: Very important. Traveling played a huge role in my career, from learning how to take care of myself to how to interact with others. I traveled to Italy, Germany, Spain, and France. When you're responsible for cleaning your own chef coat, you learn how to stay clean real fast. Back in New York, you throw your chef jacket in a laundry bag and get a new one the next day. But when you're traveling abroad, you're responsible for your own laundry. You learn how to work cleaner. You learn how to work smarter.

One of my first chefs said, "Capon, you look like you're working as a mechanic. Your chef coat is so dirty." That stuck with me. Traveling played a huge role in culinary education but also personal education—how to interact with others, how to hold myself accountable, and represent myself in the best way possible.

Sakari: I like to think of food as the final frontier.

Josh: I do too. We're living in a crazy world. Food is the final frontier. No matter what nationality, what religion, no matter where you're from, we all enjoy good food. We all celebrate around good food. We're born around good food. Food is very similar no matter what nationality—whether it's dumplings or pasta. Food transcends all boundaries.

Sakari: You're able to do so many different things. How important is it for young cooks coming out of culinary school to do every position?

Josh: One of my strongest attributes is not just relying on my culinary skills. There are a lot of great chefs out there. Being a great chef is half what you put on the plate. The other half is managing the kitchen, managing your personnel, managing your payroll, managing relations in the front of the house and back of the house. Making people feel good about where they work and who they work for. Making people feel good about coming into your restaurant multiple times and supporting you—not just enjoying good food, but enjoying your staff and the ambiance.

One of my biggest skills is putting people in the right places to make myself successful. I can't run around the dining room and light the place up if people are complaining about the food. You gotta staff your team properly. When I get rave reviews, it's always when I'm in

CHEF JOSH CAPON: THE KING OF HOSPITALITY

the dining room. People say, "Josh, this is amazing." I get a lot of credit for a lot of people's hard work.

Sakari: How important are partnerships on your journey?

Josh: Huge. Partnerships are everything. Right now, I am incredibly grateful and appreciative for the VCR Group opportunity. I'm so grateful to have lined myself with good people that support and respect the role I play. Roddy and Gary, they get it. They get that my personality is one of our biggest strengths in the VCR Group.

The most important thing is to surround yourself with people that appreciate and respect your skills and vice versa. We know what Roddy's skills are as a CEO. We know what Connor's skills are as Chief Culinary Officer. We know what my skills are as a founding chef partner. And Gary—Gary's the fucking stick right in the middle. That makes it all happen.

Since the inception of VCR Group, me, Connor, and Roddy are the three legs of a tripod, and Gary's the stick that holds it together. We all support each other. That's very important. As you build your team, you can only get so big if you have a foundation. Everybody you hire—from a dishwasher to a general manager to a sommelier—everybody's gotta be another brick in that foundation to build something that's hopefully bigger than all of us.

Sakari: People call you the king of hospitality. What does that mean to you?

Josh: I just like to make people feel good. I like to make people feel good whether they're in my house, my backyard, at the US Open, at Flyfish Club, at Little Maven, or walking down the street. I chased the general manager of Delilah down the street the other day with a shrimp cocktail. Nobody does what I do. I know how to make people feel good and appreciated in any surrounding—whether it's a restaurant or not.

Sakari's Note: This is what hospitality looks like when Josh actually shows up. This is him on the floor, second night of service at a new restaurant. This is his voice leading the team. This is what he means by making people feel good—it's not just talk. It's work.

Josh speaks to his team before service:

"Alright, places on a wonderful second night of service. People are blown away by the food. They are blown away by the service. They are literally making reservations on the way out the door. That's called winning everybody. That's pretty cool. We did 120 covers last night. Not bad for a second night of service. The training wheels are off. Okay? This place is a Ferrari. You know what that means? It's built for speed.

We did 120 covers last night. That's like in third gear. We drive a car. That's like being in third gear. We need to start revving the engine a little bit and start flexing our muscles a little bit.

Yes, we're going into fourth gear. We're gonna do 160 covers tonight, and then we're gonna go down in fifth gear, and then we're gonna be cruising down the highway doing 220 miles with the top down, with the radio blaring, with 100 on the wheel like we fucking got this. We fucking got this.

Two nights in. I feel like we've been open for three weeks. I don't know about you, this is the greatest restaurant opening I've ever been a part of. You guys all put in the work. Please continue to do so every second counts.

Table maintenance is everything.

If I see steak sauce on the table with the desserts, I get upset. If I don't see steak sauce on the table with the stakes, I get upset. If I see a puddle of chocolate ice cream on the dessert table, I get upset. Just constantly be looking. You're a hawk. You are hawks. You are flying around the table, literally. What can I do? What can I take off? A little chocolate sauce to make it that much better, right?

Everything to enhance, to get the experience better. Because on the way out, they are doing what? Future reservations. Future reservations. That's the magic of this place that's blown away from the first moment they come in the door till they leave. Yes, let's go!"

Sakari: That's it right there. That's what it looks like when somebody understands that hospitality is a sport. It's about momentum. It's about details. It's about knowing that every single interaction matters. It's about being a hawk and making sure your team is flying around that room with purpose.

CHEF JOSH CAPON: THE KING OF HOSPITALITY

Sakari: Things happen for you, not to you. Can you recall a time where a door closed but became a bigger opportunity?

Josh: Yeah. I was in situations that weren't working. But now I'm working harder than I ever have. I feel better than I ever have because I'm doing it for the right reasons with the right people. The point is to surround yourself by good people that want to see you succeed. Opportunities present themselves. You have to go get it.

Roddy and I were meeting people and tag teaming. We have each other's back. We're always building each other up, not knocking each other down. That's the difference. I was in a relationship that was going nowhere, being taken advantage of. I was miserable at 50-something years old. And now I'm fucking working harder than I ever have. I feel better than I ever have because I'm doing it for all the right reasons with the right people.

Sakari: How important has faith been on your journey?

Josh: I think you really have to believe in yourself. You have to have confidence. A year and a half, two years ago, I lost my mojo for a little while. Flyfish Club healed me. It really did. I think you have to always believe in yourself and believe in the people around you.

I don't know if you're talking from a religious aspect, but I think spirituality comes from within. You really gotta appreciate what you have every day. Roddy is stuck by my side and made me a better person, a better chef, a better partner. So yeah, I think you gotta have faith and believe in yourself. Most importantly, I think it starts there.

Sakari: One piece of advice for a young cook or chef coming out of culinary school.

Josh: Take full advantage of every opportunity that comes your way. Focus like hell. Take notes. Go home and relive it. I worked in Italy. I made pasta every day. If I don't make pasta right now, I would stumble. We're all so distracted by everything else when you go to work. Put your phone away. Just focus on what you're doing. Give it everything you got.

Time is precious. You only have so many minutes and hours in a day. How are you going to maximize them and relive them? Keep a journal. Every opportunity—whatever station you're working, whatever salad dressing you're making—make sure you make it the fucking best you can.

Be the best of what you are. There's a great poem called "The Dash." Look it up. It's about your life's work. It's about your eulogy being read. Will you be proud of how you lived your dash? Every day, man. Every fucking day. Laugh more. Tell people you love them more.

My advice is to maximize every opportunity to the fullest and really respect everybody and everything. Whether it's sun's out or rain's out, just every day. I'm grateful for everything going on around the world right now.

Sakari: What are your biggest things?

Josh: Two things. Life is about relationships. You gotta nurture them. You gotta respect them. You gotta support them and you gotta feed them. And communication is the key to life. Those are my two biggest things. Communicate with your loved ones. Communicate with your coworkers. All of that. Every relationship, you gotta feed it and you gotta communicate. That's how you build something real. And you know what? That's what drives me. That's what fuels me. Making people feel something. Making them feel welcome. Making them feel like they're part of something special.

Every second counts. Every interaction matters. If they leave happy, if they make a reservation on the way out, if they tell their friends about it—that's the legacy. That's the work.

PART III
THE TOOLKIT - THE PROMISE

For Recipe visuals and to subscribe to the SYJ Newsletter. Scan here!

CHEF SAKARI'S TOP 5 KITCHEN STAPLES

When I open my pantry, I see more than just ingredients. I see possibilities. I see the way my grandmother taught me to stretch a dollar without sacrificing flavor. I see the lessons that simple things have taught me about cooking and about life. These five staples have been my teachers. They're affordable, powerful, and full of purpose. They've shown me that you don't need fancy ingredients to create something beautiful. You just need to understand what you're working with and let each ingredient shine.

Baking Soda: is my superpower ingredient. Most people think it's just for baking cakes or keeping the fridge fresh, but this little box can do so much more. I use it for cooking, cleaning my kitchen, even whitening my cutting boards. In Chinese cooking, there's a technique called "velveting" where you coat meat in a mixture with baking soda before cooking. It makes tough, cheap cuts of meat tender and silky. That's the lesson right there: something that costs less than a dollar can transform your cooking in a dozen different ways. It taught me to look deeper at what I already have.

Coconut: reminds me of home. Whether it's the oil I cook with, the water I drink after a long day, or the sweet flesh I add to desserts, every part of the coconut gives something different. Coconut water is full of natural electrolytes that hydrate you better than most sports drinks. The oil adds richness and a subtle sweetness that connects me to my Caribbean roots. When I use coconut, I'm using all of it, wasting nothing, and that feels like honoring where I come from. It's nourishment in its truest form.

Citrus: wakes everything up. A squeeze of lemon or lime, a little grated zest, and suddenly a dish goes from flat to vibrant. That's because acid balances flavor. It cuts through richness, brightens vegetables, and makes even simple water taste alive. In cooking, citrus teaches us about balance. Too much of anything gets boring or overwhelming, but a little brightness makes everything better. I think about that in life, too. Sometimes we just need a small spark of something fresh to see things clearly again.

Fresh Herbs: are like the energy in a room. Basil, cilantro, parsley, mint—they transform heavy dishes into something light and exciting. A handful of chopped herbs on top of a stew or a salad can completely change how it tastes and how it makes you feel. Herbs have taught me that small touches bring big change. You don't need to do everything over to make something better. Sometimes all it takes is one bright, fresh addition to shift the whole experience.

Sea Salt: is the most important ingredient in my kitchen, and here's why: it enhances every single flavor. Salt doesn't just make food taste salty. It wakes up the flavors that are already there. On a scientific level, salt interacts with our taste buds and helps us taste sweetness, bitterness, and richness more fully. That's why a pinch of salt in chocolate chip cookies makes them taste more chocolatey. Salt is a reminder that simplicity can be the most powerful thing. You don't need a lot. You just need the right amount of something real.

These five staples have taught me to cook, create, and live with intention, because the smallest, simplest things often hold the most power.

SPRING

Weather: typically warm
Techniques: pan roast and other stove-top methods

artichokes (peak: March–
asparagus: green, purple white (peak: April)
beans, fava
green: green, green peak: March)
lemons, meyer
lettuces   lighter dishes
limes, key   limes, key
loquats, mushrooms
morel (peak: April)
onions: spring, Vidalia peak: May) (peak: March   soft-shell crabs
sorrfl   peak May)
spices, cooling (e.g., white peppercornns)
strawberries   maple syrup
tomatoes, heirloom
watercress

olives

oranges

watercress

zuschini blossoms

zucchini blossoms

FOOD IN SEASON

Summer

Weather: typically hot
Techniques: barbecue, grill, marinate, panfry, pan roast

apricots
basil
beans, fava
beans, green (peak: August)
blackberries (peak: July)
boysenberries (peak: June)
cherries
chilled dishes and beverages
corn
cucumbers (peak: August)
peppers
plums
plums
puddings summer
grilled dishes
ices
mengoes
melons (peak: July)
peaches (peak July/A)
pears, Bartlett (peak: August)
raspberries (peak: June, August)
salsa
ice cream
flowers edible
garlic (peak: August)
salads: fruit, green, pasta
soups, cold
tomatoes
zucchini
grapes
puddings summer
salads: fruit, green, sasta
sherbets
sorbets
tomatillos (peak: August)
watermelon
zucchini

AUTUMN

Weather: typically cool
Techniques: braise, glaze, roast

- artichokes → almonds
- basil → beach →
- bell peppers → bell peppers
- chilled dishes and bevcuages → broccoli
- → corn →
- cakes, especially served warm → cranberries
- caramel → cucumbers
- cardoons → duck
- cauliflower → eggplant
- grains → garlic (peak august)
- grapes peak september → gooseberries
- huckleberries → grains
- kale → heaver dishes
- kohlrabi → huckberrids →
- lentils → sweet potatoes
- vinegar → vinegar   red wine
- red wins   sweetbreads
- walnuts   sweet potatoes
- waterme   sweet potatoes

- → pumpkins peak: octobk
- salsa → winter
- → stuffing
- spices, sunflower, black peppercorns, cayenne, cinnamon, chill powder, clove, mustard)
- partridge → pears
- passion fruit   pecans
- pears   pheasant
- pistachios
- → pomegranates
- → pumpkins
- quinces + october
- spices, sunflower
- stuffing
- sweetbreads

WINTER

Weather: typically cold
Techniques: bake, braise, glaze, roast, simmer

Why We Cook Like This in Winter

In winter, the weather is cold al often harsh, which calls for comfort, warmthth, and nourishment. We use slow, gentle cooking methods like braising, roasting, and simmering to draw out deep flavors, and fill our homes with warmth and aroma. Winter cooking often focusos on root vegetables, hearty meats, grains, and warming spices that provide energy and grounding. Ingredients are often caramelized or browned to develop richness, bright citrus or balance se

SWEET
HEARTY CITRUS BALANCE

Seasonal Ingredients

- Bananas
- Beans
- Braiscol diches
- Broccoli
- Brussels sprouts (peak, December)
- Cabbage
- Caramel
- Chocolate
- Citrus fruit
- Dates (peak December)
- Game (e.g., December)

- Beans
- Beef
- Braiccoi (frebi)
- Brussels
- Orange (mandarin)
- Lentils
- Lobster
- Musle syrup
- Mushrooms
- Wild) (Decbmembr)
- Mussels
- Orange (peram.) (peak December)

- Game
- Grains
- Grapefruit (peak, February)
- Greens (winter greens)
- Lemons
- Peak (January)
- Mushrooms (wild) (peak December)
- Mussels
- Orange (peak, December)

- Grapefruit (peak February)
- Lentils
- Lumes (vinter greens)
- Lobster
- Maple syrup
- Mushrooms (wild)
- Mussels
- Orange (mandarin) (peak January)
- Passion fruit
- Pears (peak December)
- Plantains
- Pork

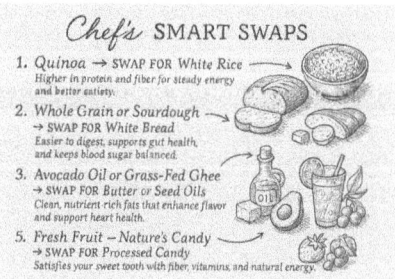

Chef's SMART SWAPS

1. **Quinoa** → SWAP FOR White Rice
   Higher in protein and fiber for steady energy and better satiety.

2. **Whole Grain or Sourdough** → SWAP FOR White Bread
   Easier to digest, supports gut health, and keeps blood sugar balanced.

3. **Avocado Oil or Grass-Fed Ghee** → SWAP FOR Butter or Seed Oils
   Clean, nutrient-rich fats that enhance flavor and support heart health.

5. **Fresh Fruit — Nature's Candy** → SWAP FOR Processed Candy
   Satisfies your sweet tooth with fiber, vitamins, and natural energy.

"You don't have to live without your favorite foods"

FARM-RAISED vs. WILD-CAUGHT FISH

FARM-RAISED FISH → **WILD-CAUGHT FISH**

- Live in crowded tanks or pens
- Eat pellets
- Less space & less movement
- May get more chemicals/antibiotics
- Softer texture, milder taste

- Swim free in oceans/rivers
- Eat natural food
- Cleaner diet, fewer chemicals
- Stronger muscles
- More nutrients (omega-3s), richer taste

Why wild is better: cleaner diet + more movement = better nutrition and flavor.

GRASS-FED & FINISHED VS CONVENTIONAL, GRAIN-FINISHED

- EATS GRASS
- RAISED ON PASTURE

- EATS GRAINS & SOY
- RAISED IN FEEDLOTS

GRASS-FED & FINISHED — IS BEST

- MORE NUTRITIOUS
- BETTER FOR THE ANIMAL
- BETTER FOR THE PLANET
- BETTER FOR THE PLANET

PASTURE-RAISED vs. ORGANIC, CAGE-FREE, CONVENTIONAL CHICKENS

Pasture-Raised Chickens
- ✓ Live outdoors in pastures
- ✓ Eat grass, bugs, worms
- ✓ Get more movement
- ✓ More nutrients, richer taste

Organic, Cage-Free, Conventional Chickens
- ✗ May live indoors
- ✗ Eat grains and corn
- ✗ May get less space to roam
- ✗ Fewer nutrients

Why pasture-raised is best: Plenty of outdoor time + natural diet = healthier chickens and flavor.

RECIPES

CONCORD GRAPE JELLY

I grew up in Long Island, but the South was always in our home. You know that saying, "You can take someone out of a place, but you can't take the place out of them"? That was my grandmother. She left the South, but the South never left her. Even after she moved to Long Island, she kept her old traditions alive. She turned our backyard into a little farm. We had fresh herbs, vegetables, and the thing I loved most—long, twisting grapevines filled with Concord grapes. Every summer, we picked those grapes right off the vine. Sometimes we ate them fresh, still warm from the sun. Other times, Grandma would turn th

em into jelly. Thick, sweet, purple jelly that smelled like pure summer.

Breakfast was a big deal in our house. It set the tone for the whole day. And that homemade Concord grape jelly turned something simple—like my peanut butter and jelly sandwich—into my first real food memory. It wasn't just jelly. It was love from the backyard straight to the table.

Chef's Note

Let the grapes break down slowly and release their juice. Strain through a fine strainer — don't rush it. The maple syrup brings natural sweetness instead of regular sugar. You'll know it's ready when a spoonful on a cold plate wrinkles when you push it with your finger.

Yield

About 4 servings

Ingredients

900 g (about 2 lbs) fresh concord grapes, stems removed

120 ml fresh lemon juice

1 tbsp lemon zest

125 ml maple syrup or honey

Pinch of salt

Procedure

Rinse the grapes and crush them gently in a heavy pot with the back of a spoon.

Add lime juice, lemon zest, and salt. Bring to a simmer over medium heat for 15–20 minutes, stirring often, until the skins break down.

Strain through a fine strainer, pushing gently to get all the juice out.

Return the juice to the pot and stir in maple syrup. Cook for 10–15 minutes longer until it's thick enough to coat a spoon.

Pour into clean jars and let cool. Put in the refrigerator until it sets completely.

Serve on warm biscuits, pancakes, or over yogurt.

WASHINGTON CARVER PEANUT BUTTER

This peanut butter is named after George Washington Carver, who discovered over 300 amazing uses for peanuts. This version keeps things simple and honest — just peanuts, oil, and a little brown sugar for sweetness.

Chef's Note

Don't skip the slow blending. The peanuts will go from crumbly to creamy to smooth — that's how you know the oils are releasing. If it feels too thick, a little bit of extra peanut oil helps. But be patient. That's the secret.

Yield

About 1 jar (serves 4)

Ingredients

400 g (about 3 cups) roasted peanuts, unsalted

15 ml avocado oil

8 g sea salt

20 g light brown sugar

Optional: 5 ml peanut oil (if you need to loosen it)

Procedure

Put roasted peanuts in a food processor and pulse until finely ground.

While the machine is running, drizzle in the avocado oil. Keep processing for 2–3 minutes until smooth and creamy.

Add salt and brown sugar. Blend until everything is mixed together smoothly.

If it's too thick, add a tiny bit of peanut oil until it spreads easily.

Transfer to a clean jar and keep in the refrigerator.

Spread on warm toast, stir into oatmeal, or eat straight from the spoon.

JAMAICAN HARD DOUGH BREAD

My grandfather was from Jamaica, so he grew up eating classics like this bread. I didn't understand how special it was until I finally tasted it myself. Instead of buying the regular white bread from the grocery store, we would go to a local Caribbean bakery. They made cocoa bread, fresh beef patties, and of course, Jamaican hard-boiled bread. The bread was a little denser than what I was used to, but still warm, soft, and slightly crispy on the outside. The flavor was rich and comforting. I had never tasted anything like it.

For me, this bread became the foundation for the perfect peanut butter and jelly sandwich. We kept it simple—just a little butter and a little Concord grape jelly. That was our thing.

There's nothing in the world like fresh bread. To me, it's one of the seven wonders of the world.

Chef's Note

This dough loves warmth — let it rise in a cozy spot. The coconut milk gives it a subtle sweetness and aroma. When it's done baking, tap the bottom. If it sounds hollow, you're good to go.

Yield

1 loaf (about 12 slices)

Ingredients

500 g all-purpose flour

40 g light brown sugar

8 g sea salt

10 g instant yeast

240 ml warm coconut milk

60 ml warm water

30 ml coconut oil, melted

15 ml unsalted butter, softened

Procedure

In a large bowl, mix flour, brown sugar, salt, and yeast together.

Add coconut milk, water, coconut oil, and butter. Mix until a dough forms.

Knead by hand for 10 minutes (or 7–8 minutes with a mixer) until the dough is smooth and stretchy.

Place in a greased bowl, cover, and let rise in a warm spot until doubled in size, about 45 minutes.

Push down the dough and shape it into a loaf. Place in a greased loaf pan and let rise again for about 30 minutes.

Preheat oven to 350°F (180°C). Bake for 30–35 minutes until the top is golden and the bottom sounds hollow when you tap it.

Let rest 10 minutes in the pan, then remove and cool on a wire rack.

This bread is soft, sweet, and smells like coconut — perfect warm with butter or jam.

SURINAMESE BARA BREAD with JAMAICAN CURRY CHICKEN & SOUTHERN CHOW CHOW

When I was cooking in the Netherlands, I fell in love with street food. One dish felt like something I'd dreamed about my whole life: fluffy fried bread soaked in curry chicken flavor. This is my take on that memory — a fusion of African, Asian, and Caribbean flavors all in one bite.

Chef's Note

The batter should be thick and spoonable, like pancake batter. Fry it like donuts — it'll puff up golden and crispy. The curry chicken should be rich and deeply seasoned, and the chow chow brings brightness and balance. Serve it all together for maximum flavor.

Yield

6 servings

Ingredients

For the Jamaican Curry Chicken:

900 g boneless chicken thighs, cut into chunks

2 tbsp Jamaican curry powder

1 tsp allspice

1 tsp salt

½ tsp black pepper

1 tsp dried thyme

2 cloves garlic, minced

1 tbsp ginger, grated

1 onion, diced

1 Scotch bonnet pepper, whole (for mild heat)

2 tbsp vegetable oil

1½ cups chicken stock

1 tbsp brown butter

For the Surinamese Bara Bread:

2 cups all-purpose flour

1 tsp baking powder

1 tsp sugar

½ tsp salt

1 egg

1 cup warm water
½ cup chopped spinach
¼ cup diced bell pepper
¼ cup diced onion
Oil, for frying

For the Southern Chow Chow:
1 cup green tomato or cabbage, finely chopped
½ cup red bell pepper, diced
½ cup onion, diced
¼ cup sugar
½ cup apple cider vinegar
½ tsp mustard seed
½ tsp turmeric
¼ tsp chili flakes
Pinch of salt

Procedure

Make the Curry Chicken Season the chicken chunks with curry powder, allspice, salt, pepper, thyme, garlic, and ginger. Let it sit for at least 30 minutes.

Heat oil in a heavy pot and brown the chicken in batches. Add diced onion and the whole Scotch bonnet. Cook until fragrant, about 2 minutes.

Pour in chicken stock, cover, and simmer gently for 25–30 minutes until the sauce is thick and rich. Stir in brown butter and set aside.

Make the Bara Bread In a bowl, mix flour, baking powder, sugar, and salt. Add the egg and warm water, stirring until you have a thick batter like pancake mix.

Fold in spinach, peppers, and onion.

Heat oil in a deep skillet to 350°F (175°C). Drop large spoonfuls of batter and fry like donuts — 2–3 minutes per side until puffed and golden. Drain on paper towels.

Make the Chow Chow In a saucepan, combine tomato or cabbage, red pepper, onion, sugar, vinegar, mustard seed, turmeric, chili flakes, and salt.

Simmer for 10–12 minutes until slightly thickened but still bright. Chill before serving.

Serve Slice open warm bara bread. Spoon in curry chicken, top with chow chow, and add a drizzle of hot sauce.

TEAM COSTA RICA WINNING DISH

This dish won me a gold medal in Costa Rica. It started with memories from my childhood on Long Island — clams, shrimp, and scallops at every meal. I wanted to take those memories and turn them into something special, something that showed skill and flavor in every bite.

Chef's Note

The roulade needs to be rolled tight and steamed gently — this keeps the seafood tender and delicate. The corn sponge cake is light and fluffy, perfect for soaking up the rich Newburg sauce. Balance is everything here: delicate seafood, sweet corn, and a silky sauce that brings it all together.

Yield

8 servings

Ingredients

For the Shrimp and Scallop Roulade:

12 large shrimp, peeled and butterflied

225 g fresh scallops

1 egg white

100 ml heavy cream

½ tsp salt

Pinch white pepper

1 tsp lemon juice

1 tbsp chopped chives

For the Corn Sponge Cake:

80 g dehydrated corn kernels

2 tbsp sugar

1 tsp baking powder

2 eggs

3 tbsp milk

2 tbsp melted butter

Pinch salt

For the Newburg Sauce:

1 tbsp butter

1 shallot, minced

1 tbsp tomato paste

¼ cup brandy

½ cup heavy cream

½ tsp paprika

Salt to taste

For the Corn and Clam Sachet:

1 tbsp olive oil

1 shallot, minced

1 clove garlic, minced

100 g fresh corn kernels

150 g clams, chopped

¼ cup white wine

1 tbsp butter

1 tbsp chopped chives

Salt and pepper to taste

Procedure

Make the Roulade Blend scallops, egg white, salt, pepper, and lemon juice in a food processor until smooth. Slowly add cream while blending until light and fluffy. Fold in chives.

Lay butterflied shrimp in a single layer on plastic wrap, overlapping slightly. Spoon the scallop mixture down the center.

Roll up tight using the plastic wrap to help form a cylinder. Twist the ends to seal.

Steam for 8–10 minutes until firm. Let rest before slicing.

Make the Corn Sponge Cake Grind dehydrated corn into powder. Mix with sugar, baking powder, and salt.

Whisk in eggs, milk, and melted butter. Pour into small molds or ramekins.

Steam for 6–8 minutes until set and springy.

Make the Newburg Sauce Melt butter and cook shallot until soft. Stir in tomato paste and cook 1 minute.

Add brandy and let it reduce by half. Pour in cream and paprika. Simmer until thick and silky.

Make the Corn and Clam Sachet Heat olive oil and cook shallot and garlic until fragrant. Add clams, corn, and white wine. Simmer until wine reduces.

Stir in butter and chives. Season with salt and pepper.

Serve Place corn sponge in the center of a plate. Arrange sliced roulade on top. Spoon Newburg sauce over and scatter the corn and clam mixture around. Garnish with chives.

DUCK BREAST with CHERRY REDUCTION & CREAMY RISOTTO

I made this dish on Chopped and it became one of my favorites. It taught me that cooking duck is about patience — starting cold, letting the fat render slowly, and letting the meat rest. When you do it right, every slice stays tender and juicy.

Chef's Note

Score the duck skin in a crosshatch pattern but don't cut into the meat. Start in a cold pan and let the heat build slowly — this gives you crispy skin and rare meat. Save that duck fat for the risotto. The cherry reduction brings brightness and a little heat. Everything balances perfectly.

Yield

4 servings

Ingredients

For the Duck Breast:

2 duck breasts (about 250 g each)

1 tsp salt

¼ tsp black pepper

1 tbsp butter

For the Cherry Reduction:

1 cup fresh or frozen cherries, pitted

1 tsp Calabrian chili paste

¼ cup chicken stock

1 tsp honey

1 tsp balsamic vinegar

Pinch salt

For the Risotto:

1½ cups Arborio rice

1 small onion, finely diced

1 shallot, minced

1 bay leaf

3 tbsp rendered duck fat

4 cups chicken stock, kept warm

¼ cup grated Parmesan cheese

2 tbsp butter

2 tbsp mascarpone

1 tbsp chopped basil

Salt to taste

Procedure

Cook the Duck Score the skin in a crosshatch pattern. Season both sides with salt and pepper. Place skin-side down in a cold, dry pan.

Turn the heat to medium. As the fat renders, spoon it off and save it for the risotto.

Cook for 8–10 minutes until the skin is deep golden and crispy. Flip and cook the other side for 1–2 minutes.

Transfer to a 400°F (200°C) oven and roast for 6–8 minutes for medium-rare.

Remove and rest for as long as it cooked — this keeps the meat juicy. Add a touch of butter and salt before slicing.

Make the Cherry Reduction Combine cherries, chili paste, chicken stock, honey, vinegar, and salt in a small saucepan.

Simmer on low heat for about 15 minutes until it gets thick and syrupy. Set aside.

Make the Risotto Heat duck fat in a saucepan over medium heat. Add onion, shallot, and bay leaf. Cook until translucent.

Add rice and toast for 1–2 minutes, stirring constantly.

Add warm chicken stock one ladle at a time, stirring constantly. Wait until the liquid is absorbed before adding more. Continue for 18–20 minutes until the rice is creamy and tender with a slight bite.

Remove from heat and stir in Parmesan, butter, mascarpone, basil, and salt. The risotto should be creamy and glossy.

Serve Spoon risotto onto each plate. Slice the duck and fan it over the rice. Drizzle with cherry reduction and garnish with basil.

BARBECUED BERKSHIRE RIBS

These ribs were inspired by my mentor's award-winning recipe. We served them at our restaurant on the Lower East Side and they became a fan favorite. The secret is that you roast, braise, chill, and glaze — so the flavor gets deep into every layer, not just the surface.

Chef's Note

Don't rush the braising. Four hours of slow cooking in liquid breaks down the meat until it's fall-apart tender. The spice rub goes on before roasting, so the flavors build in layers. That puffed rice crust at the end gives you crunch and brightness against the sticky, glossy ribs.

Yield

6 servings

Ingredients

For the Spice Rub:

2 tbsp brown sugar

1 tbsp onion powder

1 tbsp garlic powder

1 tbsp paprika

1 tbsp Spanish paprika

1 tbsp dark chili powder

1 tsp Old Bay seasoning

1 tsp curry powder

½ tsp cayenne pepper

1 tsp salt

1 tsp black pepper

½ tsp ground cumin

½ tsp crushed fennel seed

¼ tsp ground cardamom

¼ tsp Chinese five-spice powder

For the Ribs:

2 racks Berkshire pork ribs (about 2.5 kg total)

2 tbsp yellow mustard or neutral oil

For the Braising Liquid:

1 onion, chopped

1 bell pepper, chopped

2 stalks celery, chopped

1 carrot, chopped

1 orange, sliced

1 cinnamon stick

1 star anise pod

2 cardamom pods

½ cup orange juice

6 cups water or beef stock

For the Glaze:

2 cups reduced braising liquid

¼ cup ketchup

2 tbsp brown sugar

1 tbsp molasses

For the Puffed Rice Crust:

½ cup puffed rice

1 tsp lemon zest

1 tsp lime zest

¼ tsp Szechuan powder

1 tbsp chopped chives

Pinch salt

For Serving:

Pickled vegetables (turnip, radish, or carrot)

Procedure

Roast the Ribs Preheat oven to 450°F (230°C). Rub ribs with mustard or oil, then coat with the spice rub to form a crust.

Roast for 20–25 minutes until the surface darkens and smells amazing.

Braise the Ribs Place roasted ribs in a deep roasting pan. Add vegetables, aromatics, orange slices, juice, and liquid.

Cover tightly with foil. Reduce oven temperature to 325°F (160°C).

Cook for 4 hours until the meat is fall-apart tender and the bones pull out with no resistance.

Cool completely, then refrigerate overnight. Remove the solid fat from the top the next day and strain the liquid.

Make the Glaze Reduce the strained braising liquid by half. Whisk in ketchup, brown sugar, and molasses. Simmer until glossy and thick enough to coat a spoon.

Finish the Ribs Reheat the chilled ribs gently until warm. Portion as desired.

Brush generously with glaze. Finish in a 400°F (200°C) oven or on the grill for 8–10 minutes, basting as it caramelizes.

Make the Crust Toss puffed rice with lemon zest, lime zest, Szechuan powder, chives, and salt.

Sprinkle the crust over the glazed ribs just before serving for crunch and brightness.

Serve with pickled vegetables for balance.

SHRIMP STOCK

Chef's Note

Don't throw away those shrimp shells — they're liquid gold. Sauté them first so they get pink and fragrant. The rum brings depth, and the slow simmering pulls all the flavor out. This stock is the foundation that makes the curry shine.

Yield

About 500 ml (2 cups)

Ingredients

Shells from 680 g shrimp

10 ml coconut or neutral oil

5 g fresh thyme

15 g tomato paste

50 ml Jamaican dark rum

500 ml ice water

60 g yellow onion, diced

40 g carrot, diced

1 garlic clove, crushed

3 g tarragon leaves

Procedure

Heat oil in a saucepan over medium heat.

Add shrimp shells and sauté for 3–4 minutes until they turn bright pink and smell fragrant.

Add thyme, tomato paste, onion, carrot, and garlic. Cook for 3–4 minutes until lightly browned.

Carefully pour in rum and let it reduce slightly for about 1 minute.

Add ice water and bring to a gentle simmer.

Simmer for 20–25 minutes until the stock is clear, rich, and aromatic.

Strain through a fine strainer into a clean container.

Use immediately or chill for up to 3 days.

CURRY GOAT

Chef's Note

This curry goat is meant to be cooked slow and shared — the longer it simmers, the more the flavors mingle. Cleaning with vinegar keeps it fresh, while overnight marination builds layers of warmth and depth.

Yeild

8–10 Servings

Ingredients

For the Jamaican Curry Powder

30 g (4 Tbsp) cumin seeds

30 g (4 Tbsp) coriander seeds

15 g (2 Tbsp) ground turmeric

10 g (1 Tbsp) fenugreek seeds

10 g (1 Tbsp) ground black pepper

10 g (1 Tbsp) garlic powder

6 g (2 tsp) onion powder

6 g (2 tsp) ground allspice

Toast whole spices in a dry pan until fragrant, then grind and mix with the powdered ingredients.

For the Goat:

1.36 kg (3 lb) boneless goat meat (shoulder or leg), cut into 5 cm (2-inch) cubes

15 mL (1 Tbsp) white vinegar

120 mL (½ cup) neutral oil (vegetable or canola)

150 g (1 large) white onion, sliced

6 garlic cloves, minced

1 Scotch bonnet pepper, sliced (seeds removed for less heat)

3 fresh thyme sprigs

10 g (2 tsp) seasoned salt

1 g (¼ tsp) ground black pepper

600 g (3 medium) russet potatoes, peeled and cut into 2 cm (1-inch) cubes

Water or stock, as needed

Cooked white rice, for serving

Procedure:

Clean the goat with vinegar and rinse well. Pat dry. Season with 3 Tbsp of the curry powder, seasoned salt, black pepper, Scotch bonnet, garlic, onion, and thyme. Massage thoroughly and marinate overnight, covered, in the refrigerator.

The next day, heat oil in a heavy pot over medium-high heat. Add 1 Tbsp curry powder directly to the oil and stir until the oil turns golden and aromatic — this is burning the curry, an essential step for depth of flavor.

Add the marinated goat, stirring to coat in the curry oil. Sear until lightly browned on all sides. Reduce heat to medium-low, cover, and allow the goat to release its own juices. Add just enough water or stock to barely cover the meat. Simmer gently 1 ½ – 2 hours, stirring occasionally, until the meat is tender and the sauce thickens. Add potatoes during the last 30 minutes of cooking.

Taste and adjust seasoning. The sauce should be rich, earthy, and spicy with a subtle sweetness from the potatoes.

Serve hot with steamed white rice or Jamaican rice and peas.

MOTHER BELL'S SOUTHERN PICKLES

Chef's Note

These pickles take patience and sunlight, the old-fashioned way. They start sharp, but over time the sugar softens their edges into pure Southern sweetness. Perfect alongside fried chicken, collard greens, or a slice of warm cornbread.

Yield

1 Gallon

Ingredients

1 gallon glass jar

900 g (about 2 lb) cucumbers, sliced

25 g (5 tsp) fine sea salt

25 g (5 tsp) alum (helps keep pickles crisp)

15 g (1 Tbsp) pickling spice, tied in cheesecloth

1.9 L (8 cups) brown vinegar

Granulated sugar, as needed to fill the jar after pickling

Procedure:

Fill a clean 1-gallon glass jar halfway with sliced cucumbers. Add salt and alum, then tuck the pickling spice wrapped in cheesecloth into the jar. Pour in the brown vinegar until the cucumbers are fully submerged.

Seal and let sit in a cool, dark place for 8 weeks to cure. When the time is up, pour off the vinegar and discard the spice bag.

Refill the jar with sugar, covering the cucumbers completely. Leave uncovered or loosely sealed and allow it to sit so the sugar slowly dissolves and evaporates over time.

The cucumbers will turn into firm, sweet, and crisp Southern pickles — just the way Motherbell made them.

FISH & MEAT SAUCE

Yield

Two Cups (About 500 mL)

Ingredients

120 g (½ cup) tomato paste

100 g (½ cup) fresh ripe mango, peeled and cubed

250 mL (1 cup) cane vinegar

60 g (¼ cup) cane sugar

5 g (1 tsp) fine sea salt

2 Scotch bonnet peppers, seeds removed and chopped

10 g (2 tsp) onion powder

10 g (2 tsp) garlic powder

3 g (½ tsp) allspice

2 g (½ tsp) ground black pepper

3 g (1 tsp) tapioca flour (for thickening)

15 mL (1 Tbsp) neutral oil (avocado or canola)

100 mL (½ cup) water, as needed

Procedure:

In a small saucepan, heat the oil over medium heat. Add tomato paste and stir until it begins to caramelize slightly—this builds that deep, savory base. Add chopped Scotch bonnet, mango cubes, vinegar, sugar, and water. Stir well and bring to a low simmer.

Add salt, onion powder, garlic powder, allspice, and black pepper. Continue simmering 10–12 minutes, stirring occasionally until the mango softens and the sauce thickens slightly.

Whisk tapioca flour with 1 tablespoon of water to create a slurry, then stir it into the simmering sauce. Cook for another 2–3 minutes, until the mixture coats the back of a spoon.

Remove from heat and let cool slightly. Transfer to a blender and purée until smooth. Strain if desired for a glossy finish. Pour into sterilized glass bottles and refrigerate.

MOM'S FISH HEAD PUMPKIN SOUP

Yield

6 servings

Growing up, my mom used to make fish head soup from a little Grace-brand packet — the kind that came with dried noodles, pumpkin, and that bright yellow bouillon flavor. She'd add fresh pumpkin or yams, simmer it all together, and it always felt like comfort in a bowl.

This is my full homemade version — inspired by her love, but made completely from scratch. We take whole fish, simmer the heads for flavor, and pair it with fresh pumpkin, ginger, coconut, and a touch of scotch bonnet for warmth. It's rich, silky, and filled with the flavors that remind me of home.

Chef's Note:

The ginger and scotch bonnet give this soup its soul. If you want a little more kick, slice the pepper open halfway before simmering — just don't break it fully, or the heat will take over the broth. For even more depth, add okra or callaloo near the end.

Ingredients

Fish Broth

2 whole fish, heads removed and reserved (snapper, porgy, or parrotfish – about 1.2 kg total)

1 small onion, quartered (100 g)

1 thumb-sized piece of ginger, sliced (20 g)

1 stalk celery, chopped (60 g)

1 small carrot, chopped (60 g)

½ green bell pepper, chopped (50 g)

1 sprig thyme

1 teaspoon black peppercorns (5 g)

2 allspice berries (pimento)

1 scotch bonnet pepper, whole

1 tablespoon coconut oil (15 g)

1 teaspoon salt (5 g)

1.5 liters water (about 6 cups)

Soup Base

2 cups peeled pumpkin or butternut squash (300 g)

1 medium yam or sweet potato, peeled and cubed (200 g)

1 small onion, diced (80 g)

1 thumb-sized piece of ginger, grated (15 g)

½ red bell pepper, diced (50 g)

2 cloves garlic, minced (10 g)

1 sprig thyme

½ teaspoon allspice (2 g)

1 tablespoon coconut oil (15 g)

1 teaspoon salt (5 g)

½ teaspoon black pepper (2 g)

4 cups chicken stock (1 liter)

100 g thin spaghetti noodles, broken into short pieces

2 teaspoons chicken bouillon (optional, to taste)

Juice of ½ lime (10 ml)

Fresh scallions, sliced (10 g)

For the broth:

Rinse fish heads thoroughly and remove any liver or dark organs — these will make the soup bitter. In a large pot, heat coconut oil and lightly sauté onion, ginger, celery, carrot, bell pepper, thyme, peppercorns, and allspice until fragrant. Add the fish heads, scotch bonnet, salt, and water. Simmer gently for 30 minutes, skimming any foam from the surface. Strain the broth and set aside.

For the soup:

In a clean pot, warm coconut oil and sauté onion, ginger, bell pepper, garlic, and thyme until fragrant. Add pumpkin, yam, allspice, salt, and pepper. Pour in the fish broth and chicken stock. Simmer until the pumpkin and yam are tender, about 25–30 minutes.

Remove about one-third of the soup and blend until smooth. Return it to the pot to thicken naturally. Add the broken spaghetti noodles and simmer until cooked, about 8 minutes. Adjust seasoning with bouillon and lime juice.

Add the fish heads back into the soup just before serving to warm through — this keeps the meat tender and flavorful. Finish with fresh scallions and a drizzle of coconut oil on top.

GRANDMA'S CURRY SHRIMP

Chef's Note

This curry is bold and bright — a tribute to the kitchens that smelled of spice, sea breeze, and love. My grandma made something that taught me how a pinch of heat and a squeeze of lime can wake up a dish. The coconut oil gives it silk, the lime brings it to life, and the shrimp stock ties it all together.

Marinate the shrimp overnight if you can — that's where the flavor lives. Don't add too much stock or the sauce gets watery. You want it to coat the shrimp, not drown it. The butter and lime at the end are what make it sing.

Yield

4 servings

Ingredients

680 g large shrimp, peeled and deveined

15 g Jamaican curry powder

5 g sea salt

2 g black pepper

5 ml soy sauce

1 Scotch bonnet pepper, finely diced

15 ml coconut oil (for searing)

15 ml coconut oil (for aromatics)

100 g yellow onion, diced

10 g garlic, minced

10 g ginger, minced

10 g curry powder (for blooming in the oil)

250 ml shrimp stock

15 g unsalted butter

10 ml fresh lime juice and salt to taste

Procedure

Mix shrimp, curry powder, salt, pepper, soy sauce, and diced

Scotch bonnet in a bowl. Cover and marinate overnight in the refrigerator for deep flavor.

Heat 15 ml coconut oil in a medium pot over medium heat. Add diced onion, garlic, and ginger. Cook until translucent and fragrant, about 3–4 minutes.

Sprinkle in 10 g curry powder and toast it gently in the oil for about 1 minute until the oil turns golden and smells amazing.

Add the marinated shrimp and stir to coat everything in the curry oil, about 2 minutes.

Pour in shrimp stock — just enough to cover the shrimp halfway. Don't add too much or the sauce gets watery.

Simmer gently for 8–10 minutes until the shrimp are cooked through and tender.

Stir in butter and fresh lime juice. Taste and adjust salt if needed.

Serve hot over jasmine rice or with fried dumplings.

CARROT ESCOVITCH

Escovitch was something I always saw sitting on the counter growing up. It was bright, colorful, and hard to miss—pickled vegetables piled on top of a fried piece of fish. The vinegar helped keep the fish fresh at room temperature, and the fried fish soaked up all that flavor like a sponge.

Carrots were a big part of my childhood. My grandmother made her carrot punch all the time. Any carrots she didn't use went straight into her Escovitch. It was her way of never wasting anything. Sometimes the mix was spicy. Sometimes it was sweet. I like mine right in the middle—spicy, sweet, and balanced. To me, Escovitch is the perfect condiment. You can put it on almost anything, the same way people in the South use chow chow.

It brings color, crunch, and flavor to every plate.

Chef's Note

The magic is in the texture — those thin carrot ribbons feel like noodles. Don't boil the liquid; just bring it to a simmer so it stays fresh and bright. The longer it sits, the deeper the flavor. For mild heat, leave the Scotch bonnet whole instead of slicing it.

Yield

About 2 cups

Ingredients

2 large carrots, peeled and ribboned

½ red bell pepper, julienned

½ green bell pepper, julienned

½ medium onion, thinly sliced

½ Scotch bonnet pepper, thinly sliced (use less for mild heat)

2 allspice berries, lightly crushed

½ tsp salt

½ tsp sugar

½ cup carrot juice

¼ cup white vinegar

2 tbsp lime juice

1 tbsp olive oil

1 sprig thyme

Procedure

Peel the carrots, then use the same peeler to shave the flesh into long, thin ribbons.

Place carrot ribbons, bell peppers, and onions in a heatproof bowl.

In a small saucepan, combine carrot juice, vinegar, lime juice, olive oil, thyme, allspice, salt, sugar, and Scotch bonnet.

Bring just to a simmer, then remove from heat.

Pour the warm liquid over the vegetables and toss gently.

Let sit for at least 30 minutes, or refrigerate for up to 3 days. The vegetables should stay bright, crisp, and lightly tangy.

Serve with jerk, fried, or roasted dishes to bring brightness and color to the plate.

GRANDMA'S CARROT PUNCH

Growing up, this was my favorite drink — even more than the Kool-Aid sitting in the fridge. There was something about those warm spices that made it taste like eggnog any time of the year. We made it the old-school way with a blender and strained it ourselves. It was creamy, sweet, and spiced just right. Every sip brought me back to Grandma's kitchen.

Chef's Note

Don't skip the straining step — it separates the pulp from the smooth, creamy drink. The warm spices are what make this punch taste like eggnog. Use a blender, not a juicer, so everything gets blended together smoothly. The more you blend, the smoother your punch will be. Taste it as you go and add honey if you want it sweeter.

Yield

About 6–8 servings (about 1.5 liters)

Ingredients

900 g carrots, peeled and roughly chopped

240 ml whole milk

240 ml evaporated milk (or heavy cream)

100 ml sweetened condensed milk

1 tbsp vanilla extract

2 tsp ground cinnamon

1 tsp ground nutmeg

½ tsp ground ginger (optional)

¼ tsp ground cloves (optional)

30 g honey or additional sweetened condensed milk (optional, for more sweetness)

480 ml water

Pinch of salt

Procedure

Peel and roughly chop the carrots into chunks.

Add carrots and water to a blender.

Blend on high speed until completely smooth, about 2–3 minutes.

Pour the carrot mixture through a fine strainer or cheesecloth into a large bowl, pressing gently to extract all the liquid. You should have a smooth, orange juice.

Return the strained liquid to the blender.

Add whole milk, evaporated milk, sweetened condensed milk, and vanilla extract.

Add cinnamon, nutmeg, ginger, cloves, and salt.

Blend on high speed for about 1 minute until everything is smooth and well mixed.

Taste it. If you want it sweeter, add honey or a bit more sweetened condensed milk and blend again.

Pour into a pitcher or bottles and refrigerate until cold.

Stir before serving — the spices may settle at the bottom.

Serve cold in glasses. It gets thicker and creamier as it sits in the refrigerator, which is perfect.

JERK GRILLED FISH

This recipe comes from my travels and the mentors I've learned from — watching fish being cooked over open flames taught me that flavor and fire connect us to our roots. Growing up, porgy was always on the grill at backyard fish fries. The secret I learned is to brine and score the fish so every bit of seasoning reaches deep inside. Wrapping it in foil mimics the way the Maroons used to cook — burying food in the earth to cook slowly and stay moist.

Chef's Note

Score the fish deep enough for seasoning to get in, but don't cut all the way through. The brine comes first — it opens up the flesh. The jerk marinade is best overnight for deep flavor. When you wrap it in foil on the grill, the steam does the work. That's the magic.

Yield

4 servings

Ingredients

For the Fish and Brine:

2 whole porgy, snapper, or sea bream (about 450 g each, cleaned and scaled)

1 tbsp kosher salt

1 tbsp sugar

1 tbsp lemon juice

For the Jerk Marinade:

4 scallions, chopped

2 Scotch bonnet peppers, stemmed (use 1 for less heat)

1 small onion, chopped

3 cloves garlic

1 thumb-sized piece ginger, peeled

2 tbsp brown sugar

2 tsp allspice

1 tsp ground cinnamon

1 tsp dried thyme

½ tsp ground nutmeg

½ tsp black pepper

¼ cup soy sauce

2 tbsp lime juice

2 tbsp apple cider vinegar

2 tbsp vegetable or coconut oil

1 tsp salt

Procedure

Rinse and pat the fish completely dry.

Using a sharp knife, score the skin on both sides in shallow diagonal cuts.

Sprinkle both sides with salt and sugar. Let sit for 30 minutes to brine, then pat dry again.

Blend all the jerk marinade ingredients until smooth.

Rub the fish generously inside and out with the marinade. Cover and marinate overnight in the refrigerator.

Preheat the grill to medium-high. Oil the grates lightly.

Grill the fish directly over the coals for 4–5 minutes per side until the skin is charred and crisp.

Transfer the fish onto aluminum foil. Spoon some remaining marinade over it and squeeze lemon juice on top.

Wrap tightly in foil and return to the grill (or an oven at 375°F / 190°C) for 10–12 minutes until steamed through and tender.

Unwrap carefully — the aroma will be incredible — and drizzle with any juices from the foil.

Serve with fresh lemon, escovitch pickles, or rice and peas.

BUTTERNUT SQUASH & LOBSTER

When I cooked at Eleven Madison Park, one of their most elegant dishes was lobster and butternut squash draped together on a plate. It taught me that this combination is pure magic. Lobster was always my birthday treat instead of toys or games — it's a true birthday tradition for me. Once called the "cockroach of the sea," lobster is now one of the ocean's greatest delicacies. I love its salty sweetness and the way it soaks up flavor from the land and sea. This dish celebrates that: tender lobster, sweet roasted squash, and a silky sauce finished with lemon and herbs.

Chef's Note

Don't wash off the flavor from the lobster — keep all the insides, especially from female lobsters carrying eggs. That's where the deepest flavor lives. Roast the squash in the oven to let the natural sugars caramelize and bring out something magical. The lobster butter ties everything together, so don't skip making it from the shells and bodies.

Yield

4 servings

Ingredients

For the Lobster:

2 whole lobsters (about 700 g each)

1 carrot, chopped (80 g)

1 celery stalk, chopped (60 g)

1 small onion, chopped (80 g)

1 tbsp Old Bay seasoning (8 g)

1 tsp sea salt (5 g)

Water, as needed

For the Lobster Butter & Sauce:

2 tbsp unsalted butter (28 g)

2 shallots, chopped (40 g)

2 cloves garlic, crushed (10 g)

1 tbsp tomato paste (15 g)

1 sprig thyme

2 tbsp brandy (30 ml)

2 cups lobster stock or cooking liquid (480 ml)

100 ml ice water

2 tbsp butter (28 g) to finish

1 tsp lemon zest (2 g)

1 tsp lemon juice (5 ml)

2 sprigs tarragon

4 basil leaves

Salt to taste

For the Butternut Squash Purée:

1 medium butternut squash (about 1 kg)

1 tbsp olive oil (15 ml)

1 tsp salt (5 g)

For the Roasted Squash Garnish:

½ cup diced roasted squash (100 g)

1 tbsp brown butter (15 g)

1 tsp chopped chives (3 g)

½ tsp chopped thyme (1 g)

Procedure

In a big pot with carrot, celery, onion, Old Bay, and salt, steam the lobster tails for 5–6 minutes and the claws for 8–9 minutes until cooked. Take out the lobster and pull the meat away from the shells. Save everything.

In a heavy pan, cook the lobster shells with butter, shallot, garlic, tomato paste, and thyme until it smells amazing. Pour in brandy and let it bubble for a minute. Add stock and ice water, then let it simmer for 20–25 minutes. Strain it, then add tarragon, basil, lemon zest, and lemon juice. You now have a sauce.

Cut butternut squash in half, scoop out the seeds, put it cut side down on a tray, and roast at 350°F for 45 minutes until it's golden and soft. Scoop out the inside and blend it smooth with olive oil and salt.

Cut up some extra roasted squash and mix it with brown butter, chives, and thyme.

Warm up the lobster meat gently with the lobster butter.

Put squash on the plate, arrange lobster on top, pour sauce around it, sprinkle roasted squash pieces on top, and finish with chives and more lobster butter. Serve warm.

KAPSALON: ROTTERDAM FRIED with SHWARMA, GOUDA, & GARLIC SAUCE

Kapsalon was born in Rotterdam, Netherlands — a fusion of Dutch, Middle Eastern, and Caribbean flavors. A barber asked his favorite snack shop to combine his favorite foods: fries, shawarma, melted cheese, salad, and sauce. They called it "Kapsalon," which means "barbershop." It started as late-night comfort food and became a national favorite. This is my version — simpler but just as delicious.

Chef's Note

The fries need to be crispy. Don't skip that step. The shawarma spices should coat the chicken evenly — this is where the flavor lives. The garlic sauce is what ties everything together, so don't be shy with it. And make sure the cheese melts completely before you add the fresh toppings. The star of the show is the melted Dutch Gouda Cheese!

Yield

4 servings

Ingredients

For the Fries:

800 g frozen or fresh-cut fries

1 tbsp olive oil

½ tsp salt

For the Chicken Shawarma:

450 g boneless chicken thighs, sliced

2 tbsp olive oil

1 tsp paprika

1 tsp cumin

1 tsp coriander

½ tsp turmeric

½ tsp garlic powder

½ tsp onion powder

½ tsp cayenne or chili powder (optional)

½ tsp salt

½ tsp black pepper

Juice of ½ lemon

For the Garlic–Hot Sauce:

½ cup mayonnaise

2 tbsp plain yogurt

2 cloves garlic, grated

1 tsp lemon juice

1 tsp hot sauce (like Sriracha)

Pinch of salt

For Assembly:

150 g shredded Gouda cheese

1 cup shredded lettuce

½ red onion, thinly sliced

½ cucumber, thinly sliced

½ tomato, diced

Extra hot sauce to taste

Procedure

Make the Fries Preheat oven to 425°F (220°C). Toss fries with olive oil and salt. Bake for 25–30 minutes until crisp and golden.

Cook the Shawarma Toss sliced chicken with olive oil, spices, and lemon juice. Marinate for at least 15 minutes (or overnight).

Cook in a hot skillet over medium-high heat for 6–8 minutes until browned and cooked through.

Make the Garlic-Hot Sauce Mix mayonnaise, yogurt, grated garlic, lemon juice, hot sauce, and salt in a bowl. Adjust spice to your taste.

Assemble Layer crispy fries in a small baking dish or oven-safe tray. Spoon the hot shawarma over the top.

Scatter shredded Gouda cheese evenly over everything.

Bake or broil for 2–3 minutes just until the cheese melts and bubbles.

Remove from the oven and top with lettuce, onion, cucumber, and tomato.

Drizzle generously with garlic–hot sauce and extra hot sauce if you like.

Serve immediately — messy, melty, and perfect.

BROWN BUTTER CORN MADELEINES with PINK PEPPERCORN & JALAPEÑO JAM

Madeleines taught me to slow down and pay attention. When I was cooking in the Netherlands, someone got frustrated because my butter didn't mix right — it broke apart. That moment stuck with me. It taught me that small details matter. Now, whenever I make Madeleines, I listen for that perfect "helicopter" sound in the mixer. That's when I know everything has come together just right.

Chef's Note

Don't rush the brown butter. Let it turn golden and smell nutty. Pour it in slowly while mixing — this helps everything blend smoothly. You'll hear that helicopter sound when it's fully mixed in. Then refrigerate your batter so your Madeleines get that special bump on top.

Yield

About 24 Madeleines

Ingredients

For the Madeleines:

120 g butter, melted and cooled slightly

120 g sugar

3 large eggs

120 g regular flour

15 g corn flour

6 g baking powder

Pinch of salt

Zest of 1 lemon, 1 lime, and 1 orange

10 g honey (optional)

For the Jam:

1 jalapeño, finely diced (remove seeds for less spice)

1 tsp pink peppercorns, lightly crushed

150 g sugar

100 ml water

1 tbsp apple cider vinegar

Pinch of salt

Procedure

Brown the Butter Melt butter over medium heat until it's golden brown and smells nutty. Cool slightly.

Mix Eggs and Sugar Whisk eggs, sugar, honey, and citrus zest for 3–5 minutes until light and pale.

Add Dry Ingredients Mix flour, corn flour, baking powder, and salt in another bowl. Fold gently into the egg mixture.

Add the Butter Slowly drizzle in the warm brown butter while mixing. Keep going until everything is smooth and shiny — you'll hear that "helicopter" sound.

Rest Cover and refrigerate for at least 1 hour.

Bake Preheat oven to 375°F (190°C). Fill buttered Madeleine molds about ¾ full. Bake 10–12 minutes until golden with a bump on top.

Make the Jam Combine sugar, water, and vinegar in a saucepan. Add jalapeño, pink peppercorns, and salt. Simmer 8–10 minutes until thick and shiny. Cool completely.

Serve Top each Madeleine with a small spoonful of jam. Sweet and spicy!

SWEET POTATO PIE

Yeild

8 servings

My dad always loved his mother's sweet potato pie. When I first made my own version in home economics class, I knew I needed to create something that would stay with me for years to come. This one honors that memory—deeply caramelized sweet potatoes, a hint of cinnamon sugar for warmth, and a pecan streusel topping that replaces the crust entirely.

The secret? A touch of cinnamon sugar, not just cinnamon, to bring everything to life.

Ingredients

Filling

3 medium sweet potatoes (about 900 g)

2 tablespoons olive oil (30 g)

1 teaspoon sea salt (5 g)

¾ cup pitted dates (120 g)

½ cup coconut water (120 ml)

2 eggs (100 g)

¼ cup brown sugar (50 g)

¼ cup coconut sugar (50 g)

1 teaspoon vanilla extract (5 ml)

1 teaspoon cinnamon (3 g)

¼ teaspoon nutmeg (1 g)

¼ teaspoon salt (1 g)

2 tablespoons melted butter (28 g)

Streusel Topping

¼ cup buckwheat flour (30 g)

¼ cup brown sugar (50 g)

2 tablespoons coconut sugar (25 g)

2 tablespoons melted butter (28 g)

¼ cup chopped pecans (30 g)

Procedure

Preheat oven to 400°F (200°C). Line a baking sheet with parchment paper and scatter salt across the surface. Place whole sweet potatoes on top and roast for 45 minutes to 1 hour, until caramelized and tender. This step draws out their natural sweetness.

Reduce oven temperature to 350°F (175°C). Scoop the flesh from the sweet potatoes and place in a mixer fitted with a paddle. Add dates, coconut water, eggs, brown sugar, coconut sugar, vanilla, cinnamon, nutmeg, and salt. Mix until smooth and creamy. Pour mixture into a greased 9-inch (23 cm) pie dish.

In a small bowl, combine buckwheat flour, brown sugar, coconut sugar, butter, and pecans. Crumble the streusel evenly over the top of the pie. Bake in the center of the oven for 35 to 40 minutes, until set and golden brown. Cool to room temperature before serving.

GREAT GRANDMOTHER'S CAKE FOR TWO

I found my great-grandmother's recipe tucked between faded pages in North Carolina. It was simple, honest, and full of heart. This cake is her legacy living on through food. I bring it to every dinner and pop-up as a reminder of where I come from. The secret ingredient is mayonnaise — her clever way of making a rich, moist cake without butter or milk. Because mayo is just oil and eggs, it gives the batter tenderness and depth.

Chef's Note

The raisin purée is the soul of this cake — it adds moisture and sweetness. The baking soda reacts with the acid in the mayonnaise to create a light, tender crumb. Don't overmix once you add the flour, or the cake will be dense. It should come together gently and quickly.

Yield

8 servings (two 9-inch rounds)

Ingredients

150 g raisins

5 g baking soda

375 g cake flour

5 g vanilla extract

1 vanilla pod (seeds scraped)

250 g organic cane sugar

3 egg yolks plus 1 whole egg

175 g mayonnaise

50 g chopped nuts (optional)

Candied peanuts for garnish (optional)

Procedure

Soak raisins in hot water for 15 minutes, then drain and blend into a smooth purée.

Sift together cake flour and baking soda in a bowl.

In a large bowl, whisk egg yolks, whole egg, and sugar until pale and fluffy.

Add vanilla extract and the seeds from the vanilla pod.

Alternate adding flour mixture and mayonnaise in thirds, mixing just until smooth.

Fold in the raisin purée and chopped nuts if using.

Divide batter between two greased 9-inch round pans.

Bake at 350°F (175°C) for 25–30 minutes until a toothpick in the center comes out clean.

Cool in pans for 10 minutes, then turn onto a rack to cool completely.

Serve plain or topped with candied peanuts.

PERFECT GRILLED CHEESE with CITRUS HONEY & STRAWBERRY COMPOTE

Working in fine dining, I was surrounded by cheese courses with honey, fruit, and nuts. Beautiful, but sometimes too formal. I wanted to create a grilled cheese that had all those flavors but felt comforting and familiar instead of fancy.

Chef's Note

The butter-mayo mix is what makes the crust golden and crisp. Don't rush the grilling — low and slow makes sure the cheese melts completely without burning the bread. The citrus honey should be warm but not boiling, and the strawberry compote balances the richness with brightness and tang.

Yield

2 servings

Ingredients

For the Grilled Cheese:

4 slices Hawaiian bread

120 g Dutch Gouda cheese, sliced

15 g unsalted butter, softened

15 g mayonnaise

For the Citrus Honey:

120 g honey

Zest of 1 lemon

Zest of 1 orange

For the Strawberry Compote:

250 g fresh strawberries, hulled and halved

20 g sugar

5 g lemon zest

Pinch of salt

Procedure

Make the Grilled Cheese Mix softened butter and mayonnaise together. Spread one side of each bread slice with this mixture.

Place Gouda between two slices, buttered sides facing out.

Warm a skillet over medium-low heat and cook each sandwich 3–

4 minutes per side until the crust is golden and the cheese melts completely.

Cut diagonally and keep warm.

Make the Citrus Honey Warm honey gently in a small pot — do not boil. Remove from heat and stir in lemon and orange zests. Let infuse for 10 minutes.

Make the Strawberry Compote Cook half of the strawberries with sugar and salt in a small saucepan over low heat for 5–7 minutes until thick and syrupy.

Remove from heat and fold in the remaining diced fresh strawberries and lemon zest for brightness.

Serve Place grilled cheese on a plate. Drizzle with warm citrus honey and spoon strawberry compote on the side.

HOMEMADE MOLASSES (North Carolina Sugarcane)

This is slow Southern work — a nod to the fields of North Carolina where cane juice once bubbled in open kettles under the fall sun. Making molasses from scratch is about more than sweetness. It carries story, soil, and soul. Every spoonful tastes like the land itself.

Chef's Note

Don't rush this. It takes time for the cane juice to reduce down to molasses — about 1½ to 2 hours of slow cooking. Stir often so it doesn't scorch. You'll know it's ready when it coats the back of a spoon and drips slowly. As it cools, it'll get thicker and glossier.

Yield

About 500 ml (2 cups)

Ingredients

2 kg fresh sugarcane stalks (enough to make about 1 liter of cane juice)
Pinch sea salt
Optional: 5 ml lemon juice (to balance bitterness)

Procedure

Peel and chop the sugarcane into small pieces.

Crush or press the pieces to extract the juice. You can use a sugarcane press, or pulse in a blender with a little warm water, then strain through a fine strainer. You should have about 1 liter of fresh cane juice.

Pour the juice into a large, heavy pot or cast-iron kettle and bring to a steady simmer over medium heat.

Skim away any foam that rises to the top.

Continue to cook, stirring often, until the liquid gets dark and reduces by about three-quarters. This can take 1½ to 2 hours.

As it gets thicker, lower the heat and stir frequently so it doesn't scorch.

When the molasses coats the back of a spoon and drips slowly, take it off the heat.

Stir in a pinch of salt and a touch of lemon juice if desired.

Allow to cool slightly, then pour into clean jars.

The molasses will continue to thicken as it cools into a rich, glossy syrup with deep caramel notes.

Spoon it over biscuits, sweet potatoes, or warm cornbread.

CHEF SAKARI'S SIGNATURE "PANCAKE"

Pancakes go back to the Netherlands, where thin, golden cakes were shared around the table. When Dutch settlers came to New York, they brought this tradition with them. Breakfast was the first thing I learned to cook, and weekend trips to IHOP were filled with syrup, butter, and laughter. Over time, I wanted to create pancakes that felt better for your body without losing the soul of the dish. This gluten-free version uses real maple syrup instead of corn syrup, and it's lighter but still rich in flavor.

Chef's Note

Let that yeast bloom — it adds flavor even though it's not a yeast bread. The batter should rest 20–30 minutes so it hydrates and gets a little fermented flavor. Don't skip the xanthan gum — it helps everything bind together without gluten. Cook them low and slow so they stay fluffy and don't dry out.

Yield

4 servings (about 12 pancakes)

Ingredients

For the Dry Mix:

50 g tapioca starch

25 g millet flour

25 g buckwheat flour

4 g sea salt

1 g baking soda (add right before cooking)

½ g xanthan gum

For the Yeast Bloom:

55 ml warm milk

2½ g active dry yeast

1 g malt extract (optional)

For the Buttermilk:

55 ml milk

10 g apple cider vinegar

For the Emulsified Base:

30 g mayonnaise

1 egg yolk

9 g melted coconut oil

3 g vanilla extract

½ g malt extract (optional)

6 g baking powder

Procedure

Make the Yeast Bloom Warm the milk to about 100°F (38°C). Add yeast and malt extract. Let sit for about 10 minutes until foamy.

Make the Buttermilk Mix milk and apple cider vinegar. Let sit for about 10 minutes to curdle.

Mix the Emulsified Base In a bowl, combine mayonnaise, egg yolk, melted coconut oil, vanilla extract, malt extract, and baking powder. Mix well.

Add the yeast bloom and buttermilk to the emulsified base. Mix together.

Combine Everything Gently fold the wet mixture into the dry mix until smooth.

Let rest for 20–30 minutes to allow the flour to hydrate and the flavors to develop.

Cook the Pancakes Heat a non-stick skillet or griddle over medium-low heat. Scoop batter onto the hot surface.

Cook until golden brown on the bottom, about 2–3 minutes. Flip and cook the other side until golden.

Serve warm with your favorite toppings.

DAD'S CHEESE EGGS

My dad didn't cook often, even though he once owned a restaurant. But the one thing he always made was cheese eggs. Unlike diners, he'd whip the cheese into the eggs before cooking instead of melting it on top. The result was magic — soft, creamy eggs where the cheese melted invisibly inside. This recipe is dedicated to him.

Chef's Note

Grate the cheese finely so it melts evenly into the eggs — you shouldn't see it, only taste it. Cook on low heat and move the pan on and off the heat to control the temperature. The goal is creamy and softly set, never dry. That's the whole trick.

Yield

2 servings

Ingredients

4 large eggs

30 g crème fraîche

40 g smoked cheddar, finely grated

5 g butter

Salt and freshly cracked black pepper

1 tbsp chopped chives

Optional: caviar for garnish

Procedure

Crack the eggs into a bowl and add the crème fraîche. Whisk until smooth.

Fold in the finely grated smoked cheddar. Season lightly with salt and pepper.

Heat the butter in a non-stick pan over low heat.

Pour in the egg mixture and stir continuously with a spatula, moving the pan on and off the heat to control the temperature.

Cook slowly until the eggs are creamy and softly set — never dry.

Spoon onto warm plates and finish with chives and a small spoonful of caviar if desired.

SOUTHERN-STYLE BREAKFAST RICE

This is breakfast the way I grew up eating it — nothing fancy, just rice, fat, and time. No cream, no flour, no shortcuts. When you're stretching what you've got in the kitchen, this is what you make. It's creamy from the patient stirring, rich from the butter or bacon fat, and it fills you up right.

Chef's Note

Use day-old rice — fresh rice won't work the same way. The magic is in the stirring. You're releasing the natural starch from the rice grains to make it creamy, kind of like risotto but heartier. Don't rush it. Take your time and add the water or milk slowly.

Yield

4 servings

Ingredients

300 g cold, day-old cooked rice (medium-grain if you can)

30 g unsalted butter

120–180 ml warm water or milk

4 g sea salt

2 g freshly cracked black pepper

Avocado oil or bacon fat (for cooking)

To Serve:

North Carolina red sausage, fried crisp

Sliced scallions or chives (optional)

Procedure

In a heavy skillet or cast-iron pan, heat a small drizzle of avocado oil or bacon fat over medium heat.

Add the butter and let it melt gently until it foams.

Add the cold rice, breaking up any clumps with a wooden spoon.

Stir constantly, pressing and folding the grains to release their natural starch. This takes about 8–10 minutes.

Gradually add warm water or milk a few tablespoons at a time, stirring after each addition.

Keep going until the rice is glossy and coats the back of a spoon — kind of like risotto, but heartier.

Season with salt and black pepper.

Serve immediately, topped with slices of fried North Carolina red sausage

FAT BACK and UNI TOAST

Fatback was something I grew up with in the South. It was one of my mom's favorite things. She would fry up pieces of pork fat until they were crispy and salty. Even walking through the grocery store, we would see bags of crispy pork skins. That taste and smell was a big part of my childhood. As I got older, I fell in love with seafood from growing up on Long Island. That's where I discovered uni. It was creamy, sweet, salty, and briny all at the same time. I realized the saltiness of pork fat and the richness of uni were a perfect match. They balance each other like they were made to be together.

I first tasted uni in a fine-dining kitchen at Marea. One of their signature bites was uni on a crostini topped with paper-thin lardo. As a young cook, I learned how tricky it was to slice lardo the right way. If it was too warm, it melted. If it was too thick, it ruined the texture. The lardo had to be so thin you could see your fingertips through it— like a little window. This recipe is my ode to that memory. It brings my Southern roots and my seafood upbringing into one bite. Sweet, salty, creamy, and briny—all the flavors I love working together.

Chef's Note

Render the fat slowly so it's clean and golden. Toast the bread until it's crisp on both sides — this is your foundation. The fat back should soften from the warmth of the toast, and the uni sits perfectly on top. It's all about balance — salty, briny, rich, and elegant in one bite.

Yield

4 servings (appetizer)

Ingredients

1 loaf sourdough bread, sliced ½ inch thick

2 tbsp rendered pork fat

4 pieces uni (sea urchin)

4 thin slices fat back or lardo

2 tbsp crushed pork rinds

Freshly ground black pepper

Lemon zest or a few drops of lemon juice (optional)

Procedure

Slowly render small cubes of fat back in a skillet until the fat melts. Strain and reserve the pork fat.

Heat the rendered fat over medium heat and toast the sourdough slices until golden and crisp on both sides.

While still warm, top each toast with a thin slice of fat back or lardo so it begins to soften.

Place one piece of uni on top and season lightly with black pepper.

Finish with a sprinkle of crushed pork rinds and a touch of lemon zest or juice if desired.

Serve warm.

GORDON'S 5 STAR DISH - SAKARI'S OYSTER STEW

This dish is special to me because it's an ode to a man named **Thomas Downing**, the "Oyster King" of the 1800s. He was a Black entrepreneur in New York City who built one of the most famous oyster restaurants in the country. Back then, oysters were everywhere in New York Harbor, and Downing became known for serving the best of the best. So when I created this oyster stew for Chef Gordon Ramsay, I wanted to honor that history. I added **confit cod**, because cod is one of the few fish that becomes silky and perfect when slowly cooked in oil. It keeps its shape but stays soft and rich.

The flavors in this dish come together in a salty, sweet, and briny way. I added caviar on top to bring a little pop and luxury. The whole thing is also inspired by Chef Thomas Keller's signature dish, **Oysters and Pearls**, which is one of the most iconic seafood dishes in fine dining. For me, this bowl isn't just a stew. It's a mix of history, mentors, flavor, and technique—from Thomas Downing to Thomas

Keller, to Omar Tate who introduced the story, all brought into my own style.

Chef's Note

The base of this stew starts with **oyster fat**. When you chop oysters into small pieces and warm them gently, they release a natural, salty, briny fat. That becomes the foundation of the dish and gives the stew its deep ocean flavor.

Leeks are the next key. Cook them low and slow until they're soft and lightly caramelized. This adds sweetness and depth that balance the briny oysters.

For the body of the stew, use **reduced cream**. As the cream cooks down, it becomes velvety and rich. If it starts to boil over, use a **wider pan**, lower the heat, or gently **blow on the surface** to calm it. Keep it on medium-low and stir often until it reaches the texture you want. Finish with **herbs, zest, and citrus** at the very end. Adding them last keeps their bright, fresh flavor alive.

Yield

4 servings

Ingredients

For the Oyster Stew:

2 dozen fresh oysters

2 tbsp butter

2 leeks, thinly sliced

2 cups seafood stock

1 cup heavy cream

1 tsp fresh thyme leaves

½ tsp white pepper

Soy sauce to taste

Chopped fresh parsley (optional)

For the Citrus Oysters:

12 fresh oysters, shucked

¼ cup yuzu juice (or mix of lime and orange)

½ tsp salt

¼ tsp white pepper

Procedure

Make the Citrus Oysters Whisk together yuzu juice, salt, and white pepper in a small bowl.

Gently toss oysters in the citrus mixture and let marinate 10 minutes. Drain lightly before serving.

Make the Oyster Stew Shuck the oysters and reserve their liquid.

In a saucepan, melt butter over medium heat. Add leeks and cook until tender, about 5 minutes.

Pour in seafood stock and reserved oyster liquid. Bring to a gentle simmer.

Stir in cream, thyme, and white pepper.

Simmer for 10–15 minutes until slightly thickened.

Add the citrus oysters and cook 2–3 minutes just until the edges curl.

Season lightly with soy sauce.

Ladle into bowls and garnish with parsley if desired. Serve hot.

SNOW ICE CREAM WITH COCONUT GRANITA

It didn't snow often in North Carolina, but when it did, it felt magical. We'd rush outside with bowls and collect fresh snow to turn into ice cream. It was soft, cold, and sweet — the taste of childhood wonder. This recipe is a grown-up version of that memory. Instead of using food coloring, I create a golden hue naturally with turmeric. Topped with a coconut granita, this becomes my modern take on that childhood treat.

Chef's Note

Never heat the heavy cream — add it cold after warming the base. This preserves the fat structure and prevents ice crystals from forming. The xanthan gum helps keep the ice cream smooth even after days in the freezer. The granita needs to be scraped every 30 minutes to create light, icy flakes.

Yield

6 servings

Ingredients

For the Ice Cream Base:

315 ml whole milk

- 100 g sugar
- 40 g light corn syrup
- 20 g dry milk powder
- 1 g xanthan gum
- 315 ml heavy cream
- 30 g sweetened condensed milk
- 2 g turmeric powder

For the Coconut Granita:
- 240 ml coconut water
- 240 ml sugarcane water or coconut milk
- 1 g turmeric powder

Procedure

Make the Ice Cream Base In a small pot, whisk together milk, sugar, corn syrup, dry milk powder, xanthan gum, and condensed milk.

Warm gently over medium heat, stirring until smooth — do not boil.

Remove from heat and whisk in turmeric until fully dissolved.

Once cooled slightly, add the cold heavy cream and stir to combine.

Chill the mixture completely, then churn in an ice cream maker according to the directions.

Transfer to a container and freeze until firm.

Make the Coconut Granita Whisk together coconut water, sugarcane water, and turmeric.

Pour into a shallow tray and freeze. Every 30 minutes, scrape with a fork to create light, icy flakes.

Serve Scoop golden ice cream into bowls and top with coconut granita. The flakes melt softly over the top.

CYBER GREEN JUICE

As I watched Serena's final match, I thought about legacy — how she poured everything into her craft. Cyber Green Juice was born from that same energy. Green juice has always fueled athletes and creators, and this one is my take, light, refreshing, and a sneaky way to get your greens in. It's also the first product where I truly bet on myself.

Chef's Note

Juice the ingredients in order: pineapple, spinach, apple. Alternate them to get maximum juice. The honey dissolves quickly once the juice is warm. Drink it fresh within 24 hours, or sealed and chilled for up to 48 hours. A light foam may form on top — just skim it off.

Yield

About 1 quart

Ingredients

45 g fresh lemon juice

385 g pineapple, peeled and cored

365 g fresh spinach

575 g Granny Smith apple, washed

40 g honey

Procedure

Juice pineapple, spinach, and apple together, alternating ingredients for maximum juice yield.

Add fresh lemon juice and honey. Stir until fully combined.

Cool immediately and store in an airtight container.

Fill containers to the brim to remove all air and prevent oxidation.

Drink within 24 hours. If sealed airtight, it may last up to 48 hours.

If a light foam forms on top, skim it off with a ladle before serving.

For Recipe visuals subscribe to the Noble Promise Newsletter. Scan here!

SAKARI'S SECRET RECIPE FOR SUCCESS

Curiosity — stay open, experiment, keep asking "what if?"
Gratitude — remember where you came from; stay grounded
Resilience — keep going when it's not pretty, not perfect, not easy.
Consistency — show up on the days you don't feel like it.
Community — lean into people who lift you, support you, challenge you.
Integrity — do the right thing even when no one is watching.
Exposure — put yourself in rooms that stretch your imagination.
Humility — be coachable, stay learning, stay a beginner.
Courage — take shots you don't feel "ready" for.
Joy — let the process be fun; savor the small moments.

Action — don't dwell, don't overthink, build the solution.

FINAL INGREDIENT Savor Your Journey — The Journey *Is* The Reward!

CHAPTER 20: THE SECRET

GRATITUDE

It wasn't until my teens that I started to learn about one of the most important ingredients in both cooking and in life. It was, gratitude.

Everybody knows "The Fresh Prince of Bel-Air". It was one of my favorite shows growing up and I never expected to have related to it so much within my personal life. I was an only child, and like many only children, I had no idea just how good I had it. They say the one thing only children lack is gratitude. We're not bad kids, we just grow up assuming that things will always be available to us. Food, time, love, attention, and even space.

My grandfather didn't grow up that way. He was one of seven, raised in Jamaica, and nothing went to waste. He'd always finish his drink after the meal, savoring it, slowly, like a reward. When you've grown up wondering when your next meal will be, you treat everything you're given with value.

As I grappled in my early teens, there was a sense of entitlement. If I left food on my plate, he'd reach over and say, "Boy, gimme that," and scrape it clean. As a kid, I thought it was weird. I had no frame of reference for hunger, no real sense of what it meant to have been in need. I basically felt like I resonated with the character "Carlton", privileged. In need of nothing, living in Suburbia. Then everything changed.

One morning, I woke up to the sound no kid should ever have to hear. A grown man weeping from the gut. Not just crying, wailing. It echoed through the walls of the house like an alarm. My mom burst into my room, eyes swollen. "Put on your clothes, Kari," she said. "Nathan's sister just passed away."

Nathan, my dad, was a stoic man. He was stern. As a corrections officer at Rikers Island, he was used to dealing with the worst of the worst. Murderers. Abusers. The kind of men you don't flinch around, because if they smell fear, they'll use it. Nathan taught himself to stay silent. To be still and unshakeable. He even had a system, if someone from the neighborhood called out "Andre," he knew it was someone from his past life. If they said "Nathan," he kept walking. He wouldn't break. On this particular day, he broke down.

He collapsed to the floor, clutching his sister's body, begging them not to take her away. She had passed suddenly and her body was being removed and transferred into a black bag. It was the first time I saw my father become a child again, vulnerable, lost, and undone. And in the midst of that grief, a new reality took shape. My cousin Devante, her son, needed a home. No father in the picture. No fallback plan. Just like that, my dad became "Uncle Phil". Devante moved in. I was 14. I'd gone from being an only child to having to share everything—space, food, attention, life—with someone else. It was jarring. I had friends who were twins, who shared everything. That wasn't me. I wasn't used to it. But Devante? He came in with something I didn't even realize I was missing. Gratitude.

At the dinner table, every single night, he'd say thank you. Just a simple, heartfelt thank you for the meal. I never said thank you. I expected it. I assumed food was just...there. But for Devante, who had just lost his mom and moved in with a new family, food wasn't a guarantee. It was a gift. And to be thankful, every night, was a reminder and appreciation. He didn't just teach me how to share food. He taught me how to value what you have. How to cook for more than just myself. How to share with others. How to see another person's hunger—not just for food, but for love, for safety, for connection.

Devante also introduced me to hip-hop. Real hip-hop. Biggie. Tupac. Music that held pain and pride in the same verse. He'd sit on the bed, rapping along word-for-word, not just for fun, but as a way of healing. Of reclaiming.

"Who the fuck is this, pagin' me at 5:46 in the morning?

Crack of dawn and now I'm yawnin'

Wipe the cold out my eye

See who's this pagin' me and why"

And together, over shared meals and mixtapes, we learned how to be family. It wasn't always easy. But that season of my life cracked me open. I learned that food doesn't just nourish your body. It teaches you how to see beyond yourself. It connects you through conversation and shared experiences. And that is the secret ingredient I'd been missing all along. The importance of gratitude and the extension of family. Be it as a brother, a cousin, and even a father. The message and reality of gratitude in relation to family became even a bigger concept that I'd expect. Let me share with you my story. The secret.

There's something I haven't told you, to those who are reading. Something I've been carrying my whole life. Something that even now, as I'm writing this, makes me nervous as hell to share. But if I'm really gonna tell my story, I gotta tell the whole story. Identity. Man, identity is a trip, isn't it?

Some people wake up knowing exactly who they are. Me? I've been trying to figure that shit out since I was a kid. Perhaps it started when someone made a comment about my hair being too straight or when I bought a whole collection of snapbacks to hide my waves. I was trying to grow out an Afro like Ludacris when I was 10 years old. I'd spray my hair with water, pick it out, blow-dry it into this big ball. I thought I was doing something but by lunchtime, half of it would be flat again. My hair just wasn't built for that.

I wasn't Black enough for the Black kids, wasn't White enough for the White kids. Some assumed I was Spanish, but I wasn't. Where did I fit in? Nowhere. I just existed in this weird in-between space. My whole life, I never questioned why my mom and dad were both darker than me. What I have shared is that Nathan was my stepdad, that's why I called him by his first name. Cornell, my mom's first husband, must've been light-skinned. That's why I'm light-skinned, which made sense to me.

Simple, right? Wrong. Absolutely wrong.

The Day Everything Changed

When I was 16, my mom and I were going through it and argued all the time. I was rebellious and didn't like being told what to do. My mom tried to keep me in line and instill discipline. Normal parent-kid stuff, but it became more intense.

One day, out of nowhere, my grandparents flew in from North Carolina. I thought it was just a surprise visit, maybe they missed us. Maybe they wanted to check in. I had no idea they were about to drop a bomb that would change my entire life. My mom had gone to work about 2 o'clock that day. My grandparents had called me downstairs."Grandma! What are you doing here?" "Sakari, we flew in to talk to you about you and your mom." With time, patience, but an awakening, I had one of the hardest conversations with my grandparents. Instantly I assumed I had done something wrong. I was not prepared for what was to come next.

"Have you ever wondered why your mom and Nathan don't look like you? Why are they so much darker?"

"Ugh...no? I mean, I figured Cornell was my real dad and he was light-skinned."

"Boy, Cornell was darker than Nathan."

"Wait, what?"

I remembered Cornell from when I was little. He used to let me sit between his legs and pretend to drive. He gave me toys like a Beetlejuice figurine, but that memory was hazy. "Cornell?, that's not my dad?" "No, Sakari," said my grandma. My heart started racing. I didn't understand what they were trying to say to me. My grandma, who was also a social worker at the time, began to explain that in our family, it was hard for the women in the family to conceive. With that difficulty and my mom's want in the world to be a mother, a miracle happened. A young woman who was carrying a baby boy, gave my mom the greatest gift, to become a mother.

At that moment, I was told that I was adopted. There was a range of emotions that to this day it's hard to describe. Questions had been answered for these moments in my life where I was searching to fit in somewhere. Still emotionally, I felt a rage like I had been lied to. My whole world collapsed. My head literally hit the table. Tears started pouring out the kind you can't control. Everything I thought I knew about myself just evaporated.

"Boy, why are you crying?" my grandma asked.

"Because my whole life is a lie!"

"Stop that. Your life is not a lie. Your mom is still your mom. Your dad is still your dad. You just have different blood. That's it."

But it wasn't "that's it." It was everything.

All those assumptions of people making comments about my appearance, my own questions on why I didn't resemble my parents. I was adopted, and nobody told me. As I tried to stop crying, they explained more. My grandma tried to explain this issues of fertility with the women in the family. I had also found out that other family members were adopted as well. Apparently, this ran in the family. Other people in our family were adopted too because of fertility issues. I felt like I was in a movie.

When my mom got home, she had this look on her face like she knew exactly what had happened. My mom, that even though we had our disagreements, I knew she loved me. That look on her face of concern but yet had this protective essence for me to know that she was my mother. Nothing was different. She has been upset that this conversation even took place without her. .

"Ma, what am I?"

"Your biological mother was Spanish. I don't know where your father was from and the grandparents were both Black and White."

My mother had asked me how I felt. With emotions of confusion, shock, and anger, I just didn't know how to feel. It was my business that didn't need to be shared as my mother said. That didn't sit right with me. I didn't want to stay silent nor was it something I felt like I could keep inside. With everything that I had been through from dealing with kids in school, to working in restaurants, to traveling and discovering new cultures. From the conversations that I had with chefs who looked like me and even to the racism that I had faced, countless times in life, how could I hide this. This was my identity. My journey.

The first person I told was my cousin, Devante, who lived with us. His jaw hit the floor. He had thought it made so much sense. Probably trying to make light humor out of the situations, but he wasn't as surprised, but he was there for me. It felt good to tell him, like a weight had been lifted. I didn't feel confused anymore. I felt seen. Again, this moment of gratitude for having someone to be there, to listen. I appreciated that. I also told my best friend Ghil. Same reaction, who had also said that "explains everything."

The real conversation that I had was with my dad, Nathan. We sat outside Dunkin' Donuts in his red Jeep for hours. He asked me how I was feeling as I shared with him that I thought my life had been a lie. He looked at me with so much love. "I told her to tell you, man. I always wanted her to tell you. You were doing school projects about being Cherokee and I kept saying, 'Why you got that boy lying about his heritage?'"

He paused. "And what about when you go to the doctor and they ask about family history? You were saying no to everything, but you might have diabetes in your family. You need to know these things."

Then he said something I'll never forget: "If you want to tell people, tell people. It's your story. Your life. You get to decide." And that had changed everything.

From that day forward, I promised myself to own my journey. To savor the sweet, the bitter, and what was difficult to digest, like this new normal. Whenever anyone asked, I told the truth. That I was adopted, but I have two loving parents. There were apologies and shock, but I didn't need either. It was just my truth. The more I told people, the better I felt. Empowered, even. The most important thing that came from all this was becoming closer to my dad, to Nathan. Nathan was my dad. My mother was my mom. Not by blood but by bond. They raised me as their own and I was grateful. They showed up at my games, they celebrated my wins, and they watched and supported me as I became a chef.

So who am I? I wasn't sure if I could be Jamaican or tied to Caribbean roots. I grew up on curry chicken and rice and peas. I grew up listening to Martin Luther King speeches in my dad's room. I grew up at family cookouts and fish fries down South. I just was, I am Black. That's my culture. That's who I was raised to be. As I started writing this book, I got scared. What if my mom gets hurt by me telling this story? What if my family gets mad?

Close friends and those I confided in encouraged me to share it. My mission was to share my story in the event that someone could relate. Perhaps someone who had recently found out they'd been adopted or someone struggling with their identity. It's my hope that my story helps them embrace theirs.

I decided to get a DNA test. As I talked to Alexander Smalls about ancestors, and dove deeper into writing this book, I realized I needed to know. Where did I really come from? What's actually in my blood? The kit sat on my desk for two weeks and I was terrified. I took the test. Spit in the tube and send it off. When the results came back, I had my roommates look first. There was such excitement and nervousness in the room.

"Yo, Sakari, you gotta see this!" "Don't spoil it!" I opened it.

My Results:

20% Spain
19% Germanic Europe
9% Nigeria
8% Benin and Togo
7% Western Bantu peoples
6% Senegal
5% Mali
5% Cameroon, Congo, Western Bantu

3% Northern Africa
3% Dominican Republic
3% Portugal
3% England and Northwestern Europe
2% Eastern Europe and Russia
2% Central West Africa
1% North-Central Nigeria
1% Southern Bantu peoples

ALMOST 50% African. Spanish. German. Dominican. European. I'm everything. I'm a whole map of the world. Here's the wildest part: my African American ancestors? They settled in Pennsylvania. Not the South—the East Coast. I'm through and through the East Coast. And then it showed me something that stopped my heart: A DNA match. Nearly 50% from either my mother or what could have been my daughter. Since I definitely do not have kids, it had to be my biological mother, which listed her name. She'd taken the test about two years ago.

I found this out at 30 years old, months before my 31st birthday. Writing this book made me realize something: the journey never ends. As much as I understand my upbringing and the food and cuisine and the cultures I was raised on, now it is time for me to embrace other cultures that are part of my ancestors and to truly understand the food that my ancestors cooked.

The cultures in my DNA. Spain, Germany, Nigeria, Benin, Togo, Dominican Republic. I now have the next thirty years or more to go down this journey, God willing to discover it. That's what my noble promise will be. A celebration of ALL cultures. ALL stories. ALL journeys. To me, food doesn't care about blood. Food is family, through extension or connection, through love and bringing people together.

To My Mom:

Ma, if you're reading this, and I know you will, this is for you. I did this for you. I love you more than words can say. Nobody will ever replace you. You chose me, raised me, and sacrificed so much for me. I thank you for showing up for me every single day of my life. You're my hero. It was not my intention to hurt you through sharing this and I'm sorry if it has. I had to share my entire truth, not because I'm ashamed or angry, but because this could help someone else. You did a damn good job raising me, Ma. Look at me now. I love you.

To the Reader:

If you made it this far in this book, I love you too. For real. Thank you for taking this journey with me. Thank you for letting me be vulnerable. Thank you for seeing me. This book isn't about my journey to gaining a Michelin star, appearing on Hell's Kitchen or working in fancy restaurants. It's about finding identity and belonging where you are the most happy. This is about figuring out who the hell you are in a world that's constantly trying to put you in a box. It's about understanding that family isn't blood. That culture isn't DNA. Identity is something you choose to create. .

I chose to be Black. I chose to embrace Caribbean food. I chose to honor my ancestors, both the ones who raised me and the DNA I carry. That's what my Noble Promise is: a promise to honor ALL of it. ALL of me. ALL of us.

Here's what I want you to remember:

Savor your journey. The good, the bad, the ugly, the beautiful. It's all yours. Own it.

Embrace your identity. Whatever that means for you. You don't have to fit anyone's definition.

Honor your ancestors. The ones who raised you. The ones in your blood. The ones who paved the way. All of them matter.

Use your gifts to serve. Whatever you're good at—cooking, writing, teaching, building—use it to make the world better.

Tell your story. Don't wait until it's perfect. Don't wait until you have it all figured out. Tell the messy, the raw and the real.

Put love into everything. That's the secret ingredient. Love makes everything better.

So where am I now? Still cooking and creating. Noble Promise isn't just a restaurant concept anymore. It's a movement. It's a philosophy. It's a way of life. Every pop-up, every dish, every conversation with a young chef, it's all part of something bigger. I'm 31 years old. I don't have a Michelin star yet. I don't own a restaurant yet. I'm not famous, but I'm exactly where I'm supposed to be. I am learning and growing. Honoring my dad, the hopes of making my mom proud and building my legacy. Savoring every single moment of this journey that I am given.

Cheers to yours! With love,

Sakari

Noble Promise

"The journey continues..."

ACKNOWLEDGMENTS

As I'm writing this acknowledgments, I feel like I'm at the last song of an album—you know that feeling where you have a long list of people that have helped you on this path? I think of the J. Cole track, "Note to Self", and that's where I am. And if I missed you, please know it's not intentional. I'm going to do my best not to miss anyone, but I'm going to be real with you—this page can only be so long.

First and foremost, I want to start with my mother and my father. Thank you for sacrificing so much and for being great parents. Mom, you have always been my biggest fan. Thank you for showing me what true love is, for being a social butterfly with such a beautiful spirit, for being kind and funny, loud and crazy, but just beautifully and authentically yourself. That's taught me so much.

Dad, I know you're no longer here with us physically, but you're still here spiritually. Thank you for helping me become the man I am. Thank you for being a father to me when you didn't have to be—that makes you more of a man than you will ever know. You taught me about manhood, about doing hard things, about being kind and noble and a good person. Having you as my father, when so many people within our culture don't even have that blessing, meant everything to me. I love you.

To my grandparents, thank you for raising me while Mom and Dad were working to provide for us. Grandmother, you're so smart, intelligent, funny, and sweet. Thank you for teaching me to say "No, ma'am" and "Yes, sir," for teaching me the importance of gratitude and how to open a door and treat people with respect. Grandfather, thank you for showing me what it means to be a true believer in your children. You believed in me and invested in me. You rooted me on and gave me hope that I will reach my dreams and aspirations. You taught me that it just takes time—it's not going to happen overnight. Thank you for showing me what hard work looks like, how to provide as a man, and how to hold a real conversation.

To my uncles, thank you for showing me what hardship looks like. Seeing your struggles was the inspiration I needed to stay on the right track when I came across temptations, the same ones everybody faces. You influenced me to never go down that road, and I'm grateful every single day.

To my cousin Devante, who's become a brother to me: thank you for teaching me about gratitude and for helping me through grief and life's process. You're like my long-lost brother, and I love you with all my heart. To Aunt Grace and Uncle Bernard, thank you for being there and supporting me. You've always been so kind and proud of me, and that fuel keeps me going.

To my sister, Kateija: we're family no matter what. I will always have love for you. To my nieces and nephew: I love you more than words can say. I never had the best representation of what an uncle should be, and I've struggled with building that relationship. But know that I love you and I'm proud of you. Your grandfather is so, so proud of you too. Keep being a light on this journey—you're part of my story.

To my home economics teachers, thank you for introducing me to culinary arts. That gift changed my life. To all the chefs I've ever encountered throughout my career: I've worked with so many talented people, and every single one of you has left an imprint on me. Thank you to all the chefs I admire who lead teams and do the hard work every single day. It's not easy doing what we do in this industry. Thank you for giving me the confidence to write this book and share what our lives are truly like.

To my culinary arts professors, thank you for believing in me and inspiring me. From the dean to my advisor to my coach—you're all amazing. Thank you to my track coach for pushing me to new limits.

To my writing teacher in high school, Ms. Mazza: thank you for pushing me to become a better writer. I didn't know then how important that would be.

To Ian Kiowski, thank you for being there from day one and helping me develop a strategy to write this book. To my publicist, book editor, and social media strategist, Jihan Antoine: you are incredible. You're hardworking, loving, and anybody would be blessed to have you on their team. If you're reading this and looking for a publicist, hire her. She's amazing.

To every person and major figure featured in this book who gave me their time, honesty, and who extended a branch when it was scary to reach out, who believed in this crazy idea to write a memoir at 31 years old: thank you. To Todd, my former book agent, thank you for those meetings and great advice. To all the other book agents who denied this project: thank you. You helped me understand what this needed to be. To my entire team: thank you for helping me shape this into something perfectly imperfect.

To Hamza, thank you for your amazing photos throughout the QR codes in this book. You're so talented, humble, and amazing. To Kelsey Giddings for creating the Noble Promise logo and believing in my vision—we're going to keep building. To Moe, who helped with graphic design and inspired some of these recipes: you're one of the kindest human beings I know. To Yasmine, who I met in Miami and created the perfect cover: thank you for being on this journey. You're professional, talented, and I wish you nothing but success.

To all my cooks and the entire restaurant team: every dishwasher and porter I've ever encountered, you are the heartbeat of the restaurant. I wouldn't be here without you. Thank you to every server who shows up with a smile despite having other passions, making guests feel happier and allowing us to do what we do. Thank you to the hospitality managers who taught me how to host and the importance of making people feel seen.

To my Long Islanders and mentors: thank you for inspiration and resources. To Keron, my roommate and brother for so long: thank you for supporting me. To Yang, who recorded and documented all the sessions and projects for this book: thank you. To all my fraternity brothers: thank you for pushing me along the way.

And finally, to you, the reader: thank you for being here and supporting me. This journey has not been easy, and your support means the world.

If I missed you or didn't call you out, it's not because I don't appreciate you. This page can only be so long, but know that I love you all and appreciate you so, so much. Thank you for your support on this book and on my journey.

With gratitude,
Sakari